CAREERS IN HIGH TECH

Connie Winkler

An Arco Book
Published by Prentice Hall Press
New York, New York 10023

Copyright © 1987 by Connie Winkler

An Arco Book
Published by Prentice Hall Press
A Division of Simon & Schuster, Inc.
Gulf + Western Building
One Gulf + Western Plaza
New York, New York 10023

PRENTICE HALL PRESS is a trademark of Simon & Schuster, Inc.

Manufactured in the United States of America

1   2   3   4   5   6   7   8   9   10

Library of Congress Cataloging-in-Publication Data

Winkler, Connie.
    Careers in high tech.

    "An Arco book."
    Bibliography: p.
    Includes index.
    1. High technology industries—Vocational
guidance.   I. Title.
HD8039.H54W56   1986   331.7′02   86-25277
    ISBN 0-688-06537-0

CONTENTS

To *PC Magazine*

ACKNOWLEDGMENTS

This book owes much to Jean Atelsek, Martin Porter and Martin Porter and Associates who contributed to it, and Fred Klingenberg, who reviewed portions of the manuscript.

Many other individuals provided insight, references and support: Jean Barnes, Nick Basta, Charles Bermant, Linda Benson at the National Computer Graphics Association, Chick Bisberg, Richard Bolles and the entire staff of the National Career Development Project, James Donio of the Association of Systems Professionals, Posy Gering, David L. Hoffman, 9 to 5 National Association of Working Women, Fred Paul and Myrna Sameth. Also, John Buescher of North American Telecommunications Association, and Jim Weinstein, International Communications Association. And, of course, I am grateful to the other professionals whose names appear elsewhere in the book, and to my family and friends.

Special thanks to Patrick Wash at the Bureau of Labor Statistics, and to my editor, Ellen Lichtenstein, who made it happen.

1

INTRODUCTION: WELCOME TO HIGH TECHNOLOGY

High technology is a trendy, often used term. What does it really mean? How does it affect you? Common usage has turned "high technology" into more of a catchall than a term that lends insight into any specific technology. High technology refers to everything from the use of personal computers in a court administrator's office to satellites bouncing movies around the world, unmanned tanks, lasers being used in eye surgery or computer-controlled robot arms performing brain surgery.

Simply put, technology is the application of science to commercial and industrial endeavors. In this broad sense it applies to solar heating systems, population control, no-till corn plants, space shuttles, gene splicing or superlattice semiconductor chips. High technology is any technology in its most advanced form or latest state of development. It is what's on the front burner—it's hot. Possibly because of its focus on the here and now, high technology in the late 1980s has come to refer almost exclusively to the use of electronics to solve modern day tasks. The application of electronics has come to mean computers.

A high proportion of new technical developments in this country is based on the use of a computer—or its critical kernel, a microprocessor, a collection of semiconductors which electronically execute pre-programmed instructions. When it comes to finding a job, knowledge of computer technology and applications is the best key to opening doors. The skills acquired in computer-related training can be transferred to almost any hot technology, from telecommunications to health care systems. Of the 40 occupations expected to have the largest job growth between now and 1995, 20 are in the computer or health fields. Of the top 20 fastest growing occupations, 10 involve computers, and another 3 mechanical and factory engineering. Equally incredible is this Bureau of Labor Statistics (BLS) prediction: "The economy is expected to generate an additional 25.6 million jobs between 1982 and 1995. About one-half of this job growth is projected to occur in only 40 of the 1,700 occupations."[1]

Careers in High Tech looks at the broad spectrum of technologies in categories. The reality is more interconnected, but singling out disciplines chapter by chapter makes for easier study. The book is an introduction to this world, and only the most basic knowledge, interests and concerns are

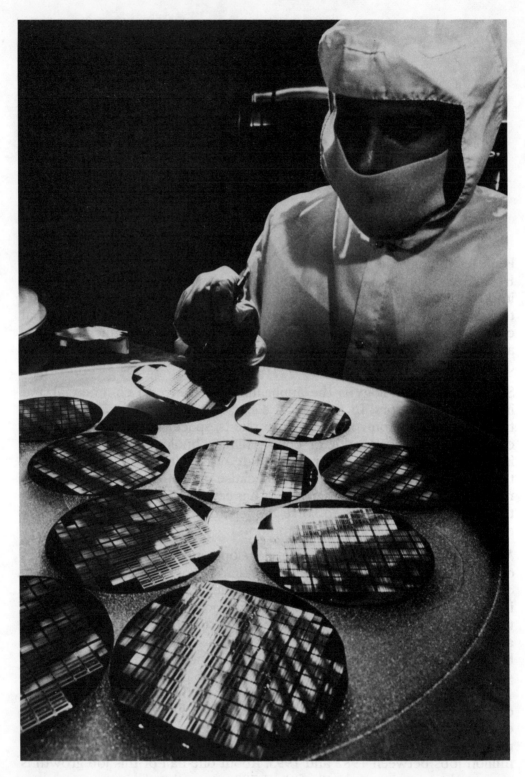

Smaller, cheaper, faster has been the story of the computer industry thanks to silicon chips, or semiconductors. Each of these silicon wafers, manufactured in dust free environments, is cut into more than 100 computer memory chips. More than 288,000 bits of data (noted as 288K—K standing for 1,000 bits) can be stored on each of these tiny squares, some of the highest capacity chips used in volume today. (Courtesy of International Business Machines Corporation)

presented. The reader of this survey book or student who's captivated even slightly by one of the disciplines will need to investigate further.

What follows is an overview of our world in the late 1980s and early 1990s, a world considerably changed from 50 or even 15 years ago. Two big changes have occurred in the economy, and, closely related, in technology. This chapter looks at those changes and then proposes how job hunters might use them to their advantage.

HIGH ON TECHNOLOGY

In the economy of the late 1980s technology is the growth edge, where the opportunities are. It's exciting. Who cannot be intrigued by possibilities such as these:

- Artificial ears that inject electrical signals developed by speech processors directly into the auditory nerve and to the brain, bypassing the ear.
- Videodiscs that show prospective home owners images of properties within their budgets and requirements before they start browsing. Such interactive videodiscs (computer-connected) might also show mechanics how to tune new carburetors by simulating their performance, complete with engine sounds.
- In-car computerized maps that allow drivers to navigate via signals beamed off satellites—you need never be lost again.
- Supercomputers that simulate air flow over an aircraft so that designers can change shapes and try new designs without long and expensive wind tunnel tests.
- The home of the future that uses 8 miles of wiring to link 13 computers, 14 telephones, 26 television monitors and many other electronic gadgets to make it a highly personalized, functional place to live.

Such developments are exciting. They're also frightening: How can ordinary people cope with such far out fantasies? The fact is that unless you choose to drop out of society, you have no choice but to take the bull by the horns. Learn to use technology to your professional benefit.

HIGH TECH IN THE U.S.

For our economy to grow, the country needs to keep moving toward more robots on the assembly line, toward lasers piercing steel, toward artificial blood; that is, towards new technologies. These are the products and processes that will keep our economy vital, technocrats tell us. Even those who believe in alternative societies tell us the information age will open

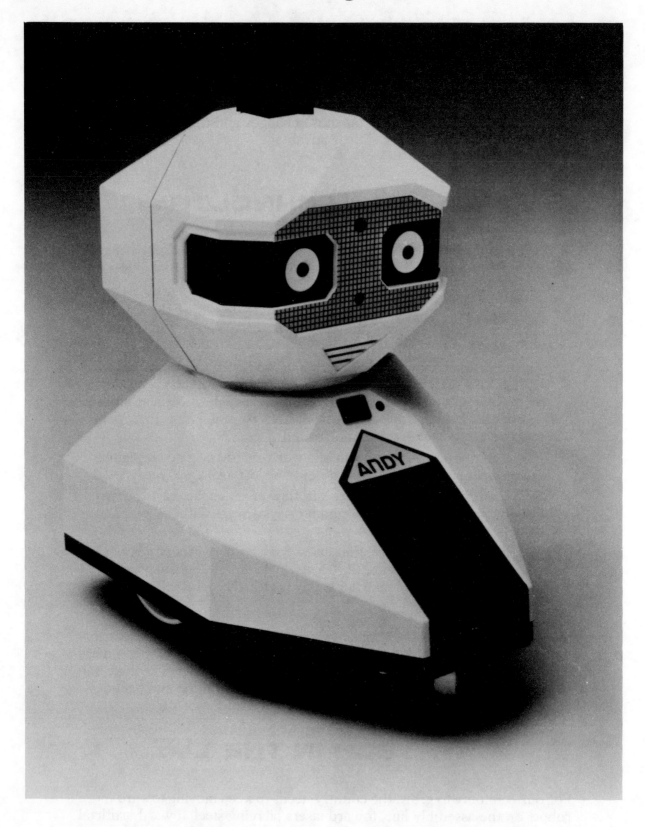

Microprocessor controlled devices like this toy robot Andy have captured the imagination of computer and electronics designers, to say nothing of users and new entrepreneurs. This home robot can be programmed through a home computer. (Courtesy of Axlon, Inc.)

new frontiers in world peace. For example, U.S. citizens at home may someday send electronic mail messages to U.S.S.R. citizens in their homes.

High technology is an elite world. It is the world of scientists, researchers, computer jocks, software company magicians, telecommunications carriers and hardware manufacturers. It is a small world. Despite the hoopla which accompanies it only a small portion of the population is involved in it. For example, the production of the entire computer industry is only 2% of the Gross National Product each year. Computer manufacturers (the category easiest defined) account for only 1% of the workforce—450,000 jobs. Thus we are faced with the long view question: Does technology create more jobs than it displaces?

Based on our experience to date, the results are disquieting. What about the workers who aren't benefitting from technology? The new America doesn't have an answer. What about the displaced auto worker, for instance, one of the 45,000 Chrysler didn't hire back? During the Chrysler bailout hearings in 1979 there was little discussion of retraining these employees or attracting new industry to Detroit. Instead, newspapers reported Michigan families living out of their campers, unable to find jobs in Dallas or Florida or other supposed meccas of employment. "We have perfected truly marvelous, ingenious ways of redeploying capital from failing firms to more successful industries. But our system of redeploying people is exceedingly harsh, inefficient, and in many cases perverse," observes Robert Reich, Harvard University economist and high tech historian.[2]

Although America invented radio and television, not one consumer radio or black-and-white television and relatively few color TVs, are made in the U.S. Almost all our video and stereo gadgets, motorcycles, and—increasingly—automobiles are manufactured overseas, especially in Japan. Fewer garments and less steel are produced in the U.S. What happened to those plants, those workers?

The world's economy no longer centers on the U.S. It's become a world economy in which more goods and services are traded internationally than domestically, and in which companies, countries and consumers are interdependent. High technology industries such as computers and electronics in which America used to dominate now are also confronted by worldwide competitors from Japan and Southeast Asia.

Jobs in the Information Age

In the early 1980s the buzzwords were Information Age, based on the concept that information was becoming more important than the production of goods. Predictions said the information industries—firms that sell information—would earn a total of $1 trillion by 1990. Such information would be stored in huge data bases, and broadcast, or distributed electronically through software and traditional print media—books, magazines, newspapers. By mid-decade that enthusiasm diminished as it

Computer circuits have been miniaturized to such an extent that an entire processor fits on a board, fittingly a microprocessor, which can be snapped in and out of systems. (Courtesy of Honeywell Test Instruments Division, Denver)

became clear that manufacturing and other segments of the economy were not disappearing. Nevertheless, jobs are shifting. BLS finds the following:

- Numbers of professional and technical workers will continue to increase faster than overall employment.
- Engineering occupations are expected to provide 600,000 new jobs by 1995 as these occupations grow faster than the average. As manufacturing rebounds with new production systems, there will be heavy demands for electrical, industrial and mechanical engineers.
- Electrical and electronic technicians, and mechanical and civil engineering technicians should experience strong growth in their occupations along with the upsurge of automation.
- Computer-aided design will make the drafter's job obsolete.
- Data entry clerks will decline in number as machines take over.
- Health care occupations will continue to grow, although perhaps not as rapidly as in the late 1970s with the increase in the number of elderly and the increased spending for health services.

Rapid Change

This is a period of rapid change in the history of our nation...and the world. Every industry is in a state of flux. The life spans of new technologies and new products shorten with each successive technology and product. For example, in the electronics industry the life of a 64K RAM is considerably shorter than the several years of popularity experienced by the 16K RAMs. Living in a period of high change is difficult because most people work toward stability and balance in their lives. High technology industries often experience the greatest changes. One year a company may introduce the greatest software package in the world and earn millions of dollars. Eighteen months later it can be declaring bankruptcy, overshadowed by the next company that's introduced an even better package. On the international front the U.S. develops and starts manufacturing the latest semiconductors only to have foreign competitors copy and then produce them in huge quantities for one-third and sometimes below cost.

Survival in such a fluctuating environment requires great flexibility. Like a tennis player one must be constantly bouncing on one's feet, prepared for what's coming across the net. At the same time, one must always be looking ahead to the next play. Who's the newest tennis whiz and what's his or her game? What's the latest thinking and variation on the technology? What's the next hot technology?

Predicting the future is impossible. The smart person adapts to future events and trends as they appear. The trick is to register changes as they occur and not to keep doing things in the same way. Those already employed in technology must continually work to stay at the forefront of what's happening in their profession. For instance, if an artificial intelligence project is being developed in your company, try to work on it or at least a related phase you're familiar with.

TECHNOLOGY IS NOT FOR EVERYONE

Just because the technology bandwagon is racing down the street doesn't mean everyone should jump on board. *Technology is not for everyone.* Working with technology does not fit everyone's skills. No amount of money or exposure to new technologies makes up for dissatisfaction with work. Don't torture yourself if technology is not for you, and only you can determine if technology is right for you.

Find out. Talk to people working in the field. Learn what skills are needed. Learn the hazards and disadvantages of the field. Find out how much or how little education is needed to work in a given area. What courses are required? Do you like those courses? Visit potential employers to evaluate the work environment.

This is the "get to know yourself and your skills" job hunting technique proposed by several job counseling books, of which probably the best is *What Color Is Your Parachute,* by Richard N. Bolles. His approach is deceptively simple but it works. If, after going through his career analysis process, nothing intrigues you, then technology is probably not for you. You're lucky to have found out early so that you don't waste any more time.

Creative Options in Technology

That's not to say that you cannot be creative in combining your skills with technical expertise and experience. For some, working as a commercial artist for a computer company is as rewarding as working for a commercial art studio—and is often more lucrative. Work as a pension specialist, secretary or audio-visual expert is the same with a high technology company as with any business. You may also combine your skills with something that's never been done before . . . and in fact have better luck applying it at high technology companies than others. The high technology industry grew from—and continues to foster—many small entrepreneurs who have new ideas or methods of doing things. As Bolles says: "I truly believe if there is a job you want to do, you ought to identify it and go out and find if it exists. If not, invent it."

No matter what their specialty, many opportunities exist for entrepreneurs in high technology. In Silicon Valley, the hotbed of semiconductors and

Making computers easier for the layman to use is one of the major challenges to realizing its potential faced by the computer industry. One of the easy-to-use techniques is a touch screen, in which users point to an easily understood symbol on the screen rather than pushing a button on a specialized control panel. (Courtesy of MicroTouch)

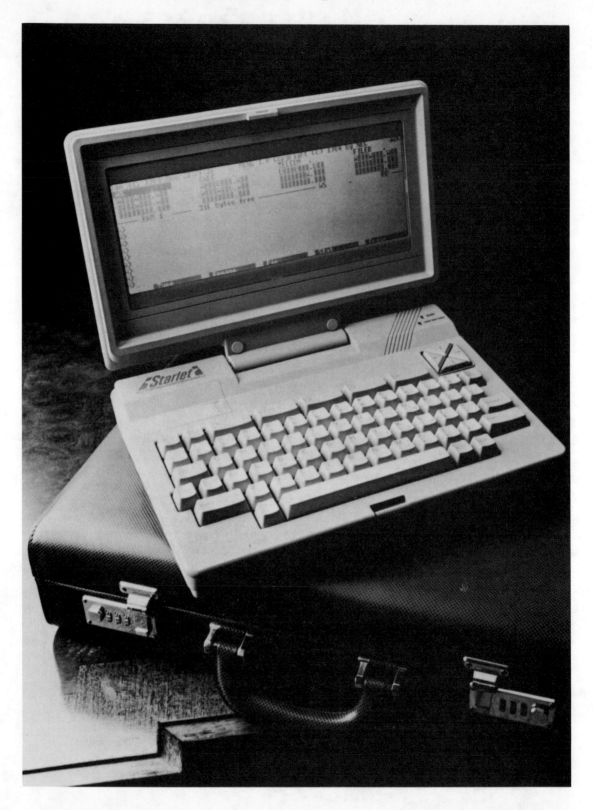

So small they fit into briefcases, today's portable computers open new ways of doing business—for example, for traveling sales agents. This lap-top computer has a built-in modem so that users can reach their main offices or on-line data bases. (Courtesy of NEC Home Electronics Inc., USA)

personal computer technologies, small service firms in public relations, advertising and personnel recruiting have been enormously successful. This doesn't include the many small electronics and components firms which originally sprouted in Silicon Valley, and helped it grow into what it is today.

Everyone is searching for answers to what's ahead tomorrow, next year, 10 years from now. Each individual has to find his or her own path through the evolution of job opportunities. You must research, talk to people and beat the pavement. You have to find out for yourself what's going on in the world, particularly your corner of it. No one can do that work except you, not even this book. You have to analyze yourself after gathering information, and decide whether or not high technology is for you. Even after that decision much more work and study is needed to find the right job for you in high technology industries. This book is a beginning in that learning process. It's also a process in which perseverance is important. Believe in your decisions, don't be discouraged, and keep moving and growing.

The good news remains: Many exciting, high-paying high tech jobs exist. Join the action—and fun.

1. George T. Silvestri, John M. Lukasiewicz and Marcus E. Einstein. "Occupational Employment Projections through 1995." *Monthly Labor Review* (U.S. Department of Labor, Bureau of Labor Statistics: Washington, DC), November 1983, pp. 44–46.
2. Betty Holcomb. "The New Economy." *The Tarrytown Letter*, April 1985, p. 13.

2

TRAINING AND EDUCATION

Education is critical for working in technology-related careers. Because technology-related jobs require special skills, it's almost impossible, even in the high tech factory, to land a good job without training and/or special education. Jobs increasingly require a four-year college degree just to get in the door. To comprehend and enjoy the work demands specialty training, usually in technical disciplines such as engineering or computer science.

The ante keeps going up. Jobs demand more and more education and exposure to the field, especially the top paying ones. It was once possible to land a good job working in computers or as a cardiology technician with as little as 6–12 months' specialized training/education. That happens less frequently today. As opportunities tighten up for various reasons, educational requirements increase.

Don't panic. There are still many jobs that only require a high school diploma. Of course, additional college training beyond high school doesn't hurt. With the deterioration of the U.S. educational system, today's junior or community college training equals high school preparation of 20 years ago.

What's important when facing a technology-related job is not to be afraid of a job just because computers are involved or because it's different from the work you know. There's nothing about jobs involving robots or personal computers or medical lasers that you can't handle.

WHICH PATH?

Identify what you like to do, what special skills you have and what tasks you are good at. Through reading about jobs, talking with people in the field and visiting possible work sites you will learn about prospective job fields and what skills you will need. The next step is to learn what training and academic credentials are necessary for which jobs. Make sure you know approximately the kind of job you want so that you can take the necessary courses. Remember also that certain positions require no training or special education. This is true of certain operations positions, word processing jobs and data entry jobs. Such positions require skills you may already possess, typing or drafting, for instance. In some cases employers provide training.

Because many technology-related career jobs do require training, however, the longer the course of study required, the more crucial the right training is. You are investing money in the program and school, and postponing earnings while you get an education. Attend the best school you can find no matter what the level or job you're after. Employers put a premium on better schools. By aiming high you may find you're more talented than you think!

LEVELS OF EDUCATION

Picking the right level of education to aim for is not only tricky, but may have ramifications later as to how much progress you make in your career. To know yourself and what each level of education qualifies you for is important. Training and education break down into these areas:

1. On-the-job training and retraining programs.
2. Vocational training (less than 2 years) at either a private school or publicly supported program. Medical-related courses at this level are often offered by public and private hospitals.
3. Two-year programs—usually vocational in orientation—available through either private schools, hospitals or public vocational or community colleges.
4. Four-year college degrees in a high tech field such as electrical engineering or computer science.
5. Four-year college programs in business in order to work within a high technology industry or with users in information processing.
6. Four-year college degrees in liberal arts.
7. Master's and Ph.D. degrees.

On-the-Job Training

It's become increasingly common for companies to transfer employees into their more technical departments by either providing training or training on the job. This is an important opportunity that job hunters shouldn't overlook. If you are now working for a company with more technical, higher paying departments, you can probably transfer to them if you're dedicated to the new field, and if your present boss can be convinced that moving you is in the company's interest. (The latter may be the more difficult point.) First find out how the transfer might be accomplished. Talk to others who have done it or to the personnel or human resources department. Of course, numerous complications may arise, but the point is to try. Your best opportunities may be in your front yard.

Vocational Training Schools

Landing a high paying job in a high technology field without having a four-year degree is still possible. The hint: The more vocational and technically oriented the job, the better. The Bureau of Labor Statistics states that an additional 160,000 computer operators will be needed by the year 1990. The number of peripheral equipment operators will rise by 63%. The number of computer technicians will double, to 108,000, by the end of the 1980s.

For most jobs in technology, vocational or basic electronics know-how leads to the entry-level jobs in the field, e.g., robot technician, computer operator, biomedical equipment technician. A robot technician or computer-aided design (CAD) system operator may find that the only training is at a specially designed program at a junior college in communities with nearby industries using robots or CAD systems.

Certain jobs do not require a college education, although a two-year program helps. You can get your training at private/proprietary schools or at local community colleges. Determining if a school is qualified is a major challenge. The problem is compounded when you are bombarded with advertisements and promotions for schools you know nothing about. Some schools are more interested in your federally insured loan payments than they are in your training and job placement. Such schools are often advertised on late-night television, matchbook covers and subway and bus posters. Other schools are highly reputable and do an excellent job of preparing students for the real job market. They have to because that's their business.

"Let the buyer beware" when picking training for high technology fields. This applies more to privately run, for-profit schools, but it is relevant as well for non-profit programs. If the program is not appropriate for you, you're wasting your time. Just because a school is "accredited," "approved," "approved for veteran's benefits" or "registered" doesn't mean it is of top quality. Such accreditation means nothing if the accreditors are irrelevant or non-existent, and so-called accrediting agencies seldom take action against a private school for not meeting quality standards. ("Approved for veterans benefits" means only that the school will take your veteran's loan check.) Despite the limitations of accreditation, however, it is important if you plan to continue your education and want to transfer credits, say from a two-year to a four-year college. The four-year college usually requires graduation from an accredited two-year school.

The most important factor about any vocational training program is whether or not it will help you get a job. The best schools give you the best odds. The low-quality schools slow you down because you may waste 6–18 months on irrelevant training. Check out the school you are interested in very carefully. If you are deciding on schools, investigate several. This is hard work, but don't be discouraged. The end result is critical to your future.

1. Visit the school. Meet the administrators and if possible the instructors. Look at the students, facilities, computer room and classrooms.
2. Talk with students at the schools you are considering. Are they satisfied with the training or education they're getting? Do they respect the teachers? Are they enthusiastic, or do they cut classes?
3. Get the names of graduates who have jobs. Contact them. What kind of job did they find? Are they satisified with their training? What salary are they earning?
4. Ask for the school's most recent results. How many students started the most recent completed term? How many graduated? How many found jobs, and what kind of jobs did they find?

Facilities

No matter what level of schooling you pursue, it's important to be trained on the latest equipment and have access to it. Make sure enough machines are available for all the students. Hands-on experience is invaluable with hardware, and waiting in line on a system is not useful. When working with equipment hands-on laboratory time or actual experience in a clinical situation with a qualified supervisor is much more valuable than books and classroom presentations. For example, anyone can sit in a classroom and write computer code. The question is whether or not it will run on the computer? To answer that a current, well outfitted computer has to be available.

Increasing numbers of corporations are donating equipment to schools in their specialities, such as medical systems or computer-aided design systems. The arrangement is mutually beneficial: The schools get the hardware they need; the employers get a pool of persons experienced on their systems.

Tuition, Grants, Loans

Next you must investigate costs and the availability of loans and other student financial aid. Find out all tuition and schooling charges. What are the terms of payment? Do you pay extra for books and equipment? Are there special fees for recreation or out of state tuition? Can tuition be refunded if for some unexpected reason you cannot attend? If you have to drop out during the term or program, can you get a partial refund? Can you make up missed classes? What government grant and loan programs are available? If you do accept a school loan through the institution, make sure you can afford it and that the terms are reasonable. Keep up with the latest policies and legislative action on loans and grants, since these change frequently.

Private or Proprietary Schools

Private or proprietary schools are the most prevalent providers of short (6, 9, 12, 18 or 24 month) courses for a set fee. In electronics these courses, usually 18 or 24 months, prepare you for basic-level electronics technician work: repair of computers, communications systems, sophisticated weapons or almost any machine with electronic circuitry. In the computer-word processing field the courses prepare you for operations jobs such as peripheral equipment operator, cardiology technician, computer operator, marketing support representative. In most proprietary schools students attend classes, although self-study courses do exist in which students work at their own speed.

Schools vary immensely in quality, so investigate them carefully and thoroughly. Proprietary schools are in business to make money. Their admissions counselors are also salespersons who may be paid based on how many students (and government backed loans) they recruit. Even if proprietary schools administer an admissions or aptitude test, be careful. This test may be only to boost your confidence that you can handle the technical material, and thus will be encouraged to sign up.

Installing new computer models such as IBM's latest 3090 mainframe is a major part of a computer technician's job. Often the work is done on weekends so that daily operations are not disrupted. (Courtesy of International Business Machines Corporation)

Although many graduates of proprietary schools receive jobs upon course completion, others spend the money, successfully complete the program, and sit at home unemployed. If your training is inadequate or inappropriate, employers will look elsewhere.

Two-year Vocational Programs

Good two-year vocational programs at private schools offer excellent training primarily in electronics and data processing. Classes are generally small and taught by good teachers, who are often better paid than their counterparts at publicly supported institutions. Good schools are likely to have the latest equipment available and, more importantly, are aggressive in helping their students find jobs.

At public vocational schools, primarily junior and community colleges, the quality of training also varies immensely. Local employers look to these electronics and computer technician programs as a source of new employees. If the schools do not yet have specialties, companies often work with the institution to initiate special programs. In the Detroit area, for instance, community colleges offer vocational training in robotics, especially robotics repair.

When looking for training in either basic electronics/computer technology or health technology, community colleges or teaching hospitals are excellent places to consider. Colleges frequently cooperate with local hospitals to train health care professionals.

Special Programs

Recognizing the need for more trained technicians and technology workers, many government agencies and institutions have run special, usually short-term courses to prepare or retrain workers for specialized fields. For example, the National Science Foundation has offered an 18 month course to retrain women with non-technical degrees for computer work. Graduates receive a certificate, and sometimes their work can be applied towards credits at the same or other institutions.

Some special programs are offered repeatedly; others are one-time only. Information about such special training usually is available from local school districts, school counselors or public librarians. Courses specially designed to bring women and minorities into technology careers are excellent entry points. Courses for women recognize that they may not have the same educational background as men. There are occasionally announcements for such programs; check your local library, school system or women's group or women's resource center. With the declining need for computer workers, and the changing stance of the federal government, these courses are not as numerous as they were in the 1970s. They're still out there, however, and bear looking into.

At one university special programs leading to a data processing diploma are given in computer technology, console operations and computer maintenance. The 16 credit program, which is available on a day, night or weekend schedule, prepares students for entry-level positions. Depending on the student's success, the credits may also be applied to a degree program at the school. Such students may have some college, but probably not a four-year degree.

This school also offers a certificate in computer programming with language specialty. This includes a basic concepts course, operating systems course and specialization in one of the business languages. There's also a certificate course in programming microprocessors, in systems programming and in data base management systems. All these courses include extensive workshop sessions.

In the past, special certificate programs were an ideal way for persons to move into technology jobs from non-technical careers. Today this is changing. Employers in some fields hold out for the best educated students, or demand experience that many don't have—except for those studying to upgrade their skills. The certificate programs thus are not as useful or relevant as they used to be.

Two-year College Degrees

For many high tech jobs a two-year or associate degree from a hospital or junior/community college provides an excellent career base. Such a degree is job oriented, and so students have worked on the skills they will need to do the work. This is especially true in data processing courses.

Two-year degrees have both positive and negative sides to them. Because students are prepared for specific jobs, employers are eager to hire them. In data processing, employers complain that four-year graduates are preoccupied with the esoterics of computer science and not interested in applying computers in business. But because of limited training, two-year-degree program graduates may find themselves stuck in low to middle range technical jobs. For many workers this is fine—they learn on the job. For those who want to grow and move ahead in the organization, however, two-year degrees may be limiting. They may need more education, perhaps by getting it on their own time, or, in rare cases, on their employer's time and bill.

Associate degree course work usually emphasizes hands-on work—programming in business data processing, for example. For more sophisticated, technical programs in computer science, the student will probably have to transfer to a four-year school to attain a computer science major. Here again, it's important to know what a program actually delivers, and most important, what you want from your schooling. Just because a community college near you offers a two-year degree in office technologies doesn't mean it's the right program for you. Some proprietary schools also offer two-year associate degrees in occupational sciences and in technical programs.

Today, it's very important that students learn a computer language that is being used in business. For example, here's a recommended mix of courses for a two-year business data processing curriculum. (Other programs should offer a similar variety.)

1. A data processing introductory course covering terminology, number systems, flowcharts, operating systems and some exposure to applications programming languages.
2. Two semesters of COBOL, the most common business programming language.
3. Two semesters of an assembler, a programming language that works closely with the computer hardware.
4. One course in an advanced topic such as project management, operating systems, data bases or systems design.
5. Courses in business principles, accounting and mathematics.

Spanish Language Programs

The universal language of computers is English. Students whose primary language is Spanish and who are interested in technology and computer-related work are often hampered and frustrated professionally until they learn more English. This doesn't need to be the case. A growing number of schools offer computer courses in Spanish, especially at the community college and certificate program level. By learning computer operations or basic programming in bilingual classes, Spanish-speaking students kill two birds with one stone: Learn data processing and English simultaneously.

In Manhattan Community College in New York City, one-third of the students enrolled in computer courses are in bilingual ones. Other universities in New York City and in other cities offer evening programming and operations certificate courses in Spanish. Students typically prepare for entry-level assignments in IBM hardware environments. One New York professor reports that Spanish-speaking students have done well in computer-related jobs, particularly in operations.

Four-year Degrees

Universities are now feeling the upheavals in computer training. The Massachusetts Institute of Technology (MIT), where computer science is closely linked to the electrical engineering degree, is limiting the number of students accepted to its highly prestigious and rigorous computer science program. In computer science and electrical engineering courses, the key courses needed for new technology careers, there are too many students and too few professors. Schools simply cannot compete with industry in salaries and even opportunities such as working on the latest equipment or forging ahead with new research. Some of these dilemmas will be alleviated as our country comes to appreciate its technology resource within its universities. Certainly the Department of Defense is once again pumping money into technological research in the universities, which always has fallout for the computer-related industries. (The early computer industry was fertilized by defense spending during and shortly after World War II.)

How much education is too much? This is a question that only you can answer. Let's examine the options. Two-year degrees generally lead to jobs that pay $20,000–35,000. Earning more than $35,000 without a four-year degree is extraordinarily difficult, although it can be done. Four-year degrees lead to higher paying professional jobs.

Choosing the Right College

Picking the right four-year program grows increasingly complicated as more students want in, options become available . . . and numbers of places lessen. The first important distinction to be made is between a business oriented program or a technically oriented program. Then the choices become boggling. The most common programs seem to be: computer science, information systems, management information systems and business information systems.

Learn what courses you'll be studying in each program, who will be teaching them, what kind of hardware and software will be available to the students, and what jobs you'll be prepared for before spending both your money and four years of your life there. Study the catalogs from programs and schools you are interested in. Compare several schools. Talk with students presently enrolled or graduates of the colleges you're studying. Talk with faculty, administrators, or counselors—after all, that's their job.

Information processing, business data processing or data processing courses are found most often in business schools. Established in the late 1970s and early 1980s, such programs are increasingly popular. They include courses in programming but are geared toward the use of computers in business.

In health care, universities are also recognizing the influx of computers and new technologies, and are starting to offer cross-discipline courses which blend computer science and medicine, or the biological sciences and technology.

The wellsprings of technical expertise for all new technologies are the engineering-computer science programs, typically engineering schools, or departments of mathematics, physics or applied mathematics. The sought-after degree is a B.S. in electrical engineering or a B.S. in computer science.

The main study routes for obtaining a technology-related degree are in the following areas:

1. Computer science
2. Computer engineering
3. Electrical engineering
4. Mechanical engineering
5. Manufacturing/industrial engineering

6. Health physics/nuclear engineering
7. Management information systems
8. Computer information systems

As noted in Chapter 1, computers are the key to many jobs in technology, and having training in computer science and/or electrical engineering and/or information management is very useful. Even if you're uncertain about which technology-related path is for you, take as many of the latest courses as possible. Stay at the cutting edge of the latest technological developments, in school as well as on the job. Today schools are adding more and more specialties to their curriculum: A current popular example is telecommunications.

Computer science: Computer science is often used as an umbrella term for everything associated with computers. In academics it is a very specific discipline of the development of software that makes the computer function, such as the operating system. Computer science majors design software such as language translators, data base management systems and other intricate programming and systems aids. Computer science generally doesn't have anything to do with business.

The degree program in computer science includes courses covering such areas as introduction to discrete structures, numerical calculus, data structures, programming languages, computer organization and systems programming. It's not uncommon for graduates of computer science programs to dream of building their own computer, as Tracy Kidder told in his *The Soul of the New Machine.* This book remains one of the best descriptions of the work of computer scientists.

Computer science students learn programming not as a vocational skill, but as a tool towards designing a computer. They're most likely to study Fortran, which is mostly used in scientific/engineering applications. At schools with artificial intelligence (AI) programs they may explore AI basics or get involved in AI research projects. Academics are still divided in their opinions as to whether such a computer science curriculum is too narrow. One side proposes computer science majors, even the most brilliant technically, should be schooled in how computers are used, and even in the ramifications of their use on society. Businesspeople certainly agree that computer science majors are not what, say, a bank data processing department needs. When businesses have hired these extremely talented, but highly technical computer experts, they have ended up with overly sophisticated systems that no average person can decipher.

Computer science programs are found under the auspices of an engineering school, within schools of arts and sciences or in departments of physics, mathematics or applied mathematics. Top computer science programs include those at MIT, Stanford, Carnegie-Mellon, University of Illinois at Champaign/Urbana and University of California at Berkeley. (The first three are also leaders in robotics research and development.)

Computer engineering: Within engineering schools the path for students who want to work on all facets of computer design is called computer

Technology is all about new processes: Here's the latest for computer printers—a flexible dot band that zips across computer printouts. (Courtesy of International Business Machines Corporation)

engineering. This encompasses the design of electronic boards, microprocessors and circuitry, as well as the architecture for the system as a whole. The computer engineering option might include courses in digital integrated circuits, computer architecture and electronic instruments such as those used for testing.

Electrical engineering: The degree most sought after by high technology companies today is the BSEE, bachelor of science in electrical engineering. As computers are introduced into almost every technology-related product, companies need electronics experts to accomplish not only the design and development, but often the initial research. This is the work of the electrical engineer, who finds many jobs centering on computers and, more recently, on telecommunications.

BSEEs work on everything from robots to semiconductor design to supercomputers to telephone switches—in fact, all the topics presented in this book. BSEEs study microprocessor design, circuit design and rotating machinery and control systems—courses that also prepare them to work with power equipment or other electrical equipment and systems not related to computers. The best engineering schools for this study include Purdue, University of Minnesota, Princeton, Cornell, University of Michigan and Northwestern.

Mechanical engineering: As computers are integrated into more machines, especially in the factory, mechanical engineers get involved in high technology projects. Mechanical engineering deals with the largest diversity of engineering problems, from the use of energy, the design and production of tools, the study of materials as they apply to design, the analysis of mechanical, thermal and fluid systems and to the automation of all of these. Practically any product with moving parts requires a mechanical engineer at some point.

This work often includes the use of computers, microprocessors and computer-aided design systems. Engineering schools are integrating mechanical engineering into programs in computer integrated manufacturing or health physics for the design of medical instrumentation. Mechanical engineers take courses covering such areas as electric circuits and fields, computer applications, dynamics of machinery, design theory and design engineering. Needless to say, mechanical engineers who understand the use of computers in the new technologies are much sought after by industry.

Manufacturing/industrial/systems engineering: Industrial/systems engineers are the links between technology and management. Manufacturing engineers emphasize the design of factories and other production systems. Their goal is to use engineering to analyze and design systems that integrate technical, economic and social behavioral factors into industrial, service, social or government systems. They specialize in fields of operations research, management science, systems engineering, methods, organization and planning. Industrial engineering programs use engineering sciences, basic sciences and social sciences for sophisticated systems analysis and systems design. Thus they are needed both by technology developers and designers and by technology users. Industrial engineers study man-machine systems, systems theory, human factors engineering and operations and facilities design.

Health/physics/nuclear engineering: Although schools differ, many offer programs that apply nuclear engineering and radiation to health problems and health care systems. The challenge is to both protect man and the environment from radiation and chemical pollutants and to develop products which use radiation beneficially. Areas studied include radiation physics, physics of radiation therapy and environmental impact of nuclear power stations.

Since nuclear engineering is in disrepute because of public disfavor and nuclear accidents and threats, the field is not growing. However, the fallout—in the public reaction sense—has heightened interest in the flip side of the coin: clean up and regulation of pollution of all kinds. The health field, of course, continues to grow, and supports the need for those who use radiation positively.

Management information systems: Management information systems (MIS) programs are most often found in schools of business or business administration. Their goal is the application of computers in business and government organizations. The MIS graduate is geared to look at the big picture, not at one computer system but at all the organization's systems—it's common for them to have many.

At the four-year level MIS programs are targeted to the person who wants to design systems and eventually manage them. MIS curricula view an organization as a complex whole composed of parts—the systems approach. The glue to this system is computer-stored information. As organizations grow, split and become more complex, people in the organization need either more, less or different information.

The primary academic emphasis is on business and organizational studies, the secondary on technical computer know-how. (Students often take basic computer courses, however, in the computer science department.) The latest topic is the use of microcomputers and data communications within large organizations. MIS courses cover organizational theory, decision theory, quantitative business analysis, systems design, data administration and informational systems policy.

Computer information systems: Trying to clear up the confusion surrounding the number, content and quality of studies in data processing and computer science, the Data Processing Management Association (DPMA) (see Appendix 1) has instituted, and continues to revise, a Computer Information Systems (CIS) curriculum. CIS combines computer expertise with an understanding of the business framework for computer applications. Graduates go on to manage computer-based information systems in large corporations.

In an institution's business school students are prepared for entry-level positions in applications programming and systems analysis. Coursework includes applications development, structured systems analysis and design, data base program development, managerial accounting principles, finance and office automation. DPMA is vigorously urging more institutions to adopt the CIS curriculum.

Advanced Degrees

Most of the above four-year programs lead to masters' or Ph.D. degrees. Advanced study is demanding and highly sophisticated, since the technology itself expands and becomes more complex. For students who are truly interested in a field an advanced degree opens many doors. Semiconductor and computer manufacturers offer salaries as high as $100,000 to experienced electronics engineers with advanced degrees.

At the doctorate level the curriculum is usually customized to the interests of the individual student, and usually involves a research specialty of the school such as robotics or artificial intelligence. Ph.D.s are primarily sought by those interested in teaching, or who want to do more theoretical research work both within the corporate and university environments.

As technology grows more complex, even organizations that have gotten along with less knowledgeable engineers have had to beef up their research and development staffs. In many cases they have raided top universities for Ph.D.-level teachers and researchers. Other corporations sponsor visiting professor programs whereby their experienced professionals and technical specialists receive sabbaticals to teach at colleges, frequently in their own communities. Other companies sponsor chair/endowments to attract more talent in particular technical fields.

PROFESSIONAL CERTIFICATION

One of the ongoing dilemmas of high technology careers is establishing levels of expertise and professionalism. The variety of course programs and job descriptions has led to disagreement about, for example, what a programmer does and what training and credentials are necessary to become a programmer.

In the health care field certification or license requirements are much more critical to advancement. In some hospitals and organizations technologists cannot be hired without certification (See Chapter 10.) Certification is a sticky issue in health care. Not only does certification maintain high education and qualification requirements, it also limits the number of professionals in the field and thus works to the advantage of those already hired. Government agencies also get involved in the qualification establishing process, especially for technologies such as radioactive treatments that could potentially injure patients.

In data processing this issue is being addressed by the Institute for Certification of Computer Professionals (ICCP), headquartered in Chicago (see Appendix 1). ICCP is an independent organization of professionals in data processing that is working to improve the industry by setting standards for professionalism. ICCP designs, sponsors and administers tests, awarding certificates or certification to those who pass. On a volunteer basis and for a fee of several hundred dollars, ICCP administers a test for data processing managers and programmers. Successful completion leads to a certificate in data processing (CDP) or a certificate in computer programming (CCP), and these initials occasionally appear after DP professionals' names.

Such certification efforts generally are undertaken by serious technicians, since few companies have come out one way or the other on the certification question. Business and technology changes so fast that certification may be an ongoing battle.

3
DATA PROCESSING

Today's world is a computer world! You cannot receive a bill or board a plane—even a train—without the assistance of a mainframe computer. You cannot make a phone call even to your mother across town without it being relayed through a message switching system run by a computer. You cannot learn the latest weather forecast or enter a state lottery without a large computer system humming somewhere, often a long distance away.

When one thinks about a career in computers, the first job that comes to mind is that of programmer. The bulk of people—and the ones most critical to production—needed to run computer centers are programmers who work with software. For the last 20 years there's been a shortage of programmers, but no more. Today supply has caught up with demand. Companies now demand experience from their junior programmers. They are unwilling to hire them directly out of a vocationally oriented program, and even out of a four-year college program in business data processing.

The other pressing demand within data processing is for operations workers who physically tend the hardware, and feed the initial data into the computer. Their ranks continue to grow as the numbers of installations increase. This chapter will first look at opportunities in operations and data entry and then in software and systems management.

Computer jobs have not gone away . . . as both the Bureau of Labor Statistics (BLS) continues to report and the stream of newspaper classified ads demonstrates. *It's the rules and requirements to entry—and what the jobs entail—that have changed.*

OPERATIONS: JOBS WITH HARDWARE

Even the most sophisticated mainframe computer equipped with efficient software programs does not function without people. Computer operations is traditionally a strong opportunity for persons without high school diplomas, although increasingly some college work is being required.

In addition, this area is buffeted by changes in technology and in data processing procedures:

- Keypunch operators (so essential to the computer room in the 1950s and early 1960s) have been almost entirely replaced by data

Business computer systems can be just as complex as those for scientific applications. Pictured is the operations center for the United Airlines Apollo travel agent management and reservations system. With 7 mainframe computers and 540 storage disks, it is one of the world's largest computer systems. (Courtesy of United Airlines and International Business Machines Corporation)

entry operators. These in turn may ultimately be replaced by voice input technologies. The Bureau of Labor Statistics (BLS) projects an increase in the number of computer operators and peripheral equipment operators, but a decline in the number of data entry operators. Between now and 1995 their numbers will decline by about 15%. They're already being replaced by other input media and devices such as optical character recognition (OCR) devices.

- Many companies are outfitting their entire staffs with computer terminals or personal computers (PCs) so that it's no longer necessary, say, for the information first to be written on paper by a customer service clerk and then encoded for the computer by the data entry clerk. That customer service representative now has a terminal, and requests are entered on-line.

- Computers are getting smarter and so have less need for human attention. Self-diagnosis systems, in which a computer reports its own problems, at least the easily detectable ones, are common.
- Computers are better engineered and easier to operate and less subject to failure.
- The increase of smaller computers (such as PCs) means that users are their own operators, eliminating the need for additional operators.

Two other trends are afoot. Many companies are getting into computers for the first time, and require operations personnel. Others are dispersing computer power via distributed systems, or networks of terminals, so that more personnel are required and in different locations.

Salary

Many factors help determine salaries in data processing, but the major ones are geography, size of installation, industry and, of course, experience. Depending on any one of or any combination of these factors, salaries vary markedly from reported averages. Also important to consider in looking at surveys of salaries is who are the ones counting? Surveys conducted by recruiting firms present higher figures than

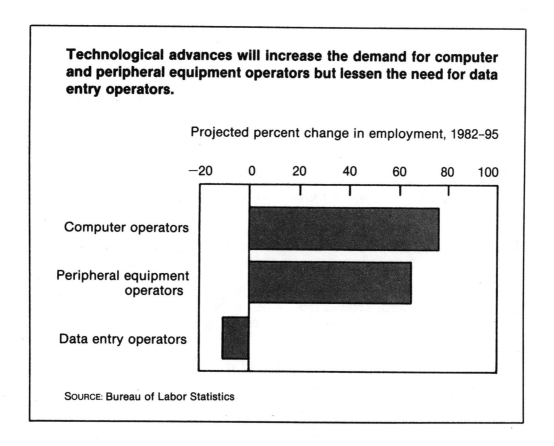

Technological advances will increase the demand for computer and peripheral equipment operators but lessen the need for data entry operators.

Projected percent change in employment, 1982–95

SOURCE: Bureau of Labor Statistics

magazine surveys compiled by traditional research methods. The recruiters are looking to attract business and candidates, and it's in their interest to report favorable salaries.

Geography: The traditional reasons why salaries are higher in certain regions and cities apply to data processing salaries: the higher cost of living and the shortage of labor. *Infosystems*, a magazine for DP managers, charted the position of junior programmer, showing a national average of $20,384. Salaries ranged from $17,524 in West North Central states (North Dakota, Minnesota, South Dakota, Nebraska and Iowa) to a high of $22,568 in the Mountain states (Utah, Montana, Idaho, Nevada, Wyoming, Colorado, Arizona and New Mexico). In the Mid-Atlantic (New York, Pennsylvania, New Jersey) pay was $21,632.[1] The pay for more experienced senior programmers ranged from a high in the Pacific states (Washington, Oregon, California) to a low in the East South Central (Kentucky, Tennessee, Mississippi and Alabama).[2]

The Robert Half International personnel organization has developed a formula for geographic variances: For salaries under $50,000, add 5% to the national average if the job is in a city with one million or more population. There's less discrepancy for salaries over $50,000.[3]

Size of Installation: The size of a DP shop is determined either by the number of employees or by the type of computer system used (these designations generally parallel IBM's range of systems). Most small shops run a small IBM system such as the System/34/36 and have less than 10 employees. The mid-sized shop is probably running an IBM mid-sized system such as the 4300 series and has less than 40 employees. A large shop usually runs an IBM 3033 or 30BX large mainframe—in many cases several—and has more than 40 employees.

At small installations the Half company reported a $16,000–20,000 range; at medium shops $19,000–23,000; and at large installations, $19,000–25,000.[4] How big the employer is, especially in data processing operations, affects employee salaries. According to *Datamation*, an average programmer earned $21,286 at a small to mid-sized installation and $25,692 at a large data center.[5]

Industry: Data processing expertise is valued less or more depending on the industry. An average programmer earned $16,500 in the services industry (for example, in retailing) and $23,000 at a bank, *Datamation* reported.[6] Industries highly dependent on computers such as banking and computer service bureau companies tend to pay their DP employees more handsomely.

There is a continual cycle in the data processing industry. In the late 1960s salaries soared. From 1969–71 business cooled and so did pay: the ups with double-digit increases and downs with sometimes minimal merit increases. The cycle continues.

Note about unions: In the late 1970s and early 1980s labor unions tried to organize programmers and low- to middle-level data center employees. In a handful of cases the unions were successful, but the general slow-down of union interest in the mid-1980s cramped that effort.

Titles

Job titles vary enormously within the data processing industry. Adding "junior" or "trainee" to the title indicates that the employee has less than six months on the job. "Junior" in a job title indicates an entry-level position either in a particular department or within the job hierarchy at a particular organization. "Trainee" at the end of a title indicates the person is new to the organization or field.

Note about promotions: How you dress is important in data processing. If men or women work, or want to work, for a conservative company, they must dress conservatively. If you want to move up the career ladder, you have to communicate that to your superiors. Dress as if you already have the next job you want, and the odds are better that you'll get it.

DATA ENTRY

Without data there's no data processing. The workers who electronically encode information into computer readable form are data entry operators. In the early days of computing, data was entered via paper cards punched with the binary combinations of "1s" and "0s"; the operators of these machines were keypunch operators. Today computers use primarily magnetic input media, tapes and disks, and keypunch operators are rare.

Companies now are doing away with intermediate data entry because of shortcut methods, or because other employees are entering the data earlier in the process. Companies found data entry labor-intensive, and encouraged manufacturers to develop machines to take over much of this work. Long term prospects for data entry clerks thus, are glum. Over the next 10 years the number of data entry operators is expected to drop by 11% from 320,000 to approximately 286,000.

Employers are cueing employees to the new situation. Salaries for inexperienced data entry operators dropped about 2% between 1983 and 1984, according to *Infosystems* magazine.[7] This doesn't mean, however, the end to jobs in data entry. Because part-time employment is so popular there's high turnover in data entry positions; one in seven workers is part-time. The need for data entry operators will thus not disappear, and computer operations keep growing. Moreover, the work of keyboarding, or typing in, information is often an entry point within an organization to other positions—word processing or computer operations, for instance.

Data entry operators work at machines with typewriter consoles and 10-key numeric pads, and transform information written in English into coded media for the computer. There may also be a VDT (Video Display Terminal) for verifying data. The data usually is put on a magnetic tape (key to tape) or on a disk or diskette (key to disk). (Diskettes are magnetic storage media that resemble flexible phonograph records.)

Data entry operators often work in shifts, and spend continuous periods in front of a terminal. Often many operators work in one large room, and such conditions have made them open to unions and other organizations. The hierarchy within data entry, which depends on experience and skill level, is junior key entry operator, data entry operator, senior key entry operator, lead key entry operator, key entry supervisor.

The **junior key entry operator,** with less than 2 years' experience, operates both the data entry machine and the verifying system—often contained in the same machine and used to verify his or her own work and others. The junior may do related clerical work.

The **data entry operator** with more than 2 years' experience is capable of handling all the machines and processes.

The **senior key entry operator** works under supervision, but may instruct other operators on routine assignments and often trains new employees.

The **lead key entry operator** assists in supervising data entry, including the scheduling of work and people. This is a big task if there are 200 data entry operators as in large insurance companies. The lead operator also trains and instructs.

The **data entry supervisor** or **key entry supervisor** plans, schedules and supervises data entry and verifying activities, and assigns people to carry out these activities. He or she maintains all the related files, and reports to the DP manager or manager in charge of data within the company.

Training: A high school diploma is usually all that's required for a data entry position, and employers provide on-the-job training or enroll operators in courses by the equipment manufacturer. Companies look for persons with good attitudes who accurately type 30 words per minute. In-house training takes from 50 to 100 hours, and be leery of any training such as that at a private school that runs longer.

Salary: Junior operators begin at $11,400 ($220 a week) with the salary range from $11,200 to $12,400. Important note: Most operators work by the hour and are eligible for overtime, in which case reported salaries may be less than what an individual takes home. Experienced operators average $13,000, but some make as much as $16,000.

PERIPHERAL EQUIPMENT OPERATORS

The two large categories of workers in hardware are peripheral equipment operators and computer operators. Peripherals are output devices for computer data, and the term includes printers, disk storage devices, magnetic tapes and many variations of these. Peripherals are usually attached to computers via heavy cables and depend on the computer to work effectively.

The number of peripheral equipment operators is expected to grow rapidly, although not in great quantities, between now and 1995. Today they number 49,000, and the estimate is for 80,000 in 10 years, a 63% jump BLS attributes to the increase in the use of computers.

New peripherals that handle several tasks are being added to today's distributed processing systems. They include laser printers that produce copies from signals sent by larger computers over telephone lines. (Courtesy of International Business Machines Corporation)

A **tape librarian** manages hundreds of tapes and disk packs that store data for future use by the computer system. (Large companies have rooms of these tapes and disks.) The tape librarian not only inventories all the tapes, but makes sure the correct tape is in the hands of the operator when he needs to run it on the computer. Librarians must work in concert with the lead operator so that the correct tapes are available at the right time in the right place. Tape librarians also must be careful that tapes are copied in the event of an emergency. (Some companies store back-up tapes safely away from the data center.) The tapes are often the only record companies have of their financial transactions. In this respect tape librarian is a highly responsible position that can be a stepping stone to a computer operator post.

Requirements: Companies look for high school diplomas from peripheral equipment operators, and additional training and/or experience in computer work. The Armed Forces are a favorite source of this training. The federal government requires a high school diploma unless applicants have had specialized training or experience. In some firms clerical workers, including data entry operators, may be transferred to computer operations. Companies may test potential operators on their ability to work quickly and accurately, and test aptitude for computer work, such as the ability to reason logically.

Salary: Tape librarians average $15,600. Some earn as little as $11,000 and others as much as $19,000.

An **input/output control manager** works closely with operators to ensure that the correct input is available for the computer. Computers also produce internal records of what has been processed, and the I/O manager makes sure that scheduled work has been completed by cross-checking reports. For instance, when 4 large mainframes are running 24 hours a day, it's no small feat to schedule and keep track of the work being processed. The control manager also supplies operators with appropriate job commands so that the work can be run. (This assumes that a tape librarian has already made necessary data tapes available.) In a smaller installation this might be handled by one production manager. In the larger shop a lead production control manager or an assistant, a production control clerk, would be in charge.

Requirements: Companies look first for loyal employees and/or those with high school diplomas and experience. Once hired there may be a two week training session; otherwise, peripheral equipment operators learn the job by working with others in the department.

Salary: I/O control managers average $19,000 with the spread from $13,500 in the Midwest to $24,000 on the West Coast.

COMPUTER OPERATIONS

Manufacturers have done much to cut the number of workers needed in the computer room, but they cannot do away with operators entirely. The BLS expects the demand to continue, especially for computer operators. They predict a 76% surge between now and 1995, from 215,000 to an estimated 371,000.

Depending on the size of the data center, a computer operator works with one or many computers and has full or partial responsibility for that operation. The job is not to be underestimated. The computer console is the command center of the data processing room and from there the operator issues commands to the system and tracks what's already underway.

Every day certain programs are scheduled on the computer, but that processing means bringing together the applications software and the actual data to process; the tape librarian and production control manager assist in this. The operator makes it happen. The operator loads the tapes and disks onto the machine which runs them. At the console he or she initiates the processing, and often queues several programs to be run. In the early days of computing, computer consoles were rows and panels of blinking lights as the movies portrayed, but today the operator works from a VDT (Video Display Terminal). Operators must know the extensive operations commands that run the computer. The computer operator, generally with 2–5 years' experience, is competent in all phases of the system and generally works without supervision. Once a program is completed the disks and tapes must be dismounted and the next program readied. Throughout this time the operator logs what's been done and any problems along the way. Operators must also monitor the computer's processing report and maintain records for stores and supplies.

Many companies run shifts, although with faster and cheaper computers they are not as common as they used to be. To staff around the clock some companies have set 3-day shifts in which operators have 3 days on and 4 days off work. This backfires when problems arise, and operators have been known to sleep overnight at the data center. A large international bank in which accounts are updated overnight is a good example of a 24-hour operation.

In the past operators moved into programming jobs, but this is changing as programming becomes more sophisticated and employers have upped the entry barriers to an oversupply of candidates. Computer operators often come from other departments within a company. Recent developments have prompted operators to complain that little career growth exists beyond operations in most companies and they have formed organizations to encourage professionalism in the field.

The typical hierarchy in computer operations runs junior computer operator, computer operator, senior computer operator, lead computer operator, manager of computer operations.

The **junior computer operator** is the newcomer who works closely with senior staffers. Though junior employees may be competent in several phases of operations, they still need guidance and instruction from others, and often work as assistants to experienced operators.

The **senior operator** usually has 5 years of experience and full command of the computer consoles. The senior operator studies program operating instruction sheets in order to determine equipment setup and run operations, and, as necessary, switches in or out auxiliary equipment. When errors are detected or changes needed, the senior operator consults technical personnel, for example, in systems programming. He or she also maintains thorough records of machine performance and production reports.

The **lead operator** is often the assistant manager of computer operations, and has supervisory duties of instructing, assigning, directing and checking the work of other operators. The lead operator assists in assigning personnel and scheduling the computer, and works with other departments to coordinate work flow, especially at the end of the month when many once-a-month programs must be run. Some companies consider this employee a shift supervisor.

The **manager of computer operations** keeps track of all personnel and hardware. In this management position operations and technical knowledge are secondary. Managers of computer operations not only schedule people, processing and hardware use, but also coordinate these with other departments. As many as 100 people report to a computer operations manager, to say nothing of the hundreds of machines under his or her control. The operations manager reports to the DP manager on the status and efficiency of all equipment.

Training: Many operators still learn on the job, but employers look more and more for computer training when hiring operators. Two-year community college or vocational school programs are ideal training grounds.

Requirements: The key to being a good operator is staying ahead of the computer—anticipating the problems, solving them as they happen or heading them off. It's not a simple job since so many things go on simultaneously. With self-diagnosis systems operators are much more involved in service. An operator must have manual dexterity, but that is increasingly a secondary consideration as more operations tasks are taken over by the computer or other machines. What's important is the operator's ability to follow detailed instructions, to listen carefully and to solve problems as they arise. As systems command languages become more complex operators are using the equivalent of a programming language. Operators generally have 2 or more years' experience. In leading installations fewer tapes are being used, and the operator is more concerned with communications systems now supplying the data and with the computer system itself. All this requires more extensive hardware *and* software skills.

Salary: Salaries for computer operators range from $10,000 to $19,000 although one recruiting agency found a high of $23,000. Salaries go as high as $30,000 for lead operators. Managers average $27,000, although one large site reported $50,000 for this management post.

HARDWARE PLANNER

This title has many variations and requirements, depending on the organization. Most hardware planners research hardware options, solicit and evaluate proposals from different vendors, recommend choices to management and then monitor the system installation. The task can be as enormous, however, as setting up an entirely new data processing center or office word processing center, or as simple as recommending the better of two versions of the same piece of equipment or two models from the same vendor. In all cases the hardware solutions must mesh with the software and operating systems being selected by or developed by the programmers and systems analysts.

The planner finds out which manufacturers make which products, usually by meeting with the manufacturers' representatives, and often attends trade shows and conventions where vendors show their wares. Based on the specific needs of the organization, the hardware planner then selects which hardware is best. Since companies keep installing new systems and adding to old ones, there seems to be no immediate end to demand for hardware planners and evaluators.

Hardware planning also offers many opportunities for consultants. For a small company to retain an expensive expert once the hardware is selected and installed doesn't make sense. Thus they hire consultants who charge premium prices because of the specialized nature of the work.

Requirements: Hardware planners must have strong background in data processing and especially be knowledgeable about hardware alternatives. In addition, the planner must listen carefully in order to understand the needs of users they're working for. Planners must also work well with the vendors, cautious of their claims but open to new ideas and processes in order to get the best options for their companies.

Salary: While staff positions usually pay $25,000–40,000, consultants earn $60,000 or more, much like software/programming consultants.

JOBS IN SOFTWARE

Programming continues to be a high growth career track. The BLS counts 226,000 programmers, and by 1995 that number will jump 75 to 80% to 471,000.

Of those 226,000 computer programmers today, 32.5% are women. That percentage will increase over the next 10 years as more and more women enter the labor force. Women are not the only ones who have recognized the potential in a career of working with computers. So many students are flocking to computer science programs that several universities have had to bar their doors to only the most prepared.

When applications programmers were more sought after in the late 1970s and early 1980s, top programmers commonly set themselves up as independent programmers, traveling from project to project. Usually they had an expertise for which companies were willing to pay from $250 to $1,500 a day. Hiring consultants also relieved companies from having to find another project for these workers once the system they were working on was complete.

What Programmers Do

Programmers are translators. They take an assigned task specified in English, and turn it into instructions that the computer/machine can process. Programming entails special languages presented in lines of code, which programmers become adept at manipulating. The popular languages are the following:

1. COBOL (Common Oriented Business Language). It is still the most popular language for business applications if only because so many applications already have been written in it. COBOL consists of about 250 businesslike key words which direct the computer. The American National Standard Institute (ANSI) regularly updates COBOL, and knowing the latest version is important.

2. FORTRAN (FORmula TRANslator). FORTRAN is the common language for developing scientific and engineering-related programs. It does what it says, allowing quick manipulation of mathematical formulas (e.g., computing how strong an airplane wing has to be for a plane to fly within a specified speed range).

3. BASIC (Beginner's All-purpose Symbolic Instruction Code). BASIC has become the language of the personal computer, and has proliferated beyond original hobbyists to the business user. It was originally designed for the small computer.

4. ADA. Named for Augusta Ada Byron (1815–1852) for her work with early mechanical computers, it is being highly promoted by the U.S. Department of Defense (DoD) as a more facile alternative to both COBOL and FORTRAN. So far, however, only DoD—and its numerous contractors—have shown much love for ADA.

5. Assembler. Assembly languages allow the programmer to get at the instructions stored inside the computer. Assembler language instructions are symbolic representations of machine instructions, the binary series of "1s" and "0s," which are translated into electrical charges and actually instruct the computer.

6. RPG II and RPG III (Report Program Generator). Used for business applications, RPG is most common on medium-sized or minicomputers, and used for simple reports that do not require complex programs and are needed quickly.

7. PL/I (Programming Language/I). Written as the definitive alternative to COBOL and FORTRAN, its proponents say it has the best features of many programming languages.

8. APL (A Programming Language). Developed by IBM, APL can also be used on PCs for scientific or more complex application development.

9. Fourth Generation Languages. The above programming languages have proven so slow and clumsy to develop systems with that

organizations have cried for better solutions. Software vendors have heard them and developed what's called the next generation in programming languages, or fourth generation languages (4GL). 4GL take over many of the tedious programming processes. For example, a 4GL programmer can instruct "create screen," and these higher-level languages fill in all the codes needed to create a screen in the program.

10. C. A newer programming language intimately connected to the Unix operating system, C has been developed by Bell Laboratories and is being pushed by American Telephone & Telegraph (AT&T). C and Unix go hand in hand, and for the most part are used on scientifically oriented systems even though C runs on all sized systems.

New Approaches

Tired of re-inventing the wheel every time they have to design and develop a new computer system, many companies now use the building blocks approach. They buy several off-the-shelf packages for portions of the desired application, and then link the package blocks. A related variation of this is the off-the-shelf 4GL programming languages noted above, which allow programmers to customize to a greater degree than strung together packages, but less than if they had written the program from scratch.

Not only does the newcomer to programming need to know the prerequisites (COBOL or FORTRAN, for example), he or she needs to understand and be able to work with these new software development tools. *It's critical to stay abreast of new developments by reading trade publications and attending courses.*

There are two broad categories of programmers (and programming in general): applications programmers and systems programmers. Simply put, applications programmers develop and code the computer programs which cause the computer to process specific jobs or applications: Print invoices, compute electricity use or design the screen on the bank's cash machine terminal. Systems programmers, on the other hand, work with the operations system itself, the internal programming that makes the computer run.

APPLICATIONS PROGRAMMER

When computer workers identify themselves as programmers, they are specifically applications programmers. They write the lines of code in one of the above programming languages that instruct the computer. Other workers such as systems analysts have done the initial design and flow of the program, i.e., the blueprints. The applications programmer builds what is specified in the plans.

Most programs today are written on a computer terminal, but in the past programmers carefully filled in the lines of code on large-sized coding sheets. Working on a terminal, or online to the computer, allows programmers to quickly test their programs and then make the necessary alterations. This fixing process is called debugging, i.e., getting the "bugs" out of the system. (The term comes from the early days of computers when an insect was found to be interfering with the then hard-wired computers. The "bug" was ceremoniously cellophane taped into the operations problem log.) Debugging not only is time consuming, it can be enormously frustrating. Curiously, it's one process that singles out the true programmer: A good programmer must have a personality that tolerates the exasperation of a program not working and persists until the problems are solved.

As noted, getting into programming used to be as simple as walking into a personnel office and doing average or better on a programming aptitude test. Such aptitude tests come in many varieties. As with any test taken more than once, prospective programmers do better on data processing aptitude tests each time they take it. [A recommended study aid is *Computer Aptitude Tests* (New York: Arco Publishing, Inc., 1985)]

Many programming positions, particularly mundane coding jobs, were initially open to high school graduates with additional vocational training in computers and/or electronics. Such courses—9 months to 2 years in length—are available either through private vocational schools, community or junior colleges or special courses at four-year colleges or universities. Another easy admission ticket to data processing was the 9 month in-depth programming course offered by a major college. Many of the students were four-year liberal arts graduates who couldn't find a job in their major, and found this 9 month program ideal vocational preparation.

The **applications programmer trainee** usually has limited or no experience as a programmer. Under the supervision of a programming manager, project leader or other manager, the trainee works or assists on routine work. Work is assigned by the day, week or at unspecified intervals by the supervisor. In this closely supervised environment the programming trainee learns programming, coding and flowcharting on the job.

The **junior programmer** has 0–2 years' experience as a programmer. On a day-to-day basis junior programmers work on all parts of the program from analysis to final product under direct supervision and most often on a team that includes other programmers and senior programmers.

Today's applications are so large that many programmers are needed in order to complete the project within a reasonable time. (Even then some applications take 2 or 3 years to complete, install and get running on the computer!) Team work also makes for better quality programming. Programmers collaborate with each other on the most efficient way to solve a problem. (There's no one or right way to program a program.) The junior programmers learn from their experienced counterparts, and the seniors may pick up new techniques from the recent graduates.

Junior programmers do the detailed analyses of the system specifications prepared by the systems analyst (see below). They develop the block diagrams and flowcharts for how the program will actually run. Then they code the program, prepare test data for the later testing process and test and debug the program. They follow up on all necessary documentation and finished program code. Juniors may also be assigned to maintain and update existing programs; that is, maintenance work.

The **programmer** usually has 2 years' experience (although junior programmers may be called programmers in some companies). The programmer is expected to be able to work alone on a programming project, although most often there is close supervision because of the need to coordinate the work of various persons on the same project. At giant companies hundreds of programmers may work in different geographical locations.

The **senior programmer** reaches his or her position after about 5 years, and works without supervision. The senior programmer works closely first with the systems analyst in setting detailed hardware and software requirements, and does the detailed design of flowcharts. To verify the program logic they do trial runs using test data. While typically not coding, the senior programmer gets involved in testing and debugging, and may be a liaison to other technical and DP departments. Senior programmers are usually expert in more than one programming language.

Most of the time the senior programmer takes on maintenance assignments of keeping the programs current and running smoothly. If small changes are to be added, the maintenance programmer makes them. (Maintenance work accounts for about 70% of all programming work in most data centers.) The catch is that it is not considered fun by eager programmers who want to solve the next programming challenge. Updating and improving existing programs written many years ago by someone long gone is considered drudgery.

This leaves companies with a dilemma: They cannot find programmers (especially senior ones) who want staff jobs doing maintenance programming. The organizations resort to bringing in freelance programmers or consultants to maintain existing programs. These consultants are self-employed, more talented than most, and command a high fee of $300 to $500 a day.

The **lead applications programmer,** the chief programmer when a programmer team is used, plans and coordinates the work of the team, and assigns and monitors portions of it. In many respects the lead programmer is the day-to-day supervisor who, depending on the size of the project, also gets involved in the actual project work. Depending on the size the lead programmer may act as project leader or project manager on a particular system. (In some companies "project leader" or "project manager" is a title which rotates depending on the project.)

The **manager of applications programming** assigns programs to programmers for development, although this manager is not always an experienced programmer. Organizations have found that a manager who understands their business needs may better determine which programs, the ones the business needs most, get written first. This underlines the increasing need for data processing professionals who understand business. More technically oriented applications managers plan and control program preparation. They set standards for the actual work: block diagramming, flowcharting and coding. Depending on the shop the manager may also get involved in writing and debugging the most complex programs. The applications manager also supervises and evaluates the quality and quantity of programmers' work.

Although non-DP managers have commonly moved into data processing, the opposite is now occurring: DP managers and professionals are moving into the mainstreams of their companies. They are moving up through traditional corporate channels because businesses have become so dependent on computers and technology that they need operations managers who understand both what computers can do to enhance the business and how to get it done.

Requirements: Depending on the sophistication and size of the organization, the junior programmer requires a high school diploma and additional training. The standard for an average to large company such as a bank or insurance company is a bachelor's degree and some computer training. That B.A. can be in computer science or almost any other field. Psychology and music majors turn out to be some of the best programmers, according to one informal study by an employment recruiter.

The straight computer-training-to-job route is not the only way into programming. Because of tremendous demands for computer employees companies have been plagued by high turnover rates, particularly among junior programmers. Once an employee was trained, he was worth an additional $2,000 or $3,000 to another employer who didn't want to have to go through the slow and expensive training process. New employees took a job for 18 or 24 months and then bailed out for an attractive raise their original employers couldn't offer because they had invested the time and money in training. Tired of getting burned, employers quickly caught on. They started looking for other sources of loyal employees, and found the ones they already had working in other departments. Thus, it's not unusual for a good administrative worker in the personnel department or mail room to be moved into data processing at these lower levels. These transferred employees become conscientious, appreciative computer workers who have a strong motivation to stay with the company. If you are working in a non-data processing job at a company that has a computer department, inquire how you go about transferring into it.

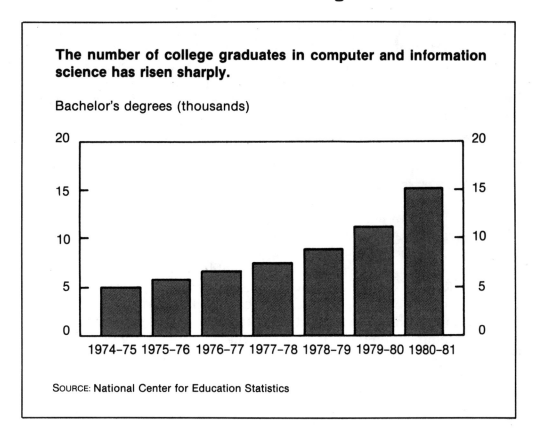

The number of college graduates in computer and information science has risen sharply.

Bachelor's degrees (thousands)

SOURCE: National Center for Education Statistics

(Often there's a line, so sign up now. Also learn how computers affect the department where you're now working in order to impress DP managers with your interest in computers.)

The beginner programmer must have academic, if not hands-on, expertise in at least one programming language and in most cases two or more. For business applications COBOL is still the most important. For scientific, FORTRAN counts most, although that is changing as engineers and scientists experiment with more powerful languages such as APL, PL/I, ALGOL or ADA. For programming jobs that are hybrids, e.g., combinations of microcomputer and mainframe applications, programmers may also need to be familiar with the operating systems, especially the popular Unix and MS-DOS. At the programmer level the employer is also looking for experience. The increased supply of persons interested in computer careers has meant an abundance of programmer candidates.

An emerging category of employee is now being sought for applications programming work, that person with dual expertise: an accounting major who's also taken programming courses. Employers and software developers have discovered that today's increasingly sophisticated computer applications require programmers with an understanding of the business they are designing systems for. This is as important if not more so for the systems analyst discussed below.

Salary: For new programmers salaries average $17,500, but the spread is from $12,000 to $30,000. Experienced applications programmers average

$22,121, although they run as high as $36,000 or as low as $16,000. With more experience more variables for setting salaries come into play: Commercial programmers with more than 5 years' experience earn as much as $40,000 or as little as $21,000. Lead applications programmers average $28,000, with a spread of $22,000–49,000. When management skills are required, salaries jump as high as $50,000, the average being $33,000.

SCIENTIFIC PROGRAMMER

Scientific programmers also develop applications programs, but because the applications are related to engineering or science, the programmer must have a specialized background and is more likely to use the programming languages designed for scientific and engineering applications (FORTRAN, Algol, APL). Scientific programmers work either alone or on teams in government funded research laboratories, universities or corporations such as the aircraft manufacturers or oil companies. Scientific programmers do the same structuring and organizing of a program, actual coding, testing and debugging that business programmers do.

Requirements: Scientific programmers are science majors first and programmers second. Many scientists, in physics or chemistry for instance, get involved in programming because the computer has become a research tool. Many of the problems the scientific programmer is called on to solve require a strong science or engineering background. Because of these high education and aptitude requirements, scientific programmers remain scarce.

Complicated science/engineering applications usually run on what are called "scientific machines" or supercomputers—computers more suitable for processing formulas and lengthy calculations than the strings of data that make up a data-intensive business application like a checking account statement. Computers more apt to run scientific applications include machines from Digital Equipment Corporation (DEC), Control Data Corporation (CDC), or Cray. Scientific programmers must know all of the hardware details of these systems that may make their programs run more efficiently. Scientific programmers may work with the most advanced processors called supercomputers. Until the late 1970s supercomputers were reserved for esoteric applications such as computing wind speed velocities for space craft in the defense and research industries. Now they're being used for more applied tasks such as searching for crude oil or processing graphics images for a science fiction movie.

Salary: Because scientific programmers are rare, they are well compensated if they work outside academia. Beginners with 1–2 years as engineering/scientific programmers and programmers analysts average $26,000 with a spread of $21,700–33,000. Salaries of experienced scientific programmers range from $26,600 to $47,300.[8]

PROGRAMMER-ANALYST

Companies use programmer-analysts in two ways. In large companies it may be considered an incremental job title between programmer and applications manager. In a variation on this, some companies expect programmer-analysts to go beyond routine programming work and to get involved in the preparatory/planning work of systems analysis. Programmer-analysts in a small company handle both tasks. They plan the project and design how the system will flow as well as do the coding, testing and implementing. The demand for such multitalented employees continues as more small companies buy computers and begin to understand what the computer means for their business.

Requirements: Depending on whether programmer-analyst is a title or a true description of responsibilities, the employee has to be an experienced programmer, or an experienced programmer and eager (or experienced) analyst.

Salary: Salaries run between $22,000 and $33,000.

SYSTEMS PROGRAMMERS

Whereas applications programmers are concerned about *what* the computer does, systems programmers are concerned with *how* the hardware and software work. They work with the programming in the computer that manages computer resources: the central processing unit, the real memory and input and output (I/O) devices. The work includes scheduling program execution and priority among multiple users and performing the complex software routines that execute the application programs.

For example, a high level application program might issue a "READ" instruction to retrieve certain data from a file on an external disk pack. The operating system interprets this instruction and then performs the hundreds of machine instructions to locate and transfer the data from the storage device, across a control unit and channel, into main memory where the application can access it. This software is the operating system—the series of programs which operate between the hardware and the applications programs. Operating systems are written in an assembly language (each hardware manufacturer has its own). Systems programmers install and maintain the operating system and the attendant utility programs. Much time is also spent reading manuals and attending classes to learn the design, logic and details of the operating systems (supplied by the vendors), which consist of millions of lines of code.

Assembly language closely approximates the binary series of "1s" and "0s" directly translated to the "on" or "off" electrical impulses the computer senses. Systems programmers write assembly programs to tailor the operating system to specific installations needs and perform specific functions that cannot be coded into higher-level languages. In addition, systems programmers must plan and fine-tune their installation's hardware and software in order to meet their company's data processing requirements.

The system programmer is concerned with the innards, especially when the computer crashes and won't process anything. In this case they put in long hours, often weekends, getting the system back up and running again. Manufacturers are continually revising their operating systems and program products in new releases that must be installed incrementally or when there are new hardware models.

Systems programmers generally become expert in one manufacturer's system. They become extremely knowledgeable about the specifics of the computer, indecipherable to a non-DP person. (It's important not to be intimidated by jargon filled conversations; the terms and acronyms are learned in time.)

Within systems programming are specialties including operating systems internals, telecommunications, data base and on-line systems. (A systems programmer specializing in one of these might be called a technical specialist in some departments.) Systems programmers are more technically expert than applications programmers or, indeed, than almost anyone in the data center. They're usually on a technical career path (within data processing) at their companies rather than one that leads to a management position within data processing.

> The **senior systems programmer** has 5–10 years' experience on one system, works at the highest levels of programming and, depending on the size of the staff, may specialize in the above topics or provide direction to junior staffers. Systems programming staffs range from 6 to 12 individuals. Senior systems programmers work with the applications developers to ensure programs are tested, debugged and actually run on the operating system. Systems requirements and configurations must be changed often to accommodate the new programs. When something goes wrong, even at 5 A.M. Saturday, the senior systems programmer hears about it.

> The **lead systems programmer,** often considered the assistant supervisor, heads the systems programming team, instructs junior staffers and assigns work. He or she works with other departments not only to schedule their applications work but the computer system as well, and insures that systems programming staffers are available to do the work.

> The **manager of systems programming** should be technically expert and have good management skills. When the computer is down because of a systems programming problem, the manager must not only ensure that the systems programmer solves the dilemma, he or she must keep other data center employees and users placated.

Requirements: Systems programming usually requires a four-year college degree, increasingly in computer science. Employers also prefer job candidates with several years' experience in writing applications programs.

Experience and strong technical skills are most important for the senior systems programmer. This requires keeping on top of the constant changes by vendors. At the managerial levels experience and managerial skills are crucial.

Salary: Systems programmers are better paid than applications programmers. An average for 2 years' experience is $27,000, although the range is $17,000–39,000. With experience the top reaches $50,000.

MINICOMPUTER PROGRAMMER

With the growing number and types of computers, programming jobs have become more varied. The best examples are the microcomputer programmer (see Chapter 5) and the minicomputer programmer.

Minicomputer programmers excel at the mid-sized systems (such as those from DEC and Data General) often used for scientific applications or in distributed processing. In distributed (or dispersed) data processing several minicomputers, usually at distant sites, are linked together via dedicated lines. Users run their smaller applications at their location, but access the computers at other locations, e.g., corporate headquarters. (Personal computers also are being used in such networks.)

Minicomputer programmers must know the languages which fully exploit the smaller but powerful minis. These include the proprietary machine languages such as Pascal, Forth and C, so popular on Unix operating systems. Because so much of the intense scientific work revolves around Department of Defense contracts, the demand for both minicomputer programmers and scientific programmers fluctuates with the level of defense spending.

Requirements: If the minicomputer programmer is working on a scientific application, he or she must be as adroit as a scientific programmer. Companies are especially looking for experts in communications, graphics and real-time control systems. Knowing about microprocessors is also useful as more powerful chips are built into these products.

Salary: Experienced minicomputer programmers or programmer-analysts and engineering/scientific programmers average $26,000, with the spread $21,700–33,000—then as high as $47,000 for experienced individuals. For programmers with expertise in minicomputer systems but not necessarily on scientific or laboratory applications, salaries are lower. The range is $21,200–34,200.

SYSTEMS ANALYSIS

Computer specialists who decide what the computer will do in the first place, and how, are systems analysts. The term systems analyst applies to anyone who studies how work is processed, be it by computer or manually or by other equipment. Systems analysis is critical to the computer operation. The larger is the system the greater the importance.

Systems analysts must ensure that the systems they design match the systems already in place. Systems analysts logically break the job to be done into a series of tasks. These tasks are further divided into the sequence of steps necessary to complete each part of the job. The systems analyst then writes a detailed narrative description of the steps necessary to complete the job from beginning to end. These are the specifications, which are then turned over to programmers for the actual coding, or in a few cases additional technical analysis. When approved by management, it's turned over to the programmers for completion. This process can take 2 or 3 years and, much to many programmers' frustration, the plans and specifications often change along the way. (Some completed systems are scratched even before they're implemented.)

Companies are now hiring systems analysts with business backgrounds rather than those with computer science backgrounds. Business graduates are more likely to see how the system will fit into and help the company. Equally important, they're better able to communicate with the non-technical users who will use the system. Before huge sums are spent it's critical that the analyst understands what the end users want to do with the computers and how sophisticated they are with them.

Until the early 1980s data processing personnel were perceived as technicians, untrained to deal with broader business questions. As organizations have embraced computers wholeheartedly, they've now learned that the same analysis skills used in DP are needed in "information age" business. The Labor Department projects that the numbers of systems analysts will grow approximately as fast as the demand for programmers, from 230,000 in 1983 to 471,000 in 1995, an 85% increase.

Like programmers, analysts are increasingly using the "building block" approach to designing systems—grouping several off-the-shelf packages together into a total system. Today's analysts must also be flexible with the hardware; in the current environment it's necessary to create combinations of PCs, telecommunications, mainframes and variable software packages.

The **systems analysis trainee** is a newcomer to this discipline, although not necessarily to data processing, the corporation or perhaps the industry. Trainees work on one project at a time under direct supervision.

The **systems analyst** works with users on project segments, usually under general supervision, and designs or redesigns projects and specifications. Systems analysts often work on teams with other analysts or with several programmers. The systems analyst title generally implies 1–2 years' experience.

The **senior systems analyst** with 3 or 4 years' experience may formulate, design and implement the system alone, but often works in consort. He or she directs junior analysts and confers with management to define data processing problems and solutions.

The **lead systems analyst** might direct at the least the analysis portion of the system or be assigned the most difficult project, often directing and supervising others. Sometimes the lead systems analyst acts as the assistant manager who schedules people, projects and resources.

The **manager of systems analysis,** also known as a project manager depending on the size of the data processing department, is an experienced analyst or sharp business manager who manages the systems analysis work. Managers of systems analysis must possess good organizational skills, good management technique and the ability to work with people at all organizational levels. The manager of systems analysis is responsible for feasibility studies, systems design and recommendations and systems analysis in general. Managers of systems analysis are usually highly experienced analysts, although there's the growing trend of assigning top business managers noted above.

Requirements: As already noted, systems analysts must have an understanding of both data processing and their organization's business and the industry. To design, say, a factory automation system a systems analyst must understand manufacturing and appreciate what the job entails for the worker on the factory floor. The critical ability is linking the capabilities of the computer and related hardware to the needs of the end-users and the business. This requires the ability to communicate with fellow employees and to learn what these needs are. Analytical ability is also important; tasks must be broken down into their components.

Companies are looking for flexibility and creativity in systems analysts. This cannot be overemphasized! Just because you've spent five years as a programmer doesn't mean you're automatically entitled to promotion to systems analyst. Increasing numbers of systems analysts have four-year degrees but not necessarily in computer science. Programming is another, and until recently was the main, route to higher paying and more prestigious systems analysis jobs. For the systems analyst working on scientific applications, the scientific understanding is as important as the business one in a corporation.

Salary: Because of the range of responsibilities salaries for systems analysts vary greatly. Junior systems analysts with less than 2 years' experience average $27,000 with a range of $19,000–30,000. Senior analysts earn between $28,000 and $40,000, although experienced analysts and managers earn as much as $51,000. Management salaries tend to improve more than staff workers because of the crunch for management talent.

PROJECT MANAGER/SENIOR ANALYST

When companies are initiating and implementing new projects they often assign one person overall responsibility. This job goes by many names—project manager, project leader, team leader—and the person assigned may have a title such as senior analyst, consultant or any of the above. The project manager is responsible for planning, organizing and controlling specific assigned projects that will become part either of the normal DP job stream or turned over to users. He or she must also bring the project in on time and on budget—two big challenges.

Requirements: Minimum requirements usually include 2 years' systems design experience and prior programming with some specialized industry experience desired. An MBA is useful.

Salary: The average salary for project/team leaders is $36,700, although a few earn as much as $60,000 or as little as $30,000.

DATA BASE ADMINISTRATOR

Think of how much information your bank has about you: your checking account balance, the checks you've written this month plus the checks you wrote last month. Add your savings account transactions. What if you have a savings deposit box? What if you have saved enough money for a savings certificate of deposit? It's quickly apparent how much data exists within large organizations. (It's also frightening to contemplate how much data exists about you and who has access to it.)

As computer systems mushroomed in the late 1960s and early 1970s, a need arose for someone to keep track of and manage all this data. The experienced employee with this responsibility came to be known as the data base administrator or, more currently, data administrator.

Besides the need for an employee responsible for the data, a filing system or framework for storing all the data in the computer was needed. What was developed is called a data base management system (DBMS), a technical term within data processing that differs from the data bases known to the public—Dow Jones News Service or *The New York Times* Information Bank. A DBMS is a cross-indexed library system. A general data base may be considered a sequential A to Z filing cabinet even though a DBMS running on the computer is used to locate the desired data. In the bank example above, should the bank have a DBMS—and they most likely do—their customer file serves as the card catalog to all the bank's data about you. This customer index file contains your vital statistics, and then notes what accounts and services you have at the bank. Managing such data masses are a handful of major DBMS, sophisticated and expensive "big systems" packages. (These are not to be confused with the simpler and considerably smaller data base management packages for PCs.)

The data base administrator reviews the data, where it is stored and which computer programs will use which files of data. This can be a monumental task when companies have huge data centers filled with high speed disk drives which hold hundreds of millions of bytes of data. The data base administrator also ensures that data files are duplicated, or backed-up, in case of emergency, and that there's a disaster contingency plan. Well managed companies store their most critical data files in vaults or underground storage facilities, often in remote communities, in event of a disaster that disables their computer center. After all, few companies could survive if they lost their computer system and had no idea how much money was owed to them, how much they owed, or any details of their employees. Some companies also have a computer security specialist who is responsible for this data backup storage and disaster recovery.

The **data base analyst** is a fast developing specialty for data processing professionals who want to remain in more technical work. Data base analysts must know applications programming and some systems programming. This knowledge is useful in planning data security and data recovery tactics.

Requirements: Data base administrators not only must have strong technical skills in order to work with the DBMS software, but must be well versed in data processing operations. Because of their tremendous responsibility, they must be conscientious, organized and relate well with people.

Salary: Because of the responsibility, data base administrators are well compensated. Salaries are $34,500–43,000, although they may reach $50,000.

USER LIAISON/INTERNAL CONSULTANT

Nowadays more and more employees at large companies either want a computer terminal or personal computer on their desk, or they want access to information stored in the giant corporate computers. The fact is that access to computers makes them more productive.

In the past DP technicians developed systems for the data processing department—essentially for themselves. Enter the naive user who knows only that he or she wants a computer or wants certain information locked up in the computer. This non-technical user, who probably isn't even in the same building with the DP department and maybe has never seen a computer, has no idea what the computer can do for him. Furthermore, the user doesn't speak DP jargon and thus is hard pressed to explain to the technical expert what he does want. On the other hand, the DP expert assumes that the user knows as much about computers as he does, and doesn't bother to make the system useable for the non-expert user. At first DP experts were asked to design systems for naive users; the results, however, were abysmal. Few systems actually worked.

At this point management realized a need for a translator between the technician and user. This go-between was called the user liaison, internal consultant or consultant. The user liaison has proved to be an effective means first of getting the appropriate systems installed and secondly of keeping them running. The more general the system to be installed and the more users on it, the greater the need for go-betweens.

Requirements: Foremost, user liaisons must be good communicators and good listeners to both the users and the data processing department. The liaison must understand data processing hardware, software and systems in order to explain it to the users.

Salary: Because these positions are recently defined and continue to change daily, salaries for consultants are wide open. Experience is a big factor, however. For those with less experience the range is $25,000–40,000. For those with more than 7 years who excel at this peacemaking job, the range is $36,000–60,000. At a certain point in their careers many DP professionals spin off as independent consultants. In most cases they are referred by word of mouth from satisfied clients and earn from $350 to $1,500 a day, although they are not ensured steady work.

TECHNICAL SERVICES MANAGER

As data processing systems keep growing in complexity, companies are finding they need specialists to keep these technical systems, for example, data base management and data communications, working together. In some departments these professionals are in the systems programming group, and a technical services specialist is comparable to a systems programmer.

Requirements: Technical services managers usually have 5 years' systems programming experience, the ability to manage junior staffers, and an understanding of where data processing technology is headed.

Salary: Because this is a rare combination of expertise and personality, salaries for technical services managers vary from $33,000 to $58,000.

EDP (ELECTRONIC DATA PROCESSING) AUDITOR

Suppose a company has a state-of-the-art computer center staffed with DP professionals who are gearing computer power to the organization. How does the company know the DP department is doing their job correctly? that data (and dollars) are not slipping through the cracks? that the department is using the appropriate hardware and software for the job?

Auditors have traditionally performed this checking function for companies. The EDP auditor does the same in data processing. The EDP auditor monitors the products of the DP operation: Do the reports report what they're supposed to beyond the fact that the subtotals balance? Are systems operated at optimum efficiency? is the appropriate computer being used for each application? Are the systems secure, internally from employees and others in the data center, and externally perhaps from hackers, (young people who want the challenge of getting inside a big computer system and "hacking" around to see what they find)?

Organizations have a tremendous financial risk in their data processing systems. In far too many cases clever employees are able to siphon funds from various systems. The classic example is the programmer who had the system round off 1/100ths of a cent to the lower figure; the difference went into his secret account. All those 1/100ths of a cent added up quickly!

The opportunities for EDP auditors grow with every new installation. At the same time systems are growing more decentralized so that more potential problem points exist for auditors to monitor. Of course, the growing number of individuals using personal computers and modems means more opportunities to illegally tap into systems. Auditors frequently find themselves confronting nightmares.

Requirements: Because auditors deal with so many aspects of a company's business to know if computer systems are being used correctly, they develop a broad and sophisticated understanding of the business. They are thus in a strong position to move on to a senior data processing spot or a general management assignment. Some companies consider the EDP auditor a stepping stone to corporate management. Auditors have more than 5 years' experience in systems analysis and programming, and at least a general knowledge of computer hardware and its capabilities. In addition, they may be trained auditors or accountants or have other experience in financial matters. Almost always they have four-year degrees. Of course, auditors themselves must be honest!

Salary: The necessary combination of DP and auditing skills required for EDP auditors is rare, and talented, experienced EDP auditors draw high salaries. For new workers, $22,600–34,600 range; experienced pros, $34,000–50,800 range.

COMPUTER SECURITY SPECIALISTS

The data processing employee concerned with security on a daily basis is the computer security specialist. The responsibilities of these jobs vary greatly—from a data center guard who makes certain that visitors sign in and out to a senior manager responsible for all DP security as well as contingency plans in the event of a disaster. Senior security staffers may help disguise data both from other employees and from competitors or interlopers.

Beyond the guard level are specialists who make the necessary security precautions for the hardware and/or software. Computer systems—especially the computer terminal or a newer personal computer—commonly require both a physical key and a software password to gain entry to the system. Nor is it enough just to assign passwords. Security specialists must assure they're used effectively. In a small to medium-sized data center, though, responsibility for passwords and keys belongs to a senior data processing professional, perhaps in data administration. In larger DP departments a computer security specialist wields broad responsibilities which may include data security, site security and contingency planning.

Data must be secured in several ways so that only authorized persons have access to it. The easiest implementation of this is keys and passwords. More sophisticated is encryption, in which data is coded, transmitted and then decoded at the receiving end. Encryption may use either hardware scramblers or formulas in the software that mathematically cause the same jumbling effect. Encryption is often used when data is transmitted over foreign borders.

Another danger to data is that it will be lost, either physically or electronically as when lightning downs a computer system's power. Companies commonly store backup computer tapes of critical data—accounts payable and receivable, for example—in secure vaults at locations distant from their computer centers. Like bank safe deposit boxes, abandoned mine shafts have been turned into tape storage locations. These backup sites are run by third-party companies in the data security business. They may also provide access to entire backup computer systems at alternative locations. In the event of a disaster, companies would transfer their data processing operation to the contingency site.

Requirements: Computer security specialists, much like EDP auditors, must be of high caliber, honest and conscientious. This is particularly true at government or defense-related computer centers. At a top-secret government installation that sends encrypted data to foreign sites DP expertise is highly sophisticated. A Ph.D. in mathematics is sometimes required for advanced encryption work. In more general business installations the level of training and knowledge is not as demanding.

Salary: Because of the varying levels of expertise required for jobs labeled computer security, salaries run a wide gamut. If the security person is on the guard level, salaries are in the $20,000 range. If the security specialist is expert in software, salaries compare to those of experienced programmers, $30,000–40,000.

MANAGEMENT INFORMATION SYSTEMS (MIS) DIRECTOR

From the overall standpoint, business computers exist for the purpose of organizing, storing and delivering information to the employees who need it. From the corporate pinnacle computers are considered information systems for managers. At the highest levels data processing is known as management information systems (MIS).

The person in charge of all computer systems is often the vice-president of MIS, information systems director or MIS director. Who this person reports to varies. The boss may be the chief financial officer or the chief operations officer, although in some cases it's the chief executive officer (CEO). The MIS director has responsibility for all the company's data systems and often the voice telecommunications ones.

Requirements: Until the 1980s data processing was considered a "staff" function that provided service to the organization. At many sites data processing employees—including executives—were considered second-class citizens because they were techies supposedly preoccupied with technical matters. With society's current economic upheaval companies now want computers closely knitted into their operations.

Although the most senior data processing executive in the past was always an experienced DP professional, that's no longer the case. Data processing, particularly at these high levels, is an excellent place to learn about a business and how to steer it in positive directions. Companies are placing their most talented executives—including many newcomers with MBAs—in top information systems positions despite the fact they don't have DP experience. (These MBAs often are computer savvy and well prepared to lead the company into the new computer age, much to the chagrin of experienced DPers.) Even for companies not using this MBA policy MIS directors and vice-presidents usually have four-year degrees and often graduate school training.

Salary: This is the top position in the data processing hierarchy and salaries are commensurate. Depending on the size of the company, salaries may exceed $100,000. Most, however, are in the $50,000–75,000 range.

EDP MANAGER

Whereas the MIS director has responsibility for the staffing, planning and strategic implications of information systems, the executive with day-to-day responsibility for specific computer systems is the EDP manager. This title varies depending on the size and sophistication of the organization, since an EDP manager may be in charge of 3 or 3,000 employees. How large the staff and the operation determines how much input the EDP manager has to daily operations. The larger the operation, the more the EDP manager is a people manager.

Requirements: EDP managers are both experienced computer professionals and good leaders and managers. They should understand their company's business and work well with employees and users. EDP managers usually have at least 5 years' experience in DP, especially in systems analysis and the positions requiring a broader view of computers. (This is not the position for technical experts, although it might have been in the past.) Today an EDP manager usually has a college degree in business and perhaps additional graduate study, or an undergraduate degree in computer science and a master's degree in business administration.

How much EDP managers are in demand depends on geographic location and their technical expertise. All managers, however, must keep up with changing technology. Too many senior managers cling to dinosaur technologies they've worked with even though more appropriate or cost-effective ones such as personal computers may have come along. Obsolescence is truly a danger at this level.

Salary: Managers' salaries have increased proportionately more than those of professionals and lower ranks in data processing. Depending on the size of the operation, DP managers earn on the average $37,500, with the range from $32,800 to $39,000.

CONSULTANTS AND SUPPORT

TECHNICAL ASSISTANT

The best example of a management adviser is the technical assistant who does an independent technical and strategic evaluation of new projects/systems. He or she can offer a new opinion and supplemental information in addition to that from the operations staff in order to make the best decision. Such a technical assistant spot is ideal for learning about both new technologies and the business.

Requirements: This can be a pass through position for employees being groomed for higher level jobs. It's also an excellent position for a highly technical person who enjoys explaining technology to less technical audiences.

Salary: Not all companies have such technical gurus, but generally they earn $35,000 a year, although salaries can be as low as $25,000.

ADMINISTRATIVE ASSISTANT

At its simplest an administrative assistant reporting to the DP manager has an excellent secretarial position. The complexity of DP, however, often requires an administrative assistant who has worked in computing, particularly in a business related area. For instance, one administrative assistant was an expert on computer leasing, and in addition to giving leasing advice often sat in at meetings and attended conferences on behalf of the DP manager. Experienced and knowledgeable administrative assistants then, are exposed to many valuable learning situations because of the broad domain of the DP manager. This job can also be a training one for up-and-comers within the corporation.

Requirements: The requirements for an administrative assistant in the DP manager's office vary with the company and the manager. Data processing employees should not discount this as a possible position, however, even if it might first appear to be a secretarial post. (Of course, don't get stuck if it doesn't offer the exposure to computers you want.)

Salary: Depending on the level of responsibility, this position pays from $15,000 to $30,000. In some large organizations the title "administrative assistant" to a top executive is a stepping stone to top management.

1. Karen Beagley and Raymond S. Winkler. "On the Rise: 26th Annual DP Salary Survey." *Infosystems,* June 1984, p. 30.
2. Ibid.
3. "Prevailing Financial and Data Processing Starting Salaries 1985." Robert J. Half International, Inc., p. 2.
4. Ibid. pp. 17–23.
5. Larry Marion. "The Big Wallet Era." *Datamation,* September 15, 1984, p. 80.
6. Ibid. pp. 84–85.
7. Beagley and Winkler, op. cit.
8. *1984 Computer Salary Survey and Career Management Guide.* Source EDP Personnel Services, p. 16.

4

THE TECHNOLOGY INDUSTRY

Businesses in the high technology industry are different, and yet the same. One may manufacture dermatologic argon lasers; another, educational software on how to write a resume; another, a warehouse-sized automatic storage system; and yet another, supercomputers used to explore for oil. What's similar is that all these products involve new technologies, and in most cases are expensive or specialized products that require training and expertise to use. You cannot walk into K-Mart and purchase these products, nor do you learn to operate them in high school courses.

High technology companies offer exciting opportunities to career seekers. There are tens of thousands of high technology firms and more are starting every day. After all, they constitute the growth edge of our economy and society—in the U.S., and abroad. Not all high tech jobs are with big manufacturers. Many are with companies that develop, produce or market products that either copy or work with other manufacturer's products.

Many companies sell customized software for the banking industry, even though the company may have only two employees, or operate out of a basement. Others sell "dumb terminals," computer VDTs with no electronics intelligence built in, that connect to large systems. "Utility software" simply makes mainframe software more efficient, or cleans and straightens up the internal software. Another lucrative segment consists of service bureau companies; they sell time on their computers for specific tasks. The lists go on and on, and such lists are what the career seeker must work through to find the right job. Be creative when looking for an employer.

For the job seeker the smaller companies are often harder to find because they do not have the large advertising budgets for national television or regular full page newspaper and magazine advertisements. They are, however, reported and do advertise in the trade magazines and newspapers listed in the appendix of this book as well as the *Wall Street Journal* and *The New York Times*. Be on the lookout for classified recruitment and product advertisements to locate suitable companies.

The work the industry has available can be grouped by the following classifications:

1. Sales and marketing
2. Product research and development, and engineering

Technology trade shows like COMDEX are some of the best places to meet those working in the industry—and to survey new technologies. It's often possible to tour the exhibits for a small admission fee. (Courtesy of the Interface Group)

3. Service technicians
4. Corporate administration

The job requirements range from a Ph.D. in computer science to a high school diploma. Many job titles may be misleading, so be sure you understand the job before you jump to the conclusion that you know what it entails.

SALES AND MARKETING

MARKETING REPRESENTATIVE

This is the elite title within marketing ranks. Especially for the mainstream computer companies, marketing representatives are well educated and technically trained (most often by their employers) salespeople. Selling a $100,000 robot for parts painting or a multi-million dollar computer system is not what is typically meant by "sales." Sales involves complicated analysis of what the robot, computer or any piece of high tech equipment will do for a company. This argument has to be convincingly presented to the company, which is most likely considering several alternatives. This is the RFP (request for proposal) process.

Marketing representatives hold numerous meetings with company officials. They make slide show presentations to evaluation committees; give presentations to financial officers or hospital administrators; play golf with vice-presidents. They also arrange visits for prospective customers to companies already using their products or running applications similar to those being proposed by the sales rep.

Marketing representatives at the most sophisticated level want to be perceived as equals to the executives of the company they're selling to. IBM founder and marketing genius, Thomas J. Watson, early on instructed his salesmen to wear white shirts, dark suits, and, if not winged-tip shoes, the general attire of the businessmen they called on. These businessmen were convinced that, despite the unknown technology of computers they were buying for their companies, IBM was trustworthy. After all, the salesmen dressed just like them. While diluted today, Watson's standards live on in the conservative tone and dress of the computer industry and the marketing community within it.

Completing a computer system sale may take a year—and often longer. Marketing representatives usually receive an adequate salary, but the real money is in commissions: the more they sell the more they earn. Their sales goals are based on "quotas," the amount assigned by their managers that they have to sell. Each vendor has its own complicated quota system, and sometimes the quota is revised during the year depending on how the industry or the company is doing.

Some reps don't meet their quota goal, in which case they are usually sidelined to a support position or, rarely, fired. Because of the investment in training and development it doesn't make sense for companies to dismiss sales reps who don't make quotas. It's simply acknowledged that they're not good at sales.

Marketing representatives most often work in teams, especially when selling to users who have many large computers. Auto makers, for instance, run dozens of the largest mainframes; utilities bank 3 or 4 giant processors together in data centers to handle all their processing. This team is managed by a senior marketing representative or an account executive.

In smaller companies the sales approach is more like that of the traveling salesperson who, once he or she has completed the sale, isn't heard from again until he has another product to sell. Competition from small firms has also forced the bigger ones to cut costs, and cutting sales amenities has been one way they've done this. Despite the changes afoot the marketing representative remains a top spot in the technology-related industries.

Salaries remain high and more women are moving into these positions with lucrative commissions because women have traditionally done well in high technology sales.

The proportion of sales representatives in the industry is growing. Salesmen will number 35,900 in 1995, 5.1% of the total industry employment, reports the BLS. That's up from 16,400 or 4.6% of the industry force in 1982.

Experienced marketing reps are well qualified to move into marketing management and even into corporate management. Top sales people are wooed by competitors, especially those new to the marketplace. Because of the opportunity to know customers and their needs, marketing representatives sometimes have the information on which to start their own enterprise.

Training: Because of the technical nature of their products, vendors recognize that they must provide specialized training needed to sell them. Large manufacturers provide extensive schooling and training periods, typically spread out over the first year of employment, during which time the intern is called a sales or marketing trainee. Trainees go to company schools at least half the time, and study and observe their branch offices for the remainder. Depending on what products they'll sell they're taught everything from the technology of their products to sales behavior to actually closing a sale.

Computer marketers must not only know inside and out the products they are selling, they must be familiar with the documentation and numerous manuals that most systems require. Furthermore, products change so frequently that this requires ongoing study and 2 or 3 weeks of additional training each year.

Requirements: The increase in the number of computer and related products to be sold combined with the difficulty of finding good people affords many opportunities for talented sales representatives. High technology companies are fast-track places that can afford to hire the top talent—and they do. An MBA is increasingly the entry requirement for top technology marketing posts. For most of these MBAs the supposition is that they will go on to management positions. It's standard for the chief executives of these companies to have come out of the sales ranks.

Vendors sometimes hire persons with four-year degrees in business or marketing. Teachers, coaches, bright college or professional athletes and music and psychology majors still squeeze into the computer marketing hierarchy. (Athletes remain popular when it comes to selling hardware.) Seldom do marketing representatives have extensive technical backgrounds although a few products require a computer science major to sell them. In the health field, when representatives call on doctors or technical health specialists, it's often useful for them to have had some job experience in medical technology.

Companies look for enthusiasm, personality and motivation. Notes recruiting firm, Source EDP: "Some organizations are willing to consider technical professionals with an aptitude for sales. This particularly includes engineers in the microcomputer and communications interface areas."[1]

Important note: Moving into sales without credentials, despite the tightening up in the industry, is still possible. Sales are a company's lifeblood. Therefore, watch for sales advertisements which indicate flexibility; often it doesn't hurt to apply for positions with defined qualifications and education. *Good sales representatives are hard to find!*

Salary: Sales representatives work on a combination of salary and commission, but the commission offers the greatest potential for earnings. Market reps are also eligible for special bonuses and cash awards during sales campaigns or for top performance. At the end of a successful sales year marketing representatives may be invited to special sales events such as combination meeting-vacation in a resort area.

Source EDP finds plump salaries for sales representatives. In the hardware segment the median salary is $50,300 with the range from $36,200 to $84,700.[2] Although salaries in the computer industry are slightly higher, they're a good indication of overall high technology salaries. For computer services marketing representatives the range was broader, $30,600–82,300 with the median $48,600. Best compensated for their efforts were software sales representatives who averaged $55,400, with the spread $40,700–89,000.

MARKETING MANAGER/SALES MANAGER/REGIONAL MANAGER

Some of the best paid marketing representatives have little contact with customers, but manage a squad of sales representatives who do. The manager receives a percentage of the reps' commission, or in some situations may have territory or key account direct sales duties. These jobs demand experienced, top producers who have excellent management skills, capable of motivating others. Such talented managers are hard to find.

Salary: Sales managers averaged $67,700, according to the Source survey, with the variation from $47,400 to $93,700.[3]

MARKETING SUPPORT REPRESENTATIVE OR SYSTEMS ENGINEER

Working closely with marketing representatives is the marketing support representative (MSR), or systems engineer. Titles vary greatly by industry, but the job is basically one of supporting marketing in making the sale. MSRs are more prevalent in office-related systems, systems engineers in computer systems. Such workers may also be called sales/technical support representatives because they provide the technical support. They may set up live product demonstrations at the customer's site, or help the client's employees install and go operational with the new equipment. For large customers support representatives may have a desk on site and spend most of their time there. These representatives give technical presentations to the customer's manager and staff, assist salespeople in studying the customer's needs, conduct feasibility studies and develop sales proposals. Like marketing reps they're looking to match their company's products to the customers' needs.

Sales/technical support representatives are salaried employees. This career route is primarily for the person who likes working with customers and wants to remain in a technical position, but it is sometimes an entry-level position for an aspiring salesperson. Many vendors have made this position a step on the technical career ladder. It is a job that can lead to management, either directly or through a sales post, or to consulting assignments as a technical, or systems, expert. In the past most MSRs and systems engineers have been women. Because of the increasing number and complexity of products in the marketplace, opportunities for support representatives are increasing, particularly in data base management systems, mini and micro computers, VDTs and custom software and systems.

Requirements: The title "systems engineer" is misleading when it describes the training for the marketing support job. Support representatives are not true engineers nor is an engineering degree required. In most cases a four-year degree is, but it may be in liberal arts as well as more technical majors. Like marketing representatives, marketing technical support representatives go through extensive initial training for as long as a year. Once on the job they regularly attend classes to learn about new products and developments. Not only must they assimilate technical information, they must translate it for their customers. Written and oral skills and interpersonal communications thus are important.

Salary: Unlike marketing reps, marketing support representatives are salaried employees. At some companies, including the growing telecommunications firms, technical support representatives share bonuses which companies award for a good year. Technical support representatives may also win cash awards and other incentives for top performance.

For newcomers with 1–2 years' experience, Source EDP reported an average salary of $28,200, with a spread from $20,700 to $38,800. For those with 2–5 years' experience the median was $33,900, with the range $25,400–47,500. Support representatives with more than 5 years' experience averaged $42,600 in a range of $34,800–50,200.

Product Research, Development and Engineering

Manufacturing high technology equipment is by no means a simple process. For one thing high tech companies are often the biggest users of their own equipment. In addition, each company has its own way of operating factories, which affects the nature and number of employees. For another, computer manufacturers are automating their own production with robots or robot-like assembler arms. For instance, at IBM's Boca Raton personal computer plant all the machines are tested automatically.

All factories employ assembly line workers, and although a high school diploma may be enough for most assembly jobs, certain spots on a computer assembly line require electronics training. Each of these jobs is special to a particular company and their production methods. Working for a high technology manufacturer is very much a factor of where you live. If there's one in your region, investigate.

High technology companies need professionals both to research and develop new products and—this is less well understood—to design the production facilities to manufacture them. Almost always these jobs require bachelor of science degrees in engineering and special study in the area of interest. The more technology-related courses, the better.

MANUFACTURING ENGINEER

How will a computer be manufactured? Manufacturing engineers determine production requirements, select tooling equipment and plan assembly stations along the production line. They must fully understand the capabilities of these automated systems to take full advantage of the benefits. Their manufacturing analysis must be done in the context of current and proposed production schedules, which is sometimes fraught with danger because new systems are often announced with long lead times. They therefore must get production up and running in time to meet shipping dates.

On an ongoing basis manufacturing engineers analyze operations, processes and manufacturing sequences, and look for improvements. Their recommendations are approved by management and often by the operations supervisors who work with factory workers to produce the computer.

Salary: Entry-level manufacturing engineers start at $22,500–30,000 and are subject to merit and periodic increases.

SYSTEM TEST ENGINEER

Computers must be operational when they come off the assembly line. When so many electronic and mechanical components are involved, this is not a simple matter. System test engineers responsible for either electronic or mechanical parts make this happen. This increasingly entails automatic test and evaluation (ATE) equipment, since companies use technology to test new technologies.

Electronic watchers plan, set up and then monitor tests of electronic equipment. This may be as simple as running the system for 24 hours, or it may involve more complicated testing equipment to monitor what's being assembled. If the product or component doesn't work, it must be fixed—another careful process. Electronic system test engineers also troubleshoot all possible problems that could arise and then solve them. One way is to randomly pull systems off the assembly line, and submit them to additional or more stringent tests than those they've already been subjected to. As part of their work test engineers develop procedures and often software and special systems to do their testing.

When testing a system for mechanical defects a mechanical systems test engineer is involved in similar processes, but with different components and different testing apparatus. Because computers are becoming so highly electronic, fewer mechanical tests are made.

Less experienced test engineers are test management engineers. Whereas system test engineers may have 5–10 years' experience, test management engineers have 2. They assist in scheduling and tracking test activities, and act as liaison engineers with other departments.

Tests within the laboratory are even more critical. Laboratory test engineers test, diagnose and repair electronic and electrical systems hardware, usually on state-of-the-art automatic test equipment (ATE). They work with systems design engineers to resolve design anomalies.

The good news about the lab work is that it's new. These posts require versatility and knowledge of a broad spectrum of digital, analog and RF equipment. Laboratory test engineers are generally experienced and have BSEEs.

Requirements: For the electronic test professionals a B.S. in electrical engineering (BSEE) is required, although equivalents are often accepted. The engineer must have strong knowledge of electrical, digital and analog computer systems.

The mechanical test engineer usually has a B.S. in mechanical engineering (BSME) or the equivalent. For jobs involving U.S. government contacts, especially defense contracts, the job candidate often must be a U.S. citizen.

Salary: Beginning salaries are in the $25,000–30,000 range.

SYSTEM SOFTWARE ENGINEER

A great deal of software is used both in running the assembly line and in conducting tests, and is necessarily highly customized. System software engineers support and manage the software and hardware with checkout computer systems during manufacture. They must not only understand ATE, but must also dissect the software that controls it.

Requirements: A computer science degree is required, as well as proficiency in FORTRAN and BASIC programming and knowledge of the scientific computer systems which do the testing.

Salary: Experience counts in software engineering. For 1–2 years' work, Source EDP found a salary range of $22,500–33,400, with the average $30,300. With 2–4 years' experience, $28,200–38,200, average $35,000; 4–7 years', $31,300–45,400, average $40,300. Software engineers with more than 7 years in the field earned $36,900–45,600, with $41,600 at mid-point.[4]

SOFTWARE DEVELOPERS

If a company develops software—the instructions that run the computer—their most critical employees are those who develop that software. Software developers must have both a streak of genius and the ability to follow through on the writing the code, testing it, and debugging it—just like applications programmers. (See Chapter 3.) They're familiar with several programming languages, especially the one they're working in, and with the relevant applications and systems their products will be running on. There's much turnover of developers and raiding among companies for such talent.

Requirements: Most software developers have BSEEs or more advanced degrees in computer science or electrical engineering. The exception is the self-taught wizard who either learns quickly or "intuits" what is necessary in order to develop a product and make it work. (If the developer has this ability companies are willing to put up with almost any behavior, no matter how weird, of their developers.)

Salary: Software developers are some of the best paid professionals in the industry, and earn $34,000–44,000, perhaps working for a personal computer software firm.[6] The person in charge of developing a software product and then readying it for market is the product manager, who earns $44,000–66,000.[7]

SERVICE TECHNICIAN/CUSTOMER SERVICE REPRESENTATIVE

Customer service representative is the fancy name for the technician or repairer. It's one of the best jobs within high technology companies yet one of the least known or appreciated. With the expanding number of machines, equipment and systems the situation is only getting better for experienced technicians and is equally promising for newcomers. In fact, bad economic times are often busier for computer and other high tech technicians; rather than purchase new systems, companies choose to keep their equipment and repair it when it breaks. The following discussion focuses on computer technicians, but it applies to all technicians of high tech equipment.

The BLS is optimistic: The number of computer technicians will nearly double from 55,000 to 108,000 by 1995 due to the increasing use of computers. The "personalization" of computers means more of them to be repaired, including those at a new and more readily accessible retail sales level.

Over the next decade service employees will make up a growing share of the computer and data processing services industry, albeit a small one. Including computer service technicians, craft workers will move from a 1.7% to 2.4% share of industry employment.

What Is Repair Work?

Repairing a computer is not much different from rewiring a light socket or squirting oil on a squeaky hinge. For example, on small systems it may entail removing a faulty microprocessor or memory board and dropping in a new one. The repairer does not have to know precisely what's wrong with the system because it's cheaper just to replace a faulty component; the repair can be done immediately at the customer's location. Repair work sometimes is nothing more than cleaning the system (this is especially true with copier systems). It may be as simple as replacing a worn connection cable by doing routine checks of either the electromechanical or mechanical parts. Technicians regularly adjust, oil and clean mechanical and electromechanical parts such as those in a high-speed printer. They also check electronic equipment for loose connections and defective components or circuits.

To save expensive service time today's computers are increasingly easy to expand by inserting color-coded plug-in memory modules. Systems also have internal diagnostics to cut down further on service calls. (Courtesy of International Business Machines Corporation)

Repairers must act quickly when expensive systems break because many workers may be immobilized waiting for the system to come back on. Determining where the system has a malfunction is the toughest job, and requires an analytical mind, technical knowledge and the ability to remain unruffled under pressure.

Of course, the repair of computer and electronic office equipment depends on the piece of hardware. The more expensive and sophisticated the system, the more trained and experienced the technician must be: In the case of mainframes the service technicians' skills are similar to those of the systems engineers. In other words service technicians must also know about software and operating systems because these are so intertwined in the big systems.

Breakdowns occur in the central processor or in one of the peripheral devices: printer, remote terminal or even another minicomputer connected to the larger system. The problem might be in the cables or data communications systems and telephone lines increasingly being used with computers. Locating such electronic or communications failures involves using tools such as voltmeters, ohmmeters, oscilloscopes and software diagnostic programs to help pinpoint problems. Locating the problem often takes longer than fixing it.

Technicians use tools such as a solder needle, needle-nosed pliers and wire strippers to replace faulty circuit boards, although manufacturers are increasingly making boards that can be readily pulled out and replaced. (The actual board diagnosis and repair may be done later at a factory if it is deemed worth doing at all.) As a time saver, technicians today automatically replace boards even if they have no idea what the malfunction is.

Besides keeping computer systems running computer technicians are responsible for the initial installation. Sometimes this is exciting, as when companies use helicopters to hoist new systems into data centers located on upper building floors. More often, however, they work one or two long weekends to take out the old system and bring in the new without disrupting work week production. Depending on the size of the system, the new installation includes laying cables (either in raised floors or stringing through ceilings or walls), making electrical connections, testing the system and correcting problems—hopefully before the customer requires the system. Overtime also occurs during the week because many large data centers keep their computers running around the clock. Like doctors, on-call computer technicians get emergency calls in the middle of the night. This occurs most often to the experienced technician who is good at repairing a certain system or locating a specific problem.

Employer Alternatives

Computer service technicians usually work for manufacturers. With the growth of small systems, however, new repair alternatives have emerged. One is an independent repair service, which provides maintenance contracts either to large users, or as third parties to smaller manufacturers. In addition, many retail stores also provide repair service, and so computer repairers find themselves working on Main Street or at nearby shopping centers. (These small repair operations are excellent entry points to better jobs with major manufacturers.)

Computer service technicians generally work out of an office for an assigned territory, usually for several companies. Some technicians, particularly for communications vendors, are assigned full time to one account.

Because computer installations run round the clock breakdowns frequently occur after workday hours, and overtime is common. In some firms technicians work rotating shifts, nights for a period, then days. Other technicians are on call 24 hours, and often wear paging beepers.

With additional training technicians move through the repair ranks. Supervisors have leadership and management skills and must work well with other people.

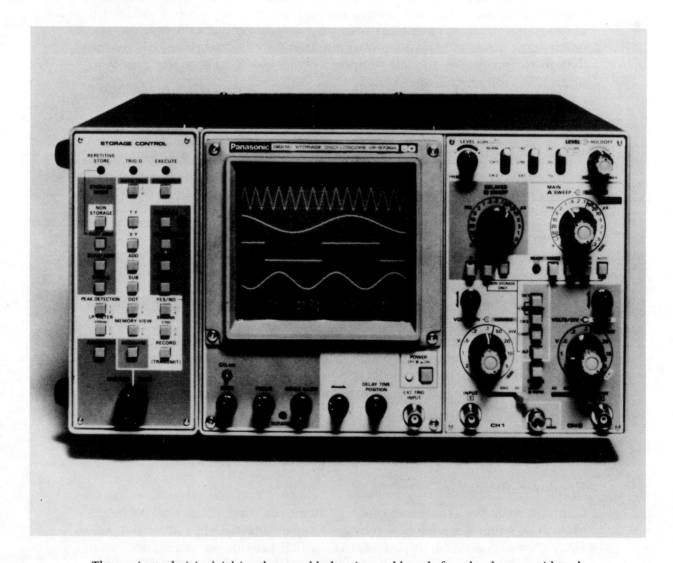

The service technician's job involves troubleshooting problems before they happen with tools such as this oscilloscope. (Courtesy of Panasonic)

If technicians are especially interested in or adroit at programming, they move into the software side of the business with either their clients or in a sales support capacity within their own company. Experienced technicians may also work with design engineers on new products. Although computer systems are conceptually all the same, in reality they are different enough so that it's difficult to move from repairing one system to another without a lot of retraining. With the pressing need for more workers technicians are seldom at a loss for new opportunities ... and this is especially true with the growth of third-party repair firms.

Women's Work

There's nothing about the computer technician's job that is unsuitable for or could not be done by women. The problem is they sometimes *think* they can't. In this case women are allowing old fashioned ideas of "women's work" and "men's work" to affect their take-home pay. This doesn't work in the interest of the woman who is working to support herself and perhaps her family.

Training: Most employers require applicants to have 1–2 years' post-high school training. This training may be from a public or private vocational school, a college or junior college, or from the Armed Forces. High school students interested in computer technician opportunities should take courses in mathematics, physics and computer programming and electronics, if available. Hobbies such as building microcomputers, stereos and ham radios are also valuable training.

Manufacturers usually provide 3–6 months' intensive training in which recruits study and expand their knowledge of basic electronics, elementary computer theory, computer math and circuitry theory. This training includes hands-on experience in repairing equipment, doing basic maintenance and using test equipment to troubleshoot and then solve malfunctions. Back at the office new employees usually work as trainees for an additional 6–24 months, initially with an experienced technician on simpler maintenance and repair assignments before they move on to more complicated equipment. Another method is to have technicians specialize in one machine, and then rotate them from one to another.

The training never ends, since the nature of technology prescribes that manufacturers improve, change or introduce new machines. Additional training is almost always provided by the company. Senior technicians may broaden their skills with advanced training in programming, systems analysis or a related field such as telecommunications. Such experienced technicians then become troubleshooters for the most difficult problems, and often travel beyond their assigned region.

Requirements: Beyond the necessary training, computer service technicians must be willing to keep up with the ever changing technical information, which means reading manuals and attending presentations and classes. As technicians become more experienced they may be asked to travel to other locations on assignments. Besides the necessary technical training applicants for trainee spots must have good vision and normal color perception—many parts and wires are color coded—and good hearing to sound out breakdowns. Since technicians often work alone they must be self-motivating and able to work alone.

Service technicians are also customer relations representatives for their company. They're often the only company representative the customer has contact with. This requires the ability to work with people and a neat appearance. In some companies employees must pass a physical examination or security clearance if they are working in restricted buildings.

Salary: Although salaries for computer technicians are slightly higher than those in other high tech industries, they are close approximations. The average computer service technician earns about $24,500, with most in the $350–600 a week salary range. The top 10% of technicians earn approximately $35,000–37,000, the lowest 10% earn about $13,000. As with all data processing professions, supply of workers and geography is important. Computer technicians are better paid in the Northeast and in the West.

CORPORATE ADMINISTRATION

All day-to-day administrative and non-technical management jobs found in any company are found in high technology companies. High tech firms are therefore a good place to begin a job hunt even if you have no technical training or experience. These companies need the same accounting, art department, mailroom, security, personnel and secretarial staffers. Even librarians, maintenance personnel and meeting planners are needed by high tech firms. Because of the sophisticated nature of their business and the need for high caliber people, high tech companies generally pay better. They also require and demand the best people. You must have good skills for whatever position you wish to attain.

Good skills may be combined with knowledge about technology to evolve a satisfying, high paying job. There's no reason a talented commercial artist can't design brochures for a computer company just as easily as for a corn flakes cereal company. Best of all, the position will be in an upbeat, thriving environment.

1. "1985 Computer Salary Survey and Career Planning Guide." Source EDP Personnel Services, p. 13.
2. Ibid. p. 17.
3. Ibid.
4. Ibid. p. 16.
5. Half, op. cit. p. 25.
6. Ibid.

5

PERSONAL COMPUTERS

Personal computers (PCs) are just that—personal, a computer designed for and most often used by one person. They've become powerful tools for individuals everywhere—at home, in a hospital operating room, in a U.S. Forest Service center or most likely in a mundane office. Compared to the mainframe computer volcano the personal computer revolution is an earthquake. The capability of putting a computer on anyone's desk has opened up tremendous opportunities. Personal computers have sent computer gurus into rhapsodies of rhetoric. Some of their predictions have proven true; others have missed the mark badly. The fact remains that PCs have opened the computer world to the masses, and the price is right. In the late 1980s it is possible to buy a "business class" PC including a monitor and good printer for $2,500–3,000. Systems less ideal from a business perspective cost under $2,000, and an adequate system for the home from $500 to $1,000. The best news: Prices keep dropping for small systems.

PCs are the quintessential example of the theory that advancing technology makes products smaller, cheaper and more powerful. For example, IBM's PC AT, the successor of the PC, has the processing power equal to a system the size of a coffin and cost hundreds of thousands of dollars that had been introduced 6 years previously. (The coffin-sized system had been a major price/performance improvement over its predecessors.) PCs are being applied to thousands of new tasks. For instance:

- Financial analysts recalculate the benefits or losses of certain investments just by plugging the respective options into an accounting "green sheet." Computations are easily made thanks to software known as "spread sheet" programs.

- Writers avoid the tedious and time-consuming process of retyping clean manuscript pages by using a personal computer running word processing programs. They get around the "paper" problem altogether by sending their manuscripts electronically over telephone lines to an editor's personal computer—electronic mail.

- Small business owners have less need for a bookkeeper and typist. Personal computers running basic accounting and word processing packages allow them to do day-to-day bookkeeping and inventory entries, and to professionally type their own correspondence and bills. Innkeepers keep their guest reservations on microcomputers.

Why not golf? The applications for the IBM PC never seem to end, and a simulated game of golf—in which players challenge the course by selecting clubs, force of swing, direction, and keep score—is as much fun as any. (Courtesy of 1 Step Software, Inc.)

- Dairy farmers know which cows on which feed combinations are producing the most milk because of tracking/output programs using a personal computer.
- A portable personal computer in the operating room was used during early artificial heart implants to monitor all ongoing processes.
- Musicians and artists either are hooking PCs to existing equipment such as synthesizers or using the computer sound capability to create new music.

Corporations have put PCs on their employees' desks. The corporate marketplace is where the early PC action has been, and companies have bought truckloads of personal computers. That's led to company stores where employees select their PC from an already approved supplier, and to "information centers" where employees get training on and help with their PCs and applications. In this exciting new PC area many new training, consulting and product jobs have evolved—especially for those who saw the PC trend coming. Lotus Development Corporation is the most amazing example of soaring success. In its first year Lotus earned $53 million. In its first 3 years of operation the Cambridge, Massachusetts-based company grew from 24 employees to 900. But Lotus is not the only one to benefit from its 1-2-3 spreadsheet, which proved to be just what financial planners and number pushers needed to run on their new IBM PCs. Training companies teaching novices (and almost everyone was) how to use 1-2-3 blossomed. Add-on product companies leaped on 1-2-3 with everything from books to plastic templates giving the functions of various keys to lay over the keyboard to specialized packages that added functions to 1-2-3.

SHAKE-OUT TIME

By the late 1980s, however, the PC action is starting to dim, in much the same way the minicomputer industry quieted in the mid-1970s and the mainframe business calmed in the late 1960s and early 1970s. This is the shake-out time long predicted for the PC industry. Firms just getting by, or making so-so products, closed their doors. "It's probably too late to go into PCs," says one corporate headhunter. He's talking about the PC as a career peg within a large organization and as a way of riding the new wave of technology. For many data processing professionals, involvement in personal computing, or end user computing, was an excellent way of staying current and lengthening their technical expertise.

The microcomputer industry is also tightening up. Starting a software company in a garage seldom occurs today. In the late 1970s and early 1980s it happened frequently. In the first half of 1985 many microcomputer hardware and software makers were shocked to find their earnings sliding. For the first time heady companies such as Apple Computer, the father of them all, and MicroPro, developers of the famous and at one time ubiquitous WordStar word processing package, laid off employees. These downturns, sudden to those not following the industry, came after bankruptcies and near-bankruptcies by many PC related firms. IBM sued IBM PC compatible manufacturers for copyright infringement of operating systems internals. VisiCalc, the software product probably most responsible for selling Apple computers, lost out totally when its parent VisiCorp was divested to the bone and then disappeared.

This doesn't mean that opportunities for working with personal computers no longer exist, just that the earthquake of tremendous growth is over—at least until a new quake of technical improvements occurs. Large numbers of PC jobs no longer exist. The barriers to entry are higher; employers expect more from PC knowledgeable workers. Both these hurdles are overcome. The dust in the industry may be settling, but PCs are not going away. By 1985 only 20% of the PC market for large corporations had been saturated, according to market research firms. New software and hardware products continue to be introduced. Knowing these new products opens many career doors. Users want the personal computer on their desk to communicate with the corporate mainframe. Few companies have accomplished this yet, but many new products are coming on the market. The world is waiting for the next VisiCalc or Lotus 1-2-3. All it takes is one person's genius.

INSTITUTIONALIZATION OF THE PERSONAL COMPUTER

In August 1981, IBM announced a baby, the IBM PC. Computer careers have not been the same since, for oldtimers or newcomers. The IBM PC has become the link for professionals, such as financial analysts and writers, and administrative workers, such as office managers and word processing operators. The IBM PC and compatibles are doing two things: They are giving users their first experiences at computing; and they are allowing non-technical, i.e., non-data processing, employees to tap directly into the organization's mainframe computer system, something they had been barred from doing by the highly protective data processing department. (Remember the locked doors on the computer room?)

The IBM PC, if only because of the logo of the largest computer company in the world, was a credible business computer. Prior to this time personal, or microcomputers as they had been commonly known until that time, were perceived as toys for intellectual misfits (or nerds, in the lexicon of the day). Microcomputers were perceived as being for electronics hobbyists, the type who until this time had had a ham radio in his basement. (Many ham radio fans have since become avid personal computer users.) The first personal computer, MITS, was more of a hobbyist assembly kit than anything useful. It was advertised and reported in the magazine *Popular Electronics*. Orders for the MITS machine flowed in, and it's still debated whether or not the machine actually worked. The more widely accepted Apple came along in 1975 when Steve Jobs and Steve Wozniak came up with the Model-T of microcomputers, the Apple II. (Only a few versions of the Apple I were built.)

By 1984 IBM had sold an estimated 2 million PCs and that number is expected to spiral throughout the late 1980s. Clever manufacturers who saw profits in the PC market produced thousands of IBM PC compatibles. PCs started appearing everywhere. One amusing way to pass time was to

Costing $5,000, the IBM Personal Computer AT puts on a desk top the processing power that eight years ago filled a large refrigerator and cost about $200,000. (Courtesy of International Business Machines Corporation)

see how many IBM PCs could be spotted through office windows on a busy commercial street.

The IBM PC has become ubiquitous for excellent reasons:

1. The price was right. For several thousand dollars users bought the same amount of computing power that used to fill a room and cost hundreds of thousands.

2. The needed "right" software was developed. The new generation of computer software developers saw immediately that workers needed software that would allow these new PCs to process text. They saw the need for software that would allow financial workers to do what sophisticated handheld calculators did . . . and go far beyond that.

3. The PC was a business machine. Until 1981 the most popular personal or microcomputer was the Apple. While the Apple, especially the Apple II, was a well built machine, its limited memory and clumsy keyboard gave it a toy-like image. Worse was the

shortage of capable business software for the Apple, a problem that continues to haunt the California manufacturer even with their subsequent computers.

4. The PC truly was "personal." The user controlled his or her machine and was less dependent on a DP guru to do computer work. For anyone who has not worked on a personal computer it is difficult to explain the one-to-one rapport that develops during the work process.

The IBM PC precipitated an entire new category of jobs and job skills. These aptitudes and skills are more likely possessed by the newcomer who's not entrenched in old ways of doing things and not afraid of touching a computer keyboard. For working with personal computers is much different than working with mainframe computers.

- They are in small businesses or in decentralized departments of large organizations. Large organizations have already dealt with their need for computing power.

- They require a jack-of-all-trades approach. Setting up a personal computer system entails not only assembling and installing the appropriate software, but plugging in cables, or even pulling out boards or defective semiconductor chips. Whereas in mainframe data processing a programmer never pulls the plug on the back of the machine, PC workers do it all the time. There's more intimacy between the PC worker, the software and the hardware.

- They involve self-contained tasks. The worker with a personal computer has two or three major jobs he or she wants to do—and that's all. Setting up a personal computer system means getting the system to run a word processing package, a spreadsheet package, a project management program and maybe a communications package that allows the user's PC to talk over telephone lines to another PC. This is especially useful for what's called electronic mail.

A large category of PC software includes word processing software, de rigeur for the PC because doing any kind of writing requires a word processing package. "Spreadsheet" is one of those catchalls that refer to accounting or accounting-like applications. The spreadsheet is the accountant's green page of numbers. This is recreated electronically instead of refiguring and then painstakingly changing figures. All the computation is handled by the software in seconds. The first spreadsheet package, VisiCalc, was responsible for Apple II's sales really taking off. An improved version, 1-2-3, was the winning one for the IBM PC.

The second large category of PC software is data base management systems, which serve as the giant filing cabinets for almost any data and allow the user to retrieve the data by category. Project management software allows the user to track the progress of various stages of a multitask, long-term project. The project management software determines what tasks need to be done by which dates in order to complete the project on time.

The personal computer industry is brimming with software to do many tasks. The latest products help one evaluate decisions, write resumes, organize thoughts, automatically dial numbers in a computer-resident address book or set type and design graphically attractive documents. PCs may even be used to develop color slide presentations.

Why You Don't Need to Learn BASIC

One of the common conversations between a person comfortable on computers and a computer illiterate goes like this:

"Oh, so you work with computers."
"Yeah."
"I wish I knew more about them. I see the kids in the stores and they all seem to know what they're doing. I really ought to take a course."

The course they often misguidedly enroll in is BASIC, until recently the only course available for persons interested in microcomputers. (This stems from the hacker days.) In few cases is it necessary to take a course in BASIC, and in most cases it's inappropriate.

BASIC is the computer language of personal computers. It was invented in the mid-1960s to be what the name says, a basic language for computer beginners that didn't require semesters of study and mental gymnastics. By comparison it is an easy-to-learn computer language if only because of its limited vocabulary.

The world has changed. When working with personal computers, writing your own computer program is rarely necessary because software packages at a reasonable price have already been written to do what you want (if not more). Serviceable packages are available at computer retail stores in the $100 range, and multifeatured ones for as high as $750. (Either the retailer or the developer provides some service, albeit often limited.)

It is this point that the person looking for a job working with personal computers finds himself. The remaining discussion looks at specific job tracks with two major distinctions: working for others or working independently—perhaps even at home.

WORKING WITH PERSONAL COMPUTERS

Because personal computers can be applied to so many tasks, workers involved with PCs find themselves in a variety of jobs. Those interested in working with PCs can apply their energy and background in at least 5 major directions:

1. Working with users, usually in larger organizations. This can be either on a staff or as an independent consultant.
2. Selling personal computers at the retail level.
3. Working for PC hardware manufacturers and software developers.
4. Using your personal computer to earn a living, which allows you to work at home. Writers are the best examples, although many companies allow their employees to telecommute.
5. Integrating a personal computer into other work and/or interests. Music projects are an interesting example of this.

In the late 1980s corporations have gobbled up personal computers, primarily the IBM PC and subsequent models. The PC is viewed as a tool for professionals and managers within the company. It's easy for these organizations to justify the benefits of putting a personal computer on an executive's desk. If the PC costs $5,000 and the manager's salary is $50,000, any productivity improvement or time the PC saves is considered well worth the cost. Ironically, too many PCs are turning into paper-weights, as executives are unwilling to take the time to learn to use them.

Since most PC users have not worked on computers before, they need help. A new group of computer workers has developed within larger companies: PC experts. They may work for companies or as independent consultants.

PC SPECIALISTS

Persons within organizations who work with personal computers go by many titles including PC specialist, microcomputer programmer or micro-computer programmer-analyst. In most cases the person is responsible for ensuring that applications run on personal computers. This entails myriad details that differ with each job.

Unlike mainframe computer specialists it's immediately assumed the PC specialist will take advantage of the existing software packages in the marketplace. The only programming from scratch is to tailor an off-the-shelf package to the needs of the organization. If custom programming is required, PC specialists may work in BASIC, but more likely one of the newer languages such as C, APL or Pascal.

Microcomputer programmers today are integrating personal computers into the organization's mainframe and/or communications systems because PC users are finding they cannot process data in isolation and need access to corporate data. This is considerably more complex than installing off-the-shelf packages.

In the past PC specialists have either started out in PCs because of their initial interest, or moved from other programming or computer specialties—many had been working as minicomputer programmers. Many PC experts-programmers have worked as independent consultants moving from small project to small project, either within one large company or among many organizations. Such consultants first meet with the potential users of the system to determine their needs. Then they usually acquire the software, install it on the PC and customize as needed for the users.

Information Centers and Company Stores

As users rushed to acquire and use personal computers, chaos developed. The purchasing department went crazy. The data processing department could not handle the deluge of questions and problems. In fact, most had never dealt with end users before and certainly not in these numbers. These were the days when companies were buying literally truckloads of PCs. Seizing the bull by the horns, enlightened data processing departments realized PCs were not going to go away . . . as they probably would have preferred. They established information centers on the "can't beat 'em, join 'em" theory. The information centers became the focal point for PC introduction within the company and were staffed by PC specialists. Information center experts trained novice users and also provided special services such as graphics. In many cases the information center also housed the more expensive graphics and printing equipment. In the same vein the purchasing departments, in order to withstand the PC onslaught, opened company stores where users could select and purchase PCs from authorized systems. In companies where the data processing department declared war on PC users, PC enthusiasts established their own centers. These wars have not been resolved in many companies.

PC jobs are mostly filled. Nevertheless, since organizations want to do more complex projects, the demand for PC specialists remains. As Source EDP projects: "Demand increasing for people with specific specialties such as teleprocessing, graphics and real-time control systems."[1]

For example, a 25-person financial services company running 7 PCs for financial analysis, accounting, word processing and communications recently required the following in a PC specialist:

1. Support operators in all software and hardware operations. Require an in-depth understanding of the software packages currently in use and familiarity with the hardware.

2. Research and report (in writing if necessary) on all hardware options available to meet the requirements of this rapidly growing company.

3. Support the next hardware structure, whether it be a micro network or mini/micro configuration.

4. Communicate with software developers writing customized packages; for example, the development of a sophisticated data base package or a highly specialized financial analysis program.

5. Ensure that the computers are used efficiently and safely by providing responsive management, advice and support.

Requirements: This firm is looking for 2 years' experience working with PCs, ability to solve hardware and software problems, some programming knowledge and the ability to communicate with non-technical colleagues and provide literate, informative summaries of research undertaken. These requirements are typical.

Because of the tremendous need for personal computer know-how several years ago, it was possible for many persons with only the vaguest notion of the technology to proclaim themselves PC specialists, and go after consulting assignments or even full-time jobs. Some consultants introduced bootlegged software or received kickbacks for the equipment and software they recommended. Once companies were stung by unqualified consultants, however, the situation tightened up. Many small companies that need a PC system but have little understanding of them remain prey for unscrupulous consultants. The fear of computers remains for these small businesses.

Portable computers—this one the size of a portable sewing machine with the keyboard flipping off the bottom—have allowed users to compute on the go, or at least from desk to desk. They've fueled the popularity of the PC. (Courtesy of COMPAQ Computer Corporation)

Large accounting firms are also employers of microcomputer consultants—one has 6,000 PC experts. These firms have found it lucrative to offer PC consulting in addition to their accounting work.

At the staff level requirements are also going up. Source EDP puts it succinctly:

"An increasing complexity of technology requires significant expertise and skills in software design and development. Most opportunities will require a minimum of one year experience with one or more high-level structured languages. Those in the greatest demand will also have direct exposure to real-time control/monitoring, operating systems, I/O drivers, compilers, interpreters, diagnostics and application software.

"The microcomputer/microprocessor explosion is creating substantial and unique opportunities for machine or Assembly Language programming in both established as well as entrepreneurial high technology organizations . . . Additionally, knowledge of two- and three-dimensional graphics, artificial intelligence and integrated telecommunications (data and voice) are needs that are rapidly increasing in demand."[2]

Salary: Salaries for PC specialists, although lower than for programmers and analysts on larger systems, vary greatly. Hourly rates range from $25 to $50 for freelance consultants. Source EDP found salaries for microcomputer programmers with 1–2 years on the job ranged from $20,500 to $34,200, with $27,800 average; 2–5 years' programming experience, $24,200–38,600, average $32,400; over 5 years, $28,900–48,200, average $39,000.[3]

PC TECHNICIANS

To alleviate always sending the systems out for repair many companies have hired in-house PC technicians. A PC technician must be a jack-of-all-trades, knowing something about software in addition to lots about hardware—down to the chip level. PCs are built so that semiconductors—chips in everyday parlance—can be popped in and out. This ease of repair and access to the machine internals is unheard of in the hands-off, larger systems business.

Unlike hardware sales, repair service revenues do not boom and bust, but tend to grow incrementally. That's good news for repairers and repair services expecting to produce almost $10 billion in revenues this year compared to $2 billion in 1972. This is for all sizes of systems. PC repair is the growth edge of this business because of the sheer numbers and because it's new. The Bureau of Labor Statistics agrees: The overall number of computer technicians in the next 10 years will almost double, from 55,000 today to about 108,000 in 1995. Again, many will work on PCs. (See Chapter 4.)

What a PC technician actually does depends on the employer. The technician may be on an in-house staff involved in putting out fires among users who have hardware, and more often, software problems with their PC. This may entail tearing the system down either in the user's office or in a shop area. The PC technician often pops out chips believed to be defective and replaces them with new ones. The in-house technician may also get involved in collecting and setting up equipment for special demonstrations for visitors as well as installing new systems as they come in. The PC technician works closely with users within the organization.

The technician working for a repair shop or third-party repair firm, spends more time diagnosing and fixing hardware problems. A technician working on repair contracts may make calls on various customers much like the computer technician on big systems. (See Chapter 4.) He or she may be called on to consult with customers, either on repairing equipment or evaluating new hardware.

Because repair work is so expensive, self-diagnostic systems are being included in new systems: When certain things go wrong, an indicator light goes on. IBM has taken the lead in providing what's called on-line diagnostics: small computers are tested by larger ones over telephone lines. Most software companies provide hot lines so that customers can find answers to technical problems. Too often, though, the printer manufacturer blames the problem on the word processing package developer and vice versa.

Requirements: Technicians need to be familiar with the PCs they work on. Most come to their jobs with a two-year vocational or electronics degree. (See Chapter 4.) Unlike large systems vendors, microcomputer vendors (with the major exception of IBM) are less likely to provide technician training or updates. Once on the job technicians on small systems are expected to teach themselves and keep abreast of the new technology. Retail sales has been one entry point to PC technicians. Salespersons with a flair for hardware and "fixing things" have moved into the shops at many retail stores.

Salary: Beginning salaries vary from $12,000 to $25,000, although most start in the $12,000–15,000 range.

PC TRAINERS

Companies that have committed themselves to the hardware/software investment provide training for their employees who are not computer-literate. PC training is hands-on and aimed at putting the user right to work. The first focus is thus on the package the user will start with. For executives with more complicated assignments PC training shows them how a software package such as Lotus 1-2-3 can be applied to their daily business problems. (Comparing pesos and dollars in a decision whether to build a new manufacturing plant in Mexico or refurbish one in Puerto Rico, for example.) Such courses usually run three days either at the company or at a special training center.

Trainers can be either on-staff or consultants. Some consultants have vans equipped with PCs that visit corporate parking lots to provide training. A new wrinkle has been the development of PC training centers, where persons from many companies attend classes to learn the use of one or several PC products.

The declining cost of memory and the improvements in memory technology have been a boon to the personal computer industry. It's easy to upgrade personal computers with add-on memory boards, which include additional features such as built-in clock and additional printer or communications ports. Boards such as this are slipped into expansion slots within the PC chassis. (Courtesy AST Research)

Requirements: Trainers must understand PCs and how they're used in business, and be able to explain that to others effectively. Such skills come from a variety of experiences. One classified advertisement added an interesting note: "Must look super corporate and be comfortable working with management."

Salary: Trainers are experienced professionals earning $25,000–35,000. If they work as independent consultants, especially with large seminars, they may earn $1,000–1,400 a day, although the majority are closer to

$350–500 a day. Trainers get paid more for working with top executives than with staff workers, although the material may be the same.

PC MANAGERS

All these PC experts report to managers. Experience is again at a premium when working with personal computers. Companies look for managers who have an understanding of the technology, but more importantly are good managers: leaders who are good communicators and who work well with people. PC managers must increasingly understand mainframe and other technologies because users want to connect their PCs to additional systems. This complex technology requires even more expertise on the part of managers and PC specialists.

The PC arena requires a bridge of communications from the technical departments to the user departments—two groups with widely divergent interests. These bridges are often difficult to build, and then precarious to maintain, especially if the system the PC specialists deliver doesn't do precisely what the users wanted. Human communication being what it is, this is almost always the case.

Requirements: PC managers must have the attributes of good managers and know about personal computers and technologies users might want to use in combination, such as communications. This all means good planning and system implementation skills. As PCs get involved in increasingly complex applications PC specialists and managers are coming from DP departments. PC challenges demand expertise on many levels.

Salary: Since responsibilities and experience for PC managers vary greatly, so do salaries. The range is $30,000–48,000.

Other PC Managers

Not to be overlooked are consulting, training and repair groups who also need management. An employment ad recently pinpointed such a need: "PC training course developer for 'Big 8' accounting firm requires an individual with three special skills to fill this 'unusual, new position' developing microcomputer training courses and materials for this firm's external courses:

1. A microcomputer buff with thorough knowledge of the terminology and concepts of IBM compatibles.
2. Familiarity with software programs such as Lotus 1-2-3 and dBase III.
3. Course design or experience in training others on micros."

PC RETAILERS

A bad joke among irreverent PC users asks, "What's the difference between a used car salesman and a computer salesman?" Answer: "The used car salesman knows he's lying."

The joke plays on the fact that many computer salespeople in the recent past have had little computer knowledge. Selling personal computers has been one of the easiest entry points into the PC arena. That is quickly changing as users get smarter and the action grows tougher in the retail marketplace. In the beginning of the PC hullabaloo retail computer stores opened in every other shopping center. Stores selling only software sprouted. With the decreased demand for business systems, the failure of the home market to materialize and the subsequent shake-out in the industry, many of those computer dealers failed. The number of stores dropped and chains such as Computerland and BusinessLand, which cater to businesses, predominated.

Even the circumspect IBM Corporation has opened PC stores, known as Retail Centers. In fact, IBM is experimenting with many new distribution schemes including working with other manufacturers who "add value" to the basic IBM box besides traditional sales representative calls to user accounts. The IBM PC has too many potential customers not to cover all the bases.

Retail sales representatives need a combination of sales ability and technical expertise. That expertise stems, from on-the-job training, personal interest in microcomputers or from formal courses. The more demanding a store's customers, the more sales personnel need to know. If the store is located in a downtown business district they need a more sophisticated understanding of business applications than a store in a suburban shopping center that emphasizes home computers and games software. Some stores catering to businesses have their own outside sales forces that call on and service area businesses. These stores are the main retail sponsors of PC training classes, often at the store in the evenings.

Requirements: Dual skills are important to PC sales positions: Sales representatives must be good at explaining their products and pulling in the sale, but to do that they require technical understanding. Retail firms prefer to get as many experienced and trained salespeople as possible on their staffs, but talented high school graduates have been also hired for these positions. They either learn on the job or attend 2–4 week training courses. PC retail chains and larger stores are better at providing training.

Retail sales is an excellent entry point to the PC business, one that still remains open despite changes in the industry.

Salary: Salaries in retail sales start as low as $12,000–15,000, but representatives almost always work on commissions, which can be lucrative.

Distributors

The existence of vibrant retail channels in the marketplace allows for growing numbers of middlemen—the distributors. Distributors handle quantities of hardware and software in order to fill orders from stores. This is unlike the large systems market in which manufacturers and software developers usually sell directly to end users. Distributors usually operate regionally. National distributors have regional offices and warehouses, making speedier deliveries possible.

Mail Order

Also specific to the PC industry are mail order companies. Although they're generally frowned on by retailers—and thus looked on less favorably by vendors—mail order firms have done extraordinarily well. More reputable mail order houses often have in-house technical experts to answer customers' questions. Most employees are involved in administrative and shipping and handling functions. Mail order firms are listed in PC magazines, their lifeline to users.

PC HARDWARE AND SOFTWARE

Success stories about young entrepreneurs who made millions in the PC industry are legend. At one point it was hard not to turn around and find a Steve Jobs, founder of Apple, or a Bill Gates, founder of Microsoft on a magazine cover. They made it sound so simple. Have a bright idea, hit up venture capitalists for seed funding, put out a product and make a million dollars.

Although it worked that way for maybe 100 players, they were a tiny minority. Even the lucky ones have encountered problems. By the late 1980s the action has slowed to routine operation of small businesses. Young entrepreneurial managers are also having to manage high growth—two dozen to 900 employees in 3 years, for instance. Their personalities and management styles are not always suited to their company's new circumstances. If the company has been a one-product success story, or a one trick pony as they're known in the industry—then management may be hard pressed to respond to a marketplace moving on to the newest hot products. This was the case with VisiCorp, which was unable to develop a successor to the enormously successful VisiCalc.

Like the mainframe companies, personal computer firms are in the business of manufacturing hardware, developing and marketing software or providing services. (Remember: These firms require the same research and development, marketing and administrative employees.) The jobs vary slightly from the established large systems firms because these newer companies are smaller or may have what author Alvin Toffler describes as a *Third Wave,* or more enlightened company philosophy. It's more likely the microcomputer companies will have Friday afternoon beer breaks, or provide swimming pools, work-out gyms and jogging tracks for their employees. Employees with these companies call them the best places they've ever worked. Often the staff is young and it's not unusual for a camaraderie to develop among employees, especially when pushing to get out a new product, project or special event. Microcomputer companies offer many good opportunities for women. Research by Cognos Associates, a non-profit research group in Los Altos, California, has found that women make more career progress at small firms within the electronics and computer industries. Once they get their foot in the door, their work speaks for itself. The smaller companies experience the greatest growth, making more opportunities available.

Financially, PC companies are more likely to offer senior managers stock options and other inducements. If the company goes public and sells shares for public trading, these employees can cash in their options for big profits. (Of course, the company may fizzle before it goes public, as did Osborne Computer.)

On the development side PC companies require the same expertise as the larger systems makers detailed in Chapter 4. The difference is that they need to understand smaller systems, most notably the IBM PC and associated languages and technologies.

BASIC is the primary language for PCs, but only a minority of commercial programs are written in this simpler programming language. More serious commercial software packages are programmed in Assembler, APL or Unix. Hardly any micro programs use the mainframe mainstay, COBOL.

Employers in the personal computer industry are more flexible about education requirements. Experience counts less in an industry that's only 10 years old; there simply aren't that many PC whizzes who have jumped through the job hoops demanded in the more entrenched mainframe business. Even hackers have found employment in the microcomputer industry. The same is true with freakers (who break through telephone systems) because the analytical and code-cracking skills used by hackers and freakers are the same as required to build products and systems.

The ultimate job in the micro industry is not work at all, but playing games. The geniuses who first dream up and then program the various video and computer games get paid for having fun—usually winning sums. Most are young men in their late teens or early 20s. Developing computer-based games requires more imagination, enthusiasm and creativity than computer knowledge, but the skills seem to go hand in hand.

MICRO MARKETERS

Marketing personal computer products requires the same skills as marketing large systems; only the specifications are different. Marketing professionals make strategies for bringing their products to a wide range of customers, as distinguished from sales representatives who visit specific companies. Because of the end user market marketing professionals also get involved in presenting a good image for their product and company at computer shows, before user groups or the media. Sales representatives for PC products have a different mission than those for mainframe products. In most instances PC sales reps have less contact with the end user and more with the retailer or decision maker (sometimes a purchase agent) at a large user.

The marketing action is more fast-paced and competitive on the PC front. Software and hardware packages come and go. Timing is all in the PC marketplace. It's important to get the product out there—through the product window, as insiders say—at the strategic moment, or your competitor will beat you. Having a terrific product too late is disastrous. Moreover, because of potential profits the competition doesn't go away. Consider this: In 1981 11 companies made 5 ¼-inch Winchester disk drives, the hard disks that have become more popular than magnetic "floppy disks" for storage on a PC. In 1985 there were 54 contenders. Simple statistics suggest that not all these hard disk manufacturers will be around next year. This is one reason for the high turnover of personnel in the PC industry, especially in the area of marketing.

PC sales representatives work on commissions. Earning a good income requires selling quantity because a commission on a $500 spreadsheet package does not compare with one for a $500,000 mainframe DBMS system. A sample advertisement for a microcomputer software salesperson states: "Selling to computer stores, software stores and distributors in the New York market. Some travel required. Must have a proven sales track record or have accounting experience with a strong desire to be in sales. Draw against commission, company car, insurance, $50–100K first year."

PC SERVICE AND SUPPORT

Some companies are excellent, others are dreadful at providing service and support for PC products. Servicing and supporting a software product is different from hardware because the software exists only on a magnetic medium (in the case of a PC on a 5 ¼-inch floppy disk). Because of the complicated nature of installing some PC products, micro firms have departments that answer customer questions, which vary greatly. One popular software developer complained that most of the questions his customer service group received related to printers, but that printer companies were less responsive.

For hardware manufacturers service means fixing. Manufacturers have set up many repair plans. Retailers have also come to a customer's aid by having service departments, although these often have to return equipment to the manufacturers.

The sheer number of personal computers requires a large number of repairers. Because the machines are less complex it's easier to break into PC technician spots. The retail store is also an ideal place to begin a career.

Third Party Service

Besides the manufacturers and retailers, a third segment of the service industry is growing: independent firms which specialize in servicing hardware. These third-parties may advertise nationwide, or just hang out a shingle.

PCS AT HOME: WORKING FOR YOURSELF

Because of the terrific capabilities and the low cost of PCs, individuals can afford microcomputers for personal and/or professional use. Writing, consulting and programming (development of other micro programs) are the most obvious and popular uses of a PC at home. Books have been written on how to earn money with your micro. Many popular writers, from playwrights to advertising copy writers, are addicted to their PCs. Newsletter editors, especially now with sophisticated word processing, typesetting and page make-up software, prepare entire editions at their computer screen.

Word processing software alleviates the need to retype manuscripts, thereby speeding a writer's production. Many writers also claim that word processing clarifies their thoughts and makes them better writers—they edit their drafts on the screen.

Communications software and modem hardware allow the writer/consultant/at-home worker to access data bases stored on-line such as Dialog

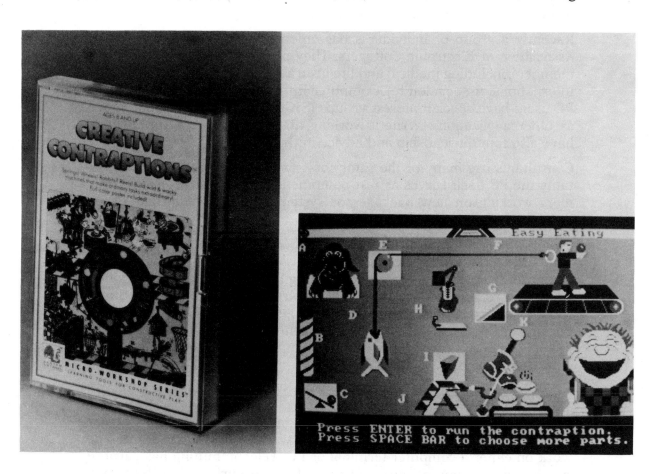

Games have been a popular application of personal computers, introducing many players to the joys of computing. (Courtesy of Bantam Electronic Publishing)

Information Services and Dow Jones News/Retrieval. Not only is this information used in consulting and writing projects, it may be the basis of a business itself—doing research with your computer.

PC users use electronic mail systems such as MCI Mail, EasyLink or CompuServe to speedily exchange information with colleagues. Many writers now beat overnight delivery services by "zapping" their manuscripts in minutes to the editor's electronic mailbox. Writers have also found uses for spelling check and dictionary software packages that grade prose for "readability" or grade-level aimed at, and even graphics packages for developing charts. Growing in popularity are outline packages and thought processors designed to organize and sequence thoughts.

Data base management packages, many of which are complicated and designed for business, are a boon for the writer. Data base managers organize data much as index cards do a term paper. Simpler data bases serve as address and telephone books. One well-known writer uses a spreadsheet package to insure that the needed elements of his thriller plots are included in each chapter—charting the flow, as it were. The newest genre of software, called desk organizers, also help the home worker manage many tasks at once.

Recently a group of individuals has emerged who work at home, The Association of Electronic Cottagers. They provide many services to their members, including medical and life insurance. The group is subtitled The International Association for Computer Entrepreneurs & Telecommuters. PC users have special interest groups (SIGs) on word processing as well as other applications. Writers working at home, and most often alone, have also found friendship and advice in the PC users' groups.

Consultants use many of the same tools as writers. If they're PC consultants the PC itself serves as test equipment for their projects. Programmers working on new packages or systems for a PC use their PCs as development tools and test systems.

Programming at home is a tremendous boon for many talented women who have relocated with their husbands to communities where their computer talents are not needed. Working at home can also be a double-edged sword. Boston sociologist Philip Kraft of the Center for Survey Research is concerned that at-home programmers are being exploited because higher-paying, satisfying programming work is not available to them. (The availability of this work is changing as games and educational software become less popular.)

Working for Others

Telecommuting is a trendy term for persons who work at home but are connected electronically to an office, or work in a satellite office. They work on either a computer terminal or PC. Telecommuting has garnered much public attention and publicity. On the surface it offers many attractive features. As telecommuting has been tested, however, it's proven less popular. In a recent survey of at-home workers Honeywell

Information Systems found that only 7% of managers and other information professionals and users would choose to work at home. They miss the camaraderie of the office!

1. Source, op. cit. p. 8.
2. Ibid.
3. Ibid. p. 16.

6

TELECOMMUNICATIONS

If any technology is breaking loose in the late 1980s it's telecommunications. The unbridled, seemingly chaotic growth that characterized the personal computer industry several years ago is now evident in communications technologies. In the wake of the deregulation of AT&T telecommunications is in turmoil. Communications companies are doubling their number of employees each year. Manufacturers with winning products one year are in trouble the next. The industry is jumping and shaking with mergers such as IBM's buying 16% of MCI. Just keeping up with the new developments, court rulings and regulatory changes surrounding American Telephone & Telegraph (AT&T) is a struggle.

Add to this the downpour of new technologies: satellites, fiber optics, communicating computers, local area networks, digital PBXs, microwave dishes, earth stations and more.

Such tumult creates career opportunities, which the experts say will probably continue through the year 2000. Most large companies today have what amounts to a small internal telephone company/system. They may have as many as 6 or 10 switches at one location. These companies regularly report that their biggest management information systems dilemma is finding qualified telecommunications talent at any level, especially managers. One estimate predicts a need for 100,000 trained people in communications. "The situation is akin to the search for space pilots in the '60's. There were none. A telecom manager by today's definition is almost as scarce," observes *Datamation*.[1]

The even better news is that, according to an A.S. Hansen telecommunications survey, telecommunications professionals are better paid and receive higher merit increases than their counterparts in other parts of organizations, such as data processing departments.[2] In addition, many communications jobs are available outside the United States. "Communications is always the first infrastructure developing countries want to improve," reports a personnel recruiter searching for persons who want to work in the Middle East.

Communications offers attractive opportunities to women. Susan A. Jarrett, an assistant vice-president of telecommunications at Bankers Trust Company in New York, is a good example. She's in charge of maintaining and operating 6 telephone switching systems within the bank. In fact, her geographical responsibility covers merely a 10 block radius in midtown Manhattan. Jarrett also operates incoming financial information services equipment such as stock market quotations from Wall Street. "I lucked

Ground stations like this one, with many microwave receiving dishes, are increasingly being used to send and receive data and voice signals via satellite links. (Courtesy of Space Communications Company)

into it; there were no undergraduate programs in telecommunications when I was in school," said Jarett. She taught elementary school for 4 years in North Carolina prior to moving to Philadelphia, where she answered a newspaper advertisement for a communications analyst at the University of Pennsylvania. Because telephone service had deteriorated so badly on campus, the job required public relations and fence mending tact as much as it did technical expertise. She got the job on tact, and quickly acquired the technical know-how. "I was always good at math," she says, although quickly adding, "You don't really need math or have to like computers to be successful in telecommunications."

Jarrett's job is keeping up with changes. "Nothing is ever static. Organizations, plans, people change . . . someone is promoted," observes Jarrett. The bank has 10,000 telephone lines and 15,000 phones, not unusual for large organizations. When those lines, phones or phone numbers need to be changed for any reason, Jarrett makes sure it happens. In one month there were 1,000 such changes, which for the most part were programmed into the switching system by a telecommunications specialist. Much of Jarrett's responsibility is as a liaison between users who need phone service, corporate administration, vendors who provide the equipment and technicians who do the work. (Technicians may work either for the vendor or for the user, in this case the bank.) Both technicians and administrative personnel report to Jarrett.

EVERYONE REACHES OUT

Despite the fact that more than 100 years have passed since Alexander Graham Bell told Thomas Watson, "Come here, Watson, I need you," communications remains in its adolescence. The explosion in telephone use, the increase in the number of new products and technologies and the revolution caused by the divestiture of AT&T all make communications a great industry in which to find a rewarding career.

From the career perspective the day that rocked the communications industry was January 8, 1982. That day the U. S. Department of Justice settled its 10-year antitrust suit against AT&T. The settlement unraveled the telephone system in this country. AT&T had been a monopoly, a sound move when the goal was to provide universal, highly reliable communications to a rapidly growing and unfolding nation. Prior to the settlement AT&T and local subsidiaries workers had always been assured of a demand for their services and products. They were "order takers" for a public who had an insatiable desire to communicate over Alexander Graham Bell's box.

As telephone service grew geometrically, especially in the 1950–70 period, other companies wanted in on this rapid growth. Beginning in 1956 a series of companies began offering alternative products to Ma Bell's. When they didn't get far selling them, these smaller firms went to court. The most famous case involved Carterfone in 1968, which allowed the sale of non-Bell equipment. A second deregulation breakthrough came when MCI Communications went to court against AT&T on antitrust violations and won.

By 1985 dozens of phone service providers were vying for the public's favor in long distance service, noticeably in television advertisements with movie stars touting or attacking AT&T's capabilities. (Providing local telephone service is expensive because of hardware and wiring and, even more costly, customer service.) Long haul transmissions between cities take advantage of high-speed computers (electronic message switches or just switches) and handle high volumes for lucrative profits. (Until the divestiture AT&T long-distance service subsidized its local service. With the divestiture into long-distance and local systems, costs for local phone service are skyrocketing. Although predicted, these changes took most citizens and certainly the federal and state governments by surprise.

Many citizens called for Humpty Dumpty to be put back together again. That's not to be. Today, phone users do the following:

- Buy telephones like toasters and in the same store.
- Choose which company switches their long-distance phone calls, often taking advantage of discounts and incentives.
- Make fewer personal phone calls from work. More sensitive to their soaring phone bills, corporations are clamping down on personal calls by their employees. (Today's computerized phone systems track long-distance phone calls, and employees must be able to reconcile these records.)

COMMUNICATIONS: VOICE AND DATA

Communications has so many meanings that readers might be uncertain exactly which meaning is pertinent here. In common usage communications is the transmittal of information. In technology it's the transference of data between people, devices or a person and a device. The device ultimately delivers the information in various forms to another person.

Telecommunications refers to the transmission or transference of voice communications. There are two types of signals. Voice signals are analog. Computers, however, produce electronic digital signals. Because it's extraordinarily useful to be able to transfer computer signals, the technology of data communications has developed. Asynchronous communications, data signals are digital as opposed to analog. Once the stepchild of both the telecommunications and computer industries, data communications is becoming a discipline in its own right.

Computers and Communications

One school of thought contends that computers and communications will become so closely entwined that there will be constantly pulsing "computing utility" (not unlike electrical circuits or a building's built-in vacuum cleaning system) that users will plug into at their homes and/or offices. Some huge computing service bureaus are not too far from this, although they've achieved less acceptance than predicted.

Telephones and maybe a PBX were formerly for communications and computers for computing. Today telephones have microprocessors and some even have computing power. The workstation of the future, the piece of equipment every worker will have, is likely to be a personal computer equipped with a telephone. Several are already on the market. Conversely, customized computers today handle almost all of the communications message switching, to say nothing of the private data transmissions from computer users.

With AT&T's divestiture and the dropping of the 13-year antitrust action against the IBM Corporation, manufacturers in both these sectors started intruding into the other's territory. AT&T introduced a family of computers including two initially disappointing personal computers. In 1985 IBM bought into MCI Communications on the heels of its 1984 purchase of the highly successful and innovative PBX maker, Rolm Corporation. AT&T and IBM have thus become the major players in today's information age, hopefully not the only ones!

Communications Employers

The communications industry is a bustling, changing, burgeoning one. Knowing who's who and where the jobs are is of the highest importance. The major employer categories are

1. Communications services providers such as AT&T.
2. Manufacturers of communications equipment, both voice and data.
3. Users of communications services. The key ones for job seekers are large corporations, but this category also includes everyone who uses a phone.

In these areas the demand for talent far outpaces the supply, and the more skilled or professional the position, the greater the gap. "Extreme shortages exist for design and development engineers with experience with any kind of current telecommunications equipment," reported Jay Jacobson of Personnel Resources, Inc. in New York. "Technicians in extremely short supply include radio and PBX installation and repair personnel." Equipment manufacturers are having similar difficulty finding systems and applications engineers, especially at the junior levels, with at least one engineering degree and experience with radio, data communications or telephone systems. This scarcity has existed for the last 15 years. "There's never the right balance between openings and people," says Jacobsen, who has been recruiting telecommunications professionals since 1969. Currently his biggest demand is for communications experts with 2–5 years' experience. Companies are becoming more stringent in their requirements.

In general, lower- and intermediate-level employees were most in demand by employers. They were also looking for one or more academic degrees, stable employment records, willingness to relocate, and state-of-the-art expertise in telecommunications. Job seekers in major centers such as Washington, DC or New York found it easier to change jobs than counterparts in Texas or Montana, observed Jacobson. "It appears," reports the Hansen survey, "the industry is hiring from wherever it can, and that the average rates of pay are strongly correlated only with years of related service and level of job in the job family."[3]

Telecommunications jobs are located around the world, just like the technology itself. Recruiters who regularly have job orders from Saudi Arabia and Third World countries, note that a telecommunications system is the first thing most developing countries want to install and/or upgrade. In addition, earth stations or switching stations are often in remote locations, and it is possible to live in Montana and have a demanding telecommunications job.

Communications Education

"Employers, even some prestigious, large ones, are frequently waiving degree requirements if job applications have appropriate experience," states Jacobson. While this is great in the short term, in the long term it's important to remember that economies and industries change. In a downturn economy or when being considered for promotions, employees without degrees will be at a career disadvantage. It's better to finish academic work, advises Jacobson.

Education and training for communications careers is constantly evolving and being upgraded. Depending on job level there are three major directions: on-the-job training, vocational electronics education and college-level communications courses. In the days before divestiture AT&T itself trained most of its semiskilled workers. After all, AT&T and its subsidiaries were the only game in town. Now communications companies want employees with some post-high school training, e.g., junior college or vocational programs. (See Chapter 2.) For technicians, installers and more skilled jobs, industry employers who are communications users are looking for employees with technical training from vocational schools or community colleges, or computer/technical training in college.

Until recently few communications courses existed at four-year schools, even at those with computer science and/or engineering programs. That began to change in 1985 when the State University of New York (SUNY) formed a Telecommunications Institute at its Utica-Rome campus. They opened degree programs in electronic information, offering a bachelor of science degree in telecommunications. Courses run the gamut of voice, video and data communications: history of telecommunications in the telephone industry, broadcasting, voice and data communications, transmission theory, principles of switching, and terminal equipment and network decision. The SUNY Institute for Telecommunications also offers non-credit courses, workshops and summer institutes.

Several organizations, including the National Telecommunications Education Committee, an arm of the North American Telecommunications Association (NATA), and the International Communications Association (ICA) are compiling directories of educational opportunities in telecommunications. (See Appendix 1.)

Communications Carriers

The giant is AT&T. Whereas its regional operating companies used to plow money back to the parent company, the Bell Operating Companies (BOC) are now separate companies making their own ways in the turbulent communications waters. (This is why your telephone bill probably lists two services—long distance from AT&T and local service from one of the BOCs.) Several are energetically establishing themselves as separate entities, buying hardware from companies other than AT&T's Western Union and offering creative services to customers.

Equally imaginative and aggressive are the independent carriers: MCI Communications, which laid much of the groundwork for today's deregulated environment; GTE, best known among consumers for Sprint service; and IT&T, also an alternative long-distance provider. Other companies offering prices too good to be true have sprung up to provide long-distance services. Some of these and other corporations that have their own telecommunications networks (including perhaps a transponder on a satellite) are selling their excess capacity, especially for computer-to-computer communications.

In 1985 at GTE more than half of the approximately 700 persons hired were technical professionals, most with four-year degrees in computer science or electrical engineering. Graduates with these degrees usually find themselves garnering as many as 10 job offers. Because many of today's communications jobs didn't exist even last year there's no existing pool of experienced employees.

Marketing Challenge

In the past, customers always called Bell companies for orders. Their product line was an evolutionary one. The introduction of color telephones in the mid-1950s created major upheavals in the company at the time. AT&T and its offspring, the Bell Operating Companies, are establishing corporate and product strategy and planning departments. If AT&T's performance with personal computers is indicative, the company is going to take time to grope its way in this competitive information age. Business majors are needed, and if the recent graduate has any technical training, so much the better. Sometimes liberal arts graduates break into the field. Job titles, responsibilities, and salaries are close to those of other technology industries. For instance, salaries are higher for computer workers, but other parameters are similar.

Manufacturers and Interconnects

The telecommunications explosion has also rocked the manufacturers of communications hardware. Telephone sets and even larger PBXs (Private Branch Exchange), the bigger phone line switches for large organizations,

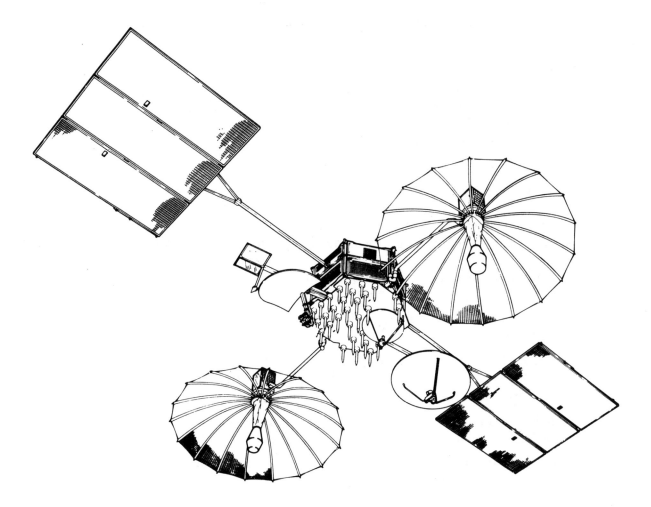

Satellites dedicated to sending voice, data and broadcast signals are growing in popularity. The satellites are launched in cooperation with the National Aeronautics and Space Administration (NASA). (Courtesy of Space Communications Company)

previously came from Western Electric, the manufacturing arm of Bell. With divestiture, supplying communications hardware became a free-for-all that included the regional operating companies, who no longer had to buy from Western Electric and who often had more innovative products. In the late 1970s Rolm offered a PBX with features customers wanted (such as call-forwarding or built-in answering machine capability) but could not get from Bell. Add to this "interconnect" companies, intermediate firms that distribute, sell and install this newly available hardware. "Twenty years ago no one ever heard of these companies," observes Jacobsen about one of his most active client groups. "The possibility still exists they will make inroads against Western Electric."

Like the carriers, the vendors need a combination of researchers, product planners, designers and marketers. When communications products incorporate computing capabilities, communications hardware manufacturers need computer experts in both hardware and software. The breadth of Northern Telecom's corporate divisions demonstrates the complexity and increasing computerization of today's communications world:

1. Data Networks
2. Advanced Telephone Products
3. Bell Northern Research
4. Transmission
5. Integrated Office Systems
6. Digital Switching
7. Carrier Networks
8. Data Systems

A recent listing of job openings at Northern Telecom's various locations showed these openings, and these needs are indicative of the industry.

Mechanical Design: Packaging of electronic systems such as computers or telephone equipment.

Plastic Component Design: Design plastic injection molds, enclosures and mechanisms.

Network Engineer: Design data networks, transmission systems and conduct traffic studies. Requires knowledge of data packet switching principles and networking.

Telephone and Modem Design: Design high quality circuitry for voice and data transmission according to FCC requirements.

Product Manager: Plan, administer, coordinate and support the overall activity of transmission product line from a marketing perspective.

Data Network Planners: Develop innovative concepts for data communication products and services to determine technical and business viabilities. In-depth experience necessary.

Sales Representatives: Requires 3–5 years' direct sales of computer/DDP products to end users. Systems selling a plus. (DDP is distributed data processing, computers at dispersed locations.)

Account Executive: Responsible for strategic marketing and business development activities to the Department of the Air Force for all NTI products and services. Extensive experience required.

Sales Engineer: Assist in preparation of proposals and systems applications. Requires BSEE and 5 years' experience in telecommunication application design.

Senior Business Methods Analyst: Consult with Business Systems users and perform preliminary analysis and design of automated systems for cost improvements. Degree and experience required.

Initial installations and ongoing maintenance are an ever-increasing demand on manufacturers. Here are additional examples from NTI's growing internal listings:

Installer: Perform initial installation.

Installation Design Engineer: Perform installation design engineering on large digital telephone switching systems, including related job specifications and drawings.

Field Service Engineer: Provide problem analysis and on-site troubleshooting on all types of NTI Digital Transmission equipment to Telcos (telephone companies) throughout the U.S.

Interconnects

Although thousands of interconnect companies exist, most are small, earning $5–10 million, and only 4 have sales of more than $100 million a year. There's even a group of companies known as "trunkers" because they sell equipment from their car trunks. Because they are small and geographically dispersed, they offer interesting job opportunities, both technical/installer positions and sales spots. Sales may be the most lucrative because sales representatives receive commissions, unlike equipment sales representatives with the giant Bell companies.

The industry association for the interconnect, North American Telecommunications Association (NATA), recently completed a compensation survey of sales representatives. It found that the majority of entry-level sales reps earned $21,000–25,000 including commissions; 12% totaled more than $35,000. Of those surveyed 90% received commissions, most often on the basis of sales. At account executive levels, 17% of the salespersons with no management responsibilities earned $26,000–30,000; 22% $31,000–35,000; 14% $36,000–40,000; 8% earned more than $70,000.

Emerging Companies

Telecommunications technologies continue to spawn new companies and new directions for the communications career seeker. Two of the latest fields are cellular radio, and buildings or campuses that are installing their own communications systems. The latter include real estate or property management companies. "As cellular radio systems are being developed in many major metropolitan areas, these companies are adding many employees," observes Jacobson. Most needed at this point are radio technicians, operation managers, systems planners (with radio and telephone experience), and marketing and administrative employees with related experience.

Real estate developers in buildings under construction are wiring their own telephone and communications switches so that the building itself contains the telephone system and computer network. Real estate developers are thus in the communications business.

New communications strategies and developments are being planned every day. One of the more recent ideas is for a "teleport," an airport for communications services such as satellite and microwave dishes. One such teleport had been planned for Staten Island, opposite the tip of Manhattan, but the project ran into stumbling blocks when the economy and interest waned.

Users of Communications

In terms of numbers, need and geography the best opportunities in communications are with corporate users. The biggest users of communications are businesses that depend on them, particularly the telephone, to conduct daily transactions.

Two or three years ago telecommunications staffers were caretakers in charge of a relatively lifeless, unchallenging PBX and perhaps a lines system to outlying offices. Ma Bell was in charge, and the biggest crisis was making sure a new executive got an additional private line installed. At one company the telecommunications manager's office was in the basement, and he was also in charge of getting the stripes painted on the parking lot each spring. Too often the manager of data processing didn't even know the name of his telecommunications manager.

The world has changed for that parking lot painter. The telecommunications job seeker can take advantage of the following:

- Only a small percentage of today's communications professionals have been trained in communications.

- Managing communications, which requires a combination of business and technical expertise, is just evolving.

- Colleges are only starting to offer quality technical communications courses. This situation is not unlike data processing; only in the past few years have colleges started to offer business courses on information management or data processing management.

- Most communications professionals are learning on the job. This is delicate because these managers may be responsible for $10 million equipment and service budgets, and in some instances as large as $90 million.

Today's systems cost millions of dollars, and that doesn't take into account monthly bills. Companies have one of the following types of telecommunications networks: Voice only (phone) network, data transmission only, integrated voice and data, or separate voice and data networks.

Analyzing, planning, designing systems, installing and then monitoring and upgrading telephone systems are the general responsibilities of telecommunications professionals. All this must be balanced against the needs of the users and the costs. Service must fulfill a customer's needs, but not provide unused capacity. Implementing too ambitious a communications system is costly, and vulnerable to obsolescence. One company installed one internal tie-line, a dedicated, less expensive long-distance line between two offices. Employees made enough business calls to the main office, however, that three tie-lines were required. Employees tried to get through on the tie-line, but found it always busy. They then used regular long-distance service. As a result the company was spending more than before on long-distance communications.

Salaries

Companies employing communications personnel—voice and data—have had to step quickly to provide competitive salaries. To bring in attractive recruits and meet their communications needs they've established separate pay schedules—even better than the data processing departments—and developed incentives such as bonuses and eligibility for a company car. In the past, data processing technicians and professionals have been paid at higher levels than their counterparts in the company. Communications managers started out with the DP salary scale, and a data communications network analyst was paid the same as the systems analyst. "As telecommunications positions have become more specialized, the premiums paid for data processing positions have become insufficient to attract and retain qualified telecommunications professionals," report the authors of the Hansen salary survey.[4]

Companies hate to lose their telecommunications employees. Although still a minority a number of companies are going beyond the premium DP salaries to pay telecommunications personnel. These companies are establishing a telecommunications pay structure that is 5–7% above the prevailing data processing/MIS structure, according to a Hansen study of 100 firms in manufacturing, finance, insurance, utilities, energy, education, service, transportation and wholesale/retail trade. If the companies were locked into the same pay scale for all employees, they gave telecommunications employees more frequent salary/performance reviews in 6-month, or even 3-month, intervals. Telecommunications employees also rated larger merit pay increases than other employees.

"Hiring, training, and compensating highly specialized telecommunications jobs has become increasingly difficult since more and more organizations are setting up private networks. Finding reliable compensation data for these jobs has been equally difficult due to the lack of accurate job descriptions, the highly technical nature of the work, and the rapidly evolving nature of the telecommunications function. Similar job titles provide little assurance that the scope of duties or levels of responsibility are comparable among various organizations."[5] (Generally, the more sophisticated the network, the higher the salary.)

TELECOMMUNICATIONS JOBS WITH USERS

Public relations and corporate internal communicators are known as "communications specialists." These communicators are concerned with the content of the communication, and work in public relations, public affairs, advertising, investor relations or corporate relations (lobbying). Their non-technical expertise is usually in writing, journalism as well as advertising.

COMMUNICATIONS OR TELECOMMUNICATIONS TECHNICIAN

Telecommunications technicians have a high level of technical expertise. At the junior level they routinely maintain, repair and often assist in the installation of telecommunications equipment (especially the "switch" or voice lines switching equipment). This is often a forbidding looking, floor-to-ceiling panel of boards and wires. Depending on the size of the operation the panel may fill a room or a closet. Technicians read and interpret circuit diagrams and electrical schematics for this hardware. They test, adjust and troubleshoot equipment as necessary. When vendors install new equipment they assist during installation, rearrangement and/or removal of equipment. If the organization has remote locations technicians frequently work with personnel at these sites.

As technicians gain experience they move up to titles such as senior technician. While under general directions from managers senior technicians are fully responsible for the switching equipment. Usually with 4 or more years' experience they supervise and/or assist less experienced telecommunications engineers.

Requirements: Technical positions in telecommunications are open to both college and non-college trained applicants. Employees without degrees necessarily have a high level of expertise often acquired in a vocational electronics program or in the military. Many good two-year electronics programs give technicians the required understanding of electronics and communications. These private or community schools are increasingly offering communications courses. (See Chapter 2.) Despite the shortage of technicians, the jobs with the most growth potential go to persons with four-year degrees, most often in electrical engineering. Four-year engineering schools are now introducing communications courses.

Salary: Entry-level telecommunications technicians average $18,300 per year. For technicians without degrees the Personnel Resources, International survey of 1,000 telecommunications professionals reported a range of $20,600–28,200. With degrees and moderate experience technicians earn $30,700–35,600. Salaries are higher in the New York City metropolitan area, followed by larger cities such as Los Angeles, San Francisco, Chicago and Boston. All salaries are up markedly over previous years.

Only 2% of the data communications technicians belong to such units as labor unions. Unions, such as the Communications Workers of America, are continuing their attempts to organize communications workers.

ENGINEERING AND OPERATIONS MANAGER

The seasoned professional responsible for the hardware and the people who install and maintain it is the engineering/operations manager. This title at a more junior level is sometimes installation manager. Titles are especially unclear in telecommunications because of the constantly changing scope of the job and the technology. For example, telephones are being built into personal computers. The chief technician is responsible for voice data and, where installed, video networks. This experienced professional—ideally with 8–10 years' experience—is responsible for the following:

1. Managing and supervising communications engineers and technicians.

2. Supervising vendors' activities, some of whom frequently have personnel at the customer's location as do some Bell operating companies.

3. Daily operation of the network(s).

4. Technical analysis of complex software, hardware and transmission systems.

5. Supervising and managing ongoing engineering projects, test and evaluation programs and normal engineering services such as transmission, circuit design and software maintenance.

Requirements: Engineering managers are experienced professionals with a minimum of 8–10 years' experience in network planning, analysis, operations and design. Almost always this requires an engineering degree.

Salary: Engineering managers can expect to earn $48,800–60,300, with the range as high as $57,300–64,500 in the New York metropolitan area. The average salary is $49,800 and an average bonus of $4,900, although only one fourth of engineering managers receive bonuses.[6] Occasionally they are eligible for a company car or other company-provided fringe benefit, what's known as a perq (for perquisite).

VOICE COMMUNICATIONS MANAGER

How big a telephone system should an organization have? Should they lease or buy the PBX and/or telephones? Should they have dedicated lines between, say, their headquarters in Houston and oil fields in Oklahoma? Should they use an alternative communications carrier to AT&T? This is a simple list of the problems and questions communications analysts face, and they require both technical and business expertise. Since only recently have these questions been asked, few individuals are trained to answer them.

The manager in charge of the planning, equipment and personnel responsible for an organization's voice communications network is the voice communications manager. Responsibilities include the following:

1. Planning for adequate and appropriate hardware—for example, phone sets and switching capabilities—for both headquarters and remote locations.

2. Implementing methodologies and procedures to analyze, install and support phone systems.

3. Coordinating analysis, acquisition and installation of headquarters and branch office phone systems—which frequently now include software as well as hardware.

4. Ensuring that internal users meet with and get their needs solved by external vendors and services suppliers.

5. Managing staff responsible for system and network planning.

6. Managing training of staff and users.

Requirements: The voice communications manager has communications credentials and 8–10 years, experience in software/hardware voice network design and analysis.

Salary: Salaries averaged $41,800 for voice communications managers with an average bonus of $4,400; 17% were eligible for such bonuses.[7]

DATA COMMUNICATIONS ENGINEER

Communications lines are electrical conduits that transmit multiple types of signals. Experts discovered no technical reason why computer electrical beeps and bleeps couldn't be transmitted as easily and readily as voice signals. These were after all, digital to analog converted signals. At the same time the technicians realized these possibilities, computer users wanted to ship information between points without having to convert it to a media such as magnetic tape, paper print-outs or punched cards. Some applications users had to consult regularly such as inquiring as to the status of a customer's outstanding balance. Company personnel at distant locations wanted to tap into the computer and get the balance immediately; they wanted "on-line" access. One way to do that was over telephone lines.

This shipping of computer signals over communications channels either on land, via satellite or other combinations is data communications. It's one of the fastest growing segments of both the computer industry and telecommunications. Because of its rapid growth and the shortage of workers, salaries are higher for data experts than voice communications professionals. Moreover, data communications is where the growth is going to be for sometime.

Because the field requires both expertise in communications and hardware and software, it's doubly hard for companies to find data communications professionals. The highest paid non-management technical positions—in the $35,000–40,000 spread—were in data communications. Examples: senior network planning analyst, $38,000; transmission engineer, $38,100; senior communications analyst, $36,200; and senior network control technician, $35,400.

NETWORK CONTROL TECHNICIAN

Network control technicians monitor and maintain an organization's data network, which spans computers, land lines, satellites, personal computers and almost any combination of them. The networks become like spider webs with the transmission computer in the middle or in the node. The webs are being connected together and layered over and under each other. Network control technicians are responsible for the following:

1. Testing and analyzing all elements of the network including power, software, communication machinery, lines, modems and terminals.
2. Monitoring and controlling the performance and status of network resources.
3. Using hardware and software evaluation tools to identify and diagnose complex problems and factors affecting network performance.

Salary: Salaries for data communications experts are higher than those for voice-only technicians. The average is $35,400. The data experts experience better salary increases: "Salary progression for the network control job family is more rapid than for telecommunications technicians: after 5 years, senior network control technicians earn about 16% more than senior telecommunications technicians. Senior network control technicians salaries reported for telecommunications departments average more than 15% above like positions for the telecommunications equipment and services firms."[9]

DATA COMMUNICATIONS MANAGER

The individual entrusted with both personnel and the equipment to keep computers and phones communicating with each other is the data communications manager, who does the following:

1. Provides adequate and appropriate planning for hardware and communications facilities at headquarters and remote locations.
2. Implements methodologies for analysis, installation and support of distributed processing systems.
3. Coordinates the analysis, acquisition and installation of terminals and computers on the network.
4. Analyzes and recommends appropriate computing terminal and data communications facilities to meet the needs of the organization.
5. Supervises and manages training of staff involved in system and network planning and analysis.

These managers have 8–10 years' experience in software/hardware network design and analysis.

Salary: Data communications managers usually are paid more than voice experts. They average $45,700, and approximately 18% are eligible for bonuses. Bonuses averaged $3,300.

TELECOMMUNICATIONS DEPARTMENT DIRECTOR/MANAGER

The manager in charge of all communications activities within an organization, voice and data, is the telecommunications department director or manager. These departments are single networks handling both voice and data transmissions or separate systems dedicated to each. This position is in transition as departments evolve. These positions are highly sensitive to the development plans of the department and the internal structure of the department. Managers of both data and voice communications usually report to them. They have significant responsibilities, especially since so much of a company's business may ride on its telecommunications systems. They're in charge of overall management of the organization's telecommunications resources as well as all telecommunications networks, activities and services used by the organization: strategic and tactical planning activities; financial, technical and usage forecasting; engineering; operations and maintenance; implementation of systems; communications security systems; telecommunications-related software and software systems.

In addition, these executives often have to develop, implement and administer billing systems for the services they provide—charge-backs to the employee departments using the system. They have the traditional people management responsibilities and must work with corporate senior and executive management to ensure telecommunications plans are coordinated with the company's business plans.

Salary: Telecommunications directors averaged salaries of $58,500, with 40% eligible for bonuses. With the bonus the average rose to $61,200. Depending on the level of responsibility and sophistication of the department, salaries ranged between $50,000 and $80,000. The more technically sophisticated the network, the higher was the salary.

NETWORK ANALYSTS

With many options available, of which several have been sketched above, companies must do careful and serious planning in order to make the most effective communications choices. All their decisions must take into account the need to balance the technical and business aspects. Technical capabilities must be considered against financial considerations, and outside factors such as system availability or overall feasibility also have to be weighed.

Networks have become strategically beneficial to major corporations beyond their technical value. Citibank considers its network a competitive advantage and advertises that fact in business magazines, and its point is well taken. The network of wires, satellites and computers allows the nation's second largest bank to do business more efficiently and effectively. Citibank takes advantage of every minute to make money on its money. They transfer funds electronically to countries where interest or exchange rates are most favorable. Customers' funds can be transferred internationally quickly! Citibank employees around the world can easily be in touch with their fellow workers so that work is accomplished efficiently. Technical communications as a competitive weapon is a new concept for corporations, but one that many are adopting in the information age.

Network analysts deal with the telecommunications choices complicated by the AT&T divestiture and the emergence of alternative carriers, equipment manufacturers and technologies. Such analysts work both for users and for vendors. Network analysts, according to their seniority:

1. Map and evaluate existing network systems and make recommendations on what's needed to maintain current service.
2. Assist in network planning, engineering and system architecture.
3. Develop technical standards and connect up (interface) several applications.
4. Evaluate new products.
5. Solve network problems.

Requirements: Network analysts have a B.S. degree or its equivalent in engineering, computer science or math. Analysts reach the senior level after 6–8 years in the field, at which time they may also work with junior analysts.

Salary: Network analysts average $38,800 and are among the most highly paid non-management technicians.[10] The Personnel Resources survey found a range of $29,900–42,200 outside New York and $31,900–45,400 in the New York area.

SATELLITE NETWORKS

A technical development that has opened up electronic communications of all kinds is the satellite. These broadcasting stations in the sky have far-reaching implications for the development of our changing world, particularly Third World nations. The first satellite was launched in 1962 and the first commercial one in 1965. Since then scientists have been finding better ways to bounce various signals off of them. With improvements and declining costs individuals place receiver dishes in their own backyards at a cost of several thousand dollars. These dishes work best in open spaces where electronic, radio and TV signals are less dense, and thus cause less interferences.

Satellites are launched into the air by launch missiles from the National Aeronautics and Space Administration (NASA). They appear to hang in space because they circle the earth in an orbit 23,000 miles over the equator, and revolve around the earth at the earth's rate of rotation. Stations on earth transmit signals to the satellite where they're received by one of many transponders and relayed to another earth station.

Originally envisioned to provide communications to remote locations, satellites are an excellent alternative to transoceanic electronic cables.

Communications has always been marked by economies of scale, and the same is true in satellite use. Once satellites are regularly launched by reusable space vehicles such as the Space Shuttle, costs are expected to decline even further.

Satellites transmit many kinds of signals: long-distance telephone calls, television, video, radio, computer data. Because computer-generated data communications are not continuous they can be what's called multiplexed, or condensed to only the actual transmission. Signals from several different computers are multiplexed together to provide even greater economy. All of this is computer-controlled.

Although not in great numbers, an ongoing demand exists for technical experts on satellite systems. Such experts work either for the developers and manufacturers of the satellite, for the operator (which may or may not be the same company) or for the user company that buys the satellite transmission capability. Such users lease channels on a transponder.

SATELLITE SYSTEMS ENGINEER

Satellite systems engineers often work at an earth station, sometimes rural, equipped with transmitters and control computers. Such satellite engineers maintain the system technically, analyze and plan for new systems and perform the tasks of the telecommunications technician and data communications engineer. Requirements and salaries are similar to those for the jobs listed above. Earth stations may be in isolated locations such as Montana or Arizona or in a foreign country.

NEW DIRECTIONS

Local Area Networks (LANS)

Data and voice communications networks encircle the earth and span space. When the network is confined to a small and defined geographic region, it is called a Local Area Network (LAN). Hard-wired LANs are strung in single buildings or over several nearby buildings in a campus arrangement. College campuses have in fact proven an ideal environment for LANs, which connect not only administrative and teaching systems but students in dormitories as well. The most sophisticated LANs connect not only telephones and computers, but also carry video signals from television-like security systems or even video conferencing signals. LANs are ideal for connecting a series of computer terminals or personal computers within an office with each other as well as to the mainframe computer—along with the assorted peripheral devices such as printers, data storage devices (large and small) and super digital laser copying machines.

With LANs the ante has been upped on required skills beyond communications and computing expertise. Employees must be familiar with the other technologies strung on a multipurpose network. Most LANs are for offices and involve terminals or personal computers running office applications. Communications professionals who work with LANs must be comfortable with PCs and office automation.

Electronic Mail

Another fast growing application in the office and at home is electronic mail—computer-to-computer or terminal-to-terminal message transmission. Electronic mail grew in popularity with the PC as more workers had a PC with communications capability (a modem attachment). In some instances electronic mail systems replace the need for telephone calls or other messages such as hard-copy Telexes. Electronic mail is one way around "telephone tag," in which callers spend all day trying to reach each other over the telephone.

Electronic mail is one of the fastest growing market segments within the computer and telecommunications industries. Speed and accuracy of communication, low cost of operation and diversity of applications are expected to make electronic mail a $4 billion industry by 1990, according to industry gurus. Since in 1984 the industry was about $148 million, almost 30-fold growth is predicted.

Electronic mail allows users to send documents composed on the PC or terminal to a central computer for receipt at any time. Over phone lines or a data network users on a dial-up line to the central computer deposit their digital messages into the intended receiver's mailbox. At his or her convenience the receiver checks the mailbox and reads whatever is being held. This independence of time is extremely useful for companies that have offices in different time zones.

The two varieties of networks are those publicly available and those available within organizations only. Organizations either develop, buy or lease their own internal electronic mail networks (usually sharing their data networks) or use publicly available electronic mail systems. IT&T's Dialcom is an example of an electronic mail network that organizations buy for internal use. Dialcom also gives these users access to other news data bases, including one prepared each day by the White House. Other companies provide internally controlled systems, which offer better security and thus are popular with corporations concerned lest information fall into a competitor's hands.

Publicly available networks have the advantage of paper copy—either Telex messages, Mailgrams or laser-printed letters—for those who do not have electronic hook-ups. Two companies in public systems are MCI Communications with MCI Mail and Western Union with EasyLink. Both MCI Mail and EasyLink receive messages electronically, convert them to paper, and then either drop them into the mail at a location nearest to the recipient or have them delivered by courier services.

Working with electronic mail applications is a growing field. Jobs exist both with product vendors and large users.

Requirements: Those working with electronic mail applications must know both the hardware of the PC or terminal and the communications system and software. As with any dual skilled position, electronic mail experts are much in demand. Technical workers need to know the computer system the electronic mailboxes are stored on as well as communications. If an internal electronic mail system such as those used internally in corporations runs on a minicomputer, the electronic mail specialist needs to know minis.

Salary: Salaries are close to or slightly above those of similar jobs dealing solely with computers or solely with communications. Since electronic mail is still rare, companies pay a premium to find workers.

Video Conferencing

Video conferencing is a technology pushed by AT&T that exploded in the late 1970s and early 1980s, but now seems to be languishing. The costs are too high, the technology too expensive and less expensive versions are ineffectual. Video conferencing is supposed to save time and money spent commuting and meeting. A video conference takes place in a room rigged with television cameras, computers and communications equipment. Conference participants in two cities gather in two such rigged rooms. Television cameras focus on each speaker and span the entire room during the conference. If need be the camera is aimed at slide shows or computer terminals projected onto large screens. The video conference is then transmitted over telephone lines and networks, including satellites.

One drawback was that many people didn't come across well to their associates on television, but the main problem was cost. Renting a video conference room for 30 minutes for a two-way conference involving eight persons cost $2,500 in the AT&T setting. Less sophisticated and less expensive conference rooms do not provide an air of authenticity. Even if the cost were manageable, the video image was not felt to be worth the effort.

The technologists have not given up, however, and new ways of packing more video capability by extracting unnecessary signals are being developed.

Video Networks

Companies building new facilities install multicapability cabling throughout to handle not only voice and data signals but video as well. A common application for these new networks is for security. Video cameras throughout the building and grounds transmit back to security control stations. It is a plus for those working with the new communications to know about video systems.

Computer Conferencing

A variant of video conferencing, computer conferencing is done on the computer with keyboard entry of comments. It is often likened to an electronic bulletin board, like those in a college dormitory, where a message is posted and observers offer comments. The collection of messages becomes an interesting, often entertaining, commentary on an issue. Computer conferencing is now being introduced in a handful of companies. Individuals have established their own bulletin boards using publicly available networks such as The Source or CompuServe, which are also known for their on-line data base services. Such a conference is extremely useful when several persons work together on a document, book, study or report. They easily react to each other's work at their convenience.

Fiber Optics

As more voice and data signals needed to be shipped, communications providers seeking alternatives to the tangled webs of copper that lie under most urban areas found fiber optics. Optical fibers are long fibers of almost pure silicon that conduct light waves at amazing speeds. An intense light like a laser beam transmitted along the fiber carries many times the amount of data sent electrically through copper. Although fiber optics technology required both the invention of the laser in 1960 and silicon optical fibers in 1970, the discovery that light energy carries more communication than electrical was made by Alexander Graham Bell shortly after he invented the telephone. His "light phone" was the photophone.

Optical fibers, now being installed over long distances in the U.S. and Canada, have as much as 100,000 times the capacity of copper cable. A ½-inch fiber has as much capacity as a 4-inch thick copper cable at 1% of the weight. One ½-inch optical cable handles as many as 40,000 telephone calls versus several of the 4-inch copper ones. The optical fiber provides greater sound fidelity and less distortion because it's immune to electromagnetic and noise interference, which are sometimes serious problems in computer communications. Fiber optics are also secure and cannot be tapped.

The biggest users of optical cables have been telephone companies and cable television broadcasters. Applications include the following: sensing devices in medicine where fibers are inserted into the body relaying images to the outside screen; in robotics, where fiber optic eyes allow the robot to "see." Predicted uses are foreseen in defense and aerospace systems, or within the body of a car. Most prognosticators see great growth for fiber optics, from sales of $300 million in 1983 to $1.5 billion in 1990. In the meantime existing systems are in the shake-down phase. "The effect fiber optics will have on the labor force is difficult to predict. While the theoretical groundwork is firmly established, many of those

Fiber optic cables offer tremendous new capacities and capabilities to the communications industries, including the connection of computers without the transmission delays experienced with current cabling. (Courtesy of International Business Machines Corporation)

intimately involved with its development can only speculate as to its future implications for workers and their jobs,"[11] observes the BLS.

AT&T has begun retraining some of its workers in fiber optics in such jobs as cable splicing and installation. The technology involved may result in loss of some jobs. Retraining efforts are hamstrung by the fast changing technology, and work techniques have to constantly be relearned. Because the technology is new, few standards exist for fiber optics work.

For the person with college-level training in physics, optics or related areas, the fiber optics future is bright. Companies also need fiber optics circuit designers with experience in computers and electronics. When buildings begin to be wired with fiber optics systems, electricians with such experience will be needed.

1. Rebecca S. Barna. "Waging the Wet Noodle War." *Datamation*, March 1, 1985, p. 21.
2. Deborah J. Thobe and John D. McMillan, A. S. Hansen, Inc. "Compensating Personnel in the Telecommunications Department." *Business Communications Review*, January–February 1985, p. 17.
3. Ibid. p. 18.
4. Ibid. p. 13.
5. Ibid.
6. Ibid. p. 16.
7. Ibid.
8. Ibid. p. 17.
9. Ibid., p. 18.
10. Ibid., p. 18.
11. Mike Stanton. "Fiber Optics: Careers in the New Technologies." *Occupational Outlook Quarterly* (U.S. Department of Labor, Bureau of Labor Statistics: Washington, DC), Winter 1984, p. 28.

7
MANUFACTURING TECHNOLOGY

At first glance the factory of the future appears to be the wrong place to look for the jobs of the future. Economic and employment statistics for industrial centers of the Midwest are bleak. Consumer preference for imported goods is at a record high. Unemployment is high in cities like Detroit and Cleveland. The picture through the 1990s doesn't show any let up of this dark scenario, for factory employment is expected to drop by 40% over the next 10 years.

The author Richard Bolles, head of the National Career Development Project in Walnut Creek, California, has some startling figures. Only 26% of the work force is in goods-producing industries versus 52% in the 1960s. In 1983 the average manufacturing worker earned $21,469 versus $10,000 for the retail worker, $15,350 for a service worker and $18,154 for a government employee. "The jobs that pay the most in this country are precisely the ones being terminated," he observes.

The growth of a world economy no longer dominated by the U.S. is also taking its toll. Several years ago the average assembly line worker earned $16 per hour. Today the average industrial worker earns $9 per hour, the average laborer $7.53. U.S. workers are up against robots amortized at a cost of $4 per hour; a South Korean worker, $1.53; a Taiwanese worker, $1.43. What's more, in the U.S. the $16 per hour worker takes 31 hours to turn out a car; the Japanese factory equipped with robots takes 9 hours!

RAPID CHANGE

American manufacturing is undergoing tremendous upheavals. Smoke-stack America has crashed. Job hunters, especially those displaced by dying industries, have two alternatives. They can continue to identify as "auto worker" or "steel worker," and cling to the old. Or they can accept that the old jobs don't exist, but new ones are out there for the finding. The manufacturing sector continues to offer opportunities for those already in the factory and for newcomers, and recent graduates should not eliminate the factory from their job hunt. Be forewarned that geography has much to do with manufacturing opportunities. If no heavy manufacturing exists in your area and you don't plan to move, forget about opportunities in robotics and CAD or CAM.

116

This discussion details possible job opportunities in the new factory. Understanding the interconnectedness of various new processes—most computer-controlled—is the beginning of understanding what's going on in the so-called factory of the future.

American industry is not about to roll over and die because of foreign competition. The healthy signs on the factory floor all point to high technology as the cure. Each company, each industry is at a different stage in automated manufacturing. The action fronts from the initial design of products to the loading for shipment include the following:

1. Computer-integrated manufacturing (CIM)
2. Computer-aided design (CAD) or computer-aided design and drafting (CADD)
3. Computer-aided engineering (CAE)
4. Computer-aided manufacturing (CAM)
5. Robotics
6. Numerically-controlled (N/c) tools
7. Lasers

These are all parts of what will ultimately be the automated factory. Each segment creates new jobs and displaces existing ones. The catch is that the skills required of new workers are seldom those held by the old. After all, that's the nature of change and new technologies.

WHAT IS THE FACTORY OF THE FUTURE?

The totally integrated and automated manufacturing plant envisioned for the future goes far beyond speeding up the assembly line. The new factory will rely heavily on computers. Data developed in the beginning of the design cycle will not be recreated, but only passed down the chain: from drafters and designers to testing engineers to the factory floor with robot tools, to the warehouse and the loading dock. Almost every manufacturing worker will use a computer.

The professionals who oversee the production process and design the products will someday feed their data into factory-wide computer networks; communicate with each other via VDT screens; and pass designs down the factory pecking order until they are physically created on the plant floor. Once design data is digitized, it will be used in every production process thereafter.

Pieces of this new manufacturing world are already being installed, but today computerized manufacturing systems exist as islands in the manufacturing chain. The goal is to connect these islands into a new world that is being called computer-integrated manufacturing (CIM). A

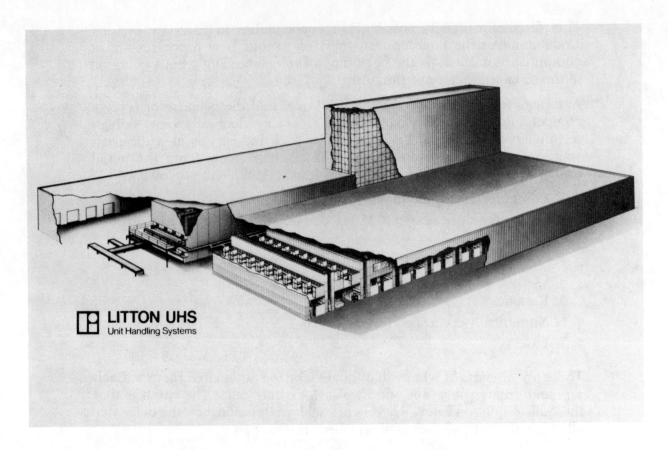

LITTON UHS
Unit Handling Systems

Warehouses offer time and labor savings when huge "unit handling systems" are installed to speed parts handling and material control for later transfer to assembly lines. (Courtesy of Litton)

look at the Coors Brewery in Colorado gives a good indication of the possibilities of a computer automated manufacturing plant. Many of the rooms are virtually abandoned but for computer consoles and VDTs. A single employee works in a huge room overlooking the brewing vats. He tests (not tastes) the brew, times the process and adjusts the temperature and mixture to perfection. All he must do is shut down the system if a warning alarm rings and watch the VDT readouts to make sure they match predetermined figures. The job of the brewmeister is all but extinct.

Not to be forgotten in this coming factory is unknown new technology that may further radicalize changes in manufacturing. Robots are increasingly equipped with vision—cameras that direct the controlled limbs in selecting and picking up various parts on the assembly line. Touch sensitive sensors in the robot recognize when two parts are correctly aligned. If the parts are off slightly, the robot arm, or wrist in this instance, works the pieces until they do fit together. The next step for robotics will be the addition of artificial intelligence. If a procedure doesn't work, the robot will start running through a list of possible problems, testing each solution as it goes. A human technician currently has to fix the problem.

Japan: Seeing the Future

Frightening and at the same time amazing is the present day Japanese factory. The Japanese have committed themselves to the new manufacturing world. One gets a good picture of what tomorrow's factories will look like by seeing Japan's "flexible manufacturing system" (FMS), the corporate rule for nearly 20 years. Many believe that Japan has succeeded because of commitment and financial investment, not from necessarily superior technology, knowledge or skill. Using FMS one Japanese producer has reduced the number of machines in its factory from 68 to 18, the number of employees from 215 to 12, the space requirements from 103,000 square feet to 30,000 and the processing time from 35 days to 1½.

A look at Detroit—at one time America's industrial showplace—gives an idea of the changes to come in the American factory. These changes directly result from the fact that the American auto industry was clobbered during the 1970s and early 1980s by the superior marketing efforts and improved automation of the Japanese auto manufacturers (coupled with a consumer preference for gas-cheap cars). Detroit is changing and is taking a high tech tack. Whenever planning a career for the future one approach is to follow corporate capital expenditures. Here are numbers to consider:

- Chrysler has linked 16 large scale computers processing a total of 64 million design questions per second at its Technical Computer Center in Detroit. Chrysler had already installed a Control Data Cyber 205 supercomputer that services almost 1,000 separate terminals, half of which are designed exclusively for CAD/CAM purposes. By 1986 almost 600 terminals should be added for controlling factory robots.

- At the recent opening of the Ford Robotic and Automation Consulting Center Ford President, Donald Peterson, indicated that Ford would have almost 7,000 robots by 1990.

- General Motors has installed 2,500 robots and expects to install 15,000 more in its 18 assembly plants by 1990. The company's 2,500 CAD terminals will double to 5,000 by that time. GM's interest in high tech factories was emphasized by its $2.5 billion acquisition of Electronic Data Systems (EDS) in 1984 and by its launch of the Saturn Corporation—a high tech pilot program to design and manufacture a new automobile using strictly computer and automated procedures by 1988.

- The Upjohn Institute for Employment Research estimates that although robots will eliminate 24,000 jobs in Motor City by 1990, there will be 18,000 new blue collar jobs plus 3,500 openings for robotics engineers.

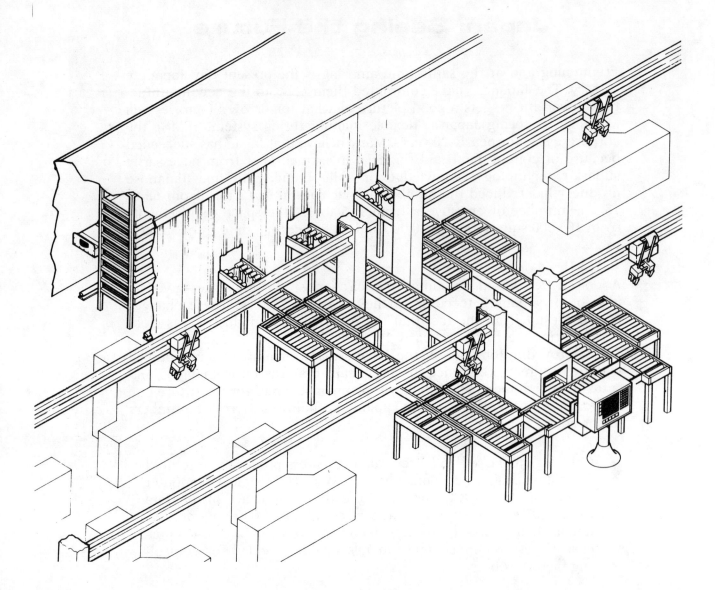

This computer-controlled and -monitored "flexible manufacturing system" is being installed in a large automobile manufacturing plant. It features a computer system to control the flow of material from its introduction as a bar of forged steel through machining, finishing and inspection processes until it emerges as a precision, polished camshaft. (Courtesy of Litton)

CIM:
COMPUTER-INTEGRATED
MANUFACTURING

What will make automated factory flourish is computer-integrated manufacturing (CIM), in which automation controls the production in addition to the assembly process. In other words computers not only control the

In the new factory, computer-controlled automated storage and retrieval systems regulate small parts handling and keep track of inventory. This crane delivers replacement parts to the assembly line, stores work-in-process, moves subassemblies between stations and keeps track of inventory. (Courtesy of Litton, by Mark Joseph Corporate Photography, Inc.)

robots but match warehouse inventory with the schedule of the production cycle. Computer-integrated manufacturing hardware and software products, a $25 billion market in 1982, is growing at a rate of 14% per year, and is expected to reach $100 billion by 1992, estimates the Arthur D. Little consulting firm in Cambridge, Massachusetts.

From an employment standpoint this means that within the next ten years machine tooling, assembly, robotics, engineering, design and production engineering will be computer terminal occupations. Information needed at each stage of the production process will be stored in data bases and accessed as needed. Operators will control the laser die cutters by typing instructions on a computer keyboard. Robots will be programmed while on-line by computer control. Product designs and instructions will be supplied directly from the computer-aided design systems directly to the factory floor by product engineers and designers. The FMS factory will be an integrated network of VDTs tracking and adjusting the robotic activities and automated flow of parts from the warehouse, through assembly, and to the market. All work orders and inventory lists will be on computer printouts.

In automated warehouses inventories will be tracked on computers and moved on automated lifts and conveyor belts without forklift drivers. Nor will it be necessary to stockpile raw materials. The Japanese have been successful with Just in Time (JIT) systems wherein the manufacturing system is so finely tuned that necessary parts and/or materials arrive at the loading dock the day they're needed on the production line, and eliminates expensive storing and wasteful overstock.

Productivity and profitability will become as much the result of an efficient control of information resources—with networked computers tying all factory offices—as it is the result of hardware, labor and marketing expenditures.

American manufacturers are following the Japanese lead toward automation. In 1967 they spent $1.9 million on automated machine tools and controllers. In 1987 they will spend an estimated $7.9 billion. In 1995 they will spend more than $18 billion, according to Predicasts, a Cleveland market research house. Not everyone is convinced, however, that the love affair with CIM is progressing fast enough. "Manufacturing fell out of vogue in the U.S. about 30 years ago. American business fortunes are currently made through high technology, service, banking, finance and the information revolution. Manufacturing remains behind the scenes. Everyone knows it's there, but no one wants to take responsibility. After all, what type of cocktail chatter would setting a new record in reducing quality defects make? Nothing exciting here. Henry Ford stories are passe."[1]

This is in sharp contrast to the Japanese who are 100% committed to manufacturing. Adds this robotics consultant: "The battle for today's consumer's dollar is being won by perfecting the manufacturing process. Automation and quality control are the battle cries of new-wave manufacturing. U.S. manufacturers continue to retreat to the high ground of volume products, clever advertising, promotions and balance sheet restructuring through consolidation and depreciation of obsolete manufacturing capacity."[2]

What everyone is coming to realize is that there's no quick fix for the new factory. CIM will evolve as the islands of automation within the manufacturing chain are linked together via computer networks and an integration of the processes. No one manufacturer will supply all the parts. It will be a slow process of each company pulling together the various pieces required: numerical control machines, process controllers, computers, quality inspection systems, robots, automated material handling and warehousing systems.

CAD: COMPUTER-AIDED DESIGN

Factory engineering centers are starting to look more like typing pools than art or drafting rooms. Engineers, architects, designers and draftsmen are all seated before VDTs equipped with a form of electronic pointing device—an optical pencil, graphics tablet or mouse. The engineering tool of the future is CAD—hardware and software. CAD is computer-aided design or sometimes CADD, computer-aided design and drafting. CAD-customized workstations put computer power in the hands of the engineer, architect, designer or drafter.

Although the National Science Foundation may be overly enthusiastic when it says CAD may represent the "greatest increase in productivity since electricity,"[3] CAD has meant dramatic changes for manufacturing. It's created a high growth business unto itself. First introduced in 1964 CAD systems sales grew 40-fold between 1973 and 1981, from $25 million to $1 billion. By 1987 it's expected to reach $6.9 billion, growing at a 40% annual rate. Most of these systems were developed and built by firms specializing in CAD. The systems included sophisticated $25,000 workstations/VDTs connected, usually in clusters, to powerful minicomputers running powerful software (probably on the Unix operating system). Today, however, the CAD market is using personal computers. Although current CAD systems for PCs are limited in use to simpler projects, they are quickly growing more powerful.

Think of the CAD computer as an engineer's word processor. What was once painstakingly plotted with drafting pencils, erased and reworked is all simulated hundreds of times electronically. The CAD computer not only has infinite patience and absolute accuracy but it provides massive storage for data bases of past designs and design elements. CAD systems, which typically have industry design software embedded, allow the user to do the following:

1. Replicate an image or design, and use it again within the same part or within a related part. This gives companies the opportunity to cut down the number of parts they use in designing a product. This also helps to keep the inventory down.

2. Transfer or translate features from one part of the product to another. If the first-class part of the airplane has certain touches, so can the coach class.

3. Upsize or downsize a part, product or design. The system works on scaling, but because all the data is stored digitally, size is readily changed. If the production and marketing data are available, product development managers use this scaling to compare how much it would cost to produce a product at one size versus another.

4. Rotate the design/product visually to inspect it from different angles and perspectives. Systems are offering designs viewed in three dimensions.

One third of design time is saved with CAD modeling, according to CAD proponents. Most products can be changed without having to start over from scratch.

Although great strides have been made in CAD/CAM software for individual desktop microcomputers, most current systems are attached to a central processor that stores a large information data base, and coordinates the work flow between draftsmen, designers and engineers. Attached to the computer system is a device that transfers the computerized designs onto paper—dot matrix or laser printers and plotting devices. The digitized data is ultimately shipped to a laser or computerized tool maker that automatically replicates the electronic design in the physical product (computer-aided manufacturing). The next logical step is to network the CAD system with the automated factory floor—CAE, CAM and CIM.

CAD Applications

CAD has been applied to almost every predictable manufacturing activity and then to some unexpected ones. Cartography lends itself to computer aid. Such maps might be used for environmental impact statements or for land use planning documents. Artificial heart valves are also designed on the CAD table. Architects and landscapers can design away to their heart's content, or they can do more precise renderings. Process industries such as the oil industries or chemical manufacturers can plot their pipelines or electrical grids. Even garment makers can use the system to lay out and cut fabric.

The computer/electronics industry is always one of the primary users of its own products. Semiconductor manufacturers have embraced CAD for design of printed circuit boards and integrated circuits. Much of their work and development is tedious and time-consuming and would be prohibitively expensive without CAD and CAM.

One CAD company insider estimates the need for CAD operators may reach 100,000 by 1990,[4] although that depends on what happens to the economy as a whole, especially the manufacturing sector. In the automotive industry, the need for trained CAD/CAM engineers should double by 1995. "Computer graphics and CAD/CAM aren't doing away with anybody," said Rosemary Russo, a people finder for Grumman Engineering/Manufacturing Systems. "It's changing jobs, making things easier and more efficient. But I don't think you'll see a day when there are people-less factories."

The demand for CAD/CAM equipment and trained personnel is at an all-time high. Industry analysts predict that companies like Computervision will be billion-dollar firms by the 1990s because of their head start in CAD/CAM equipment manufacture and systems design. A study by the Office of Technology Assessment (OTA)—a congressional advisory body—recently concluded: "Programmable automation industries are likely to become increasingly important to the industrial base and national security of the U.S. because of increasing dependence on programmable automation both to enhance manufacturing productivity and to manufacture defense equipment."

Human Implications

Whether CAD will create or displace more jobs in the long run is debatable. The drafter has been made obsolete by CAD systems. "Drafting is one important occupation . . . to fall victim to new technology. As computer-assisted design equipment gains more widespread use, the growth of this occupation will be virtually nil."[5] How many jobs there will be as CAD engineers, designers and operators remains to be seen, for the estimates change monthly. In 1983 there were an estimated 32,000 CAD workstations in U.S. companies. Most of the employers are in aerospace and electronics and integrated circuit design. The Office of Technology Assessment maintains that "CAD will eventually reduce the demand for draftsmen—unless trends in product markets lead design activity to grow substantially." The easier and quicker a final design rendering is produced, the fewer drafters will be required. Anticipated improvements in equipment will reduce the need for programming. For example, CAD stations are being developed that will automatically generate designs.

Another concern is that the drafter-level or operator-level CAD position may disappear. Engineers are able to do all the work themselves because of the computer-based systems. Proponents of the CAD/CAM system disagree, however, and maintain that CAD/CAM will simply cause a shift of trades to the computer equivalent of their current job description. In fact, the experts say, there is now a tremendous shortage of trained CAD/CAM engineers, draftsmen and related technicians.

Unlike the traditionally all-male drafting ranks, women are finding employment working on CAD systems. Of 700 recent graduates of the drafting and design program at Fullerton Community College in Fullerton, California (the heart of engineering, especially aerospace), one-third have been women. A similar program at San Jacinto Community College in Pasadena, Texas, has been successfully training handicapped persons, including paraplegics. Steve Horton, chairman of the engineering and drafting technology department, reports, "With a firm grounding in drafting and design theory and training in CAD techniques, a handicapped person can be as productive as any other drafter or designer."

Work Changes

The revolution in design/drafting work has received mixed reviews. The manufacturers argue that the systems enhance the creativity and skills of the designer. Others say that because of CAD less professional, less educated and, of course, less well-paid workers now do the work. Those concerned with the loss of creativity and individuality refer back to Karl Marx, who found imagination one of the things that distinguishes us from animals: "A bee puts to shame many an architect in the construction of its cells; but what distinguishes the worst of architects from the best of bees is namely this: The architect will construct in his imagination that which he will ultimately erect in reality. At the end of every labour process, we get that which existed in the consciousness of the labourer at its commencement."[6]

Although more attention has been paid to the complaints of office workers, perhaps because of their active organizations, the worker at a CAD system is vulnerable to many of the same stresses as the office VDT user. Both are stuck in front of a screen for long periods. Office workers often work night shifts. One concern of CAD operators is that they will also be assigned night shifts, although that is not yet common place.

CAD proponents counter that since CAD stimulates creativity, stress is less likely because operators enjoy their work. Many CAD/CAM systems are just being implemented, and so the full effects are not understood. Office systems have been around longer. However, companies are seeing that "Once the system is in place, most of the decisions are made. Whoever's involved downstream is working in a much more controlled environment."[7]

Putting professionals behind a terminal means their work can be monitored, just as office workers have their keystrokes counted. Such monitoring is sure to affect a worker's sense of autonomy and control over his or her work.

It's impossible to hold back progress. The above concerns are all valid, and have been little dealt with in the U.S. and probably won't be if the economy, and especially the manufacturing sector, continue to drag. It may be well to heed the comments from those further along the automation trail: "The alternatives are stark. Either we will have a future in which human beings are reduced to a sort of bee-like behaviour, reacting to the systems and equipment specified for them; or we will have a future in which masses of people, conscious of their skills and abilities in both a political and technical sense, decide that they are going to be the architects of a new form of technological development which will enhance human creativity and mean more freedom of choice and expression rather than less. The truth is, we shall have to make the profound political decision as to whether we intend to act as architects or behave like bees."[8]

CAD Training and Retraining

Many CAD operator positions require a two-year associate degree. Responding to industry's need in this area, many junior, community and vocational colleges offer such programs. At the engineering level CAD will continue to demand four-year graduates as CAD product designers. Schools such as the Georgia Institute of Technology already offer specialized engineering courses in such CAD areas as human factors engineering and computer graphic design.

Requirements: CAD work requires good design sense, ability to work accurately with details, to grasp spatial relationships and to work closely with engineers, designers and other professionals. It is important to note that CAD draftsmen are not designers. They may take rough sketches on paper or even vague written descriptions of a product and convert them to a "first draft" on the computer screen. There will be a considerable demand for individuals who can make this computer transfer. Those employers who have a great demand for CAD draftsmen include those who are involved in electronics or mechanical manufacturing, CAD/CAM systems manufacturing and design, and computer graphics.

What exactly does a CAD draftsman do? The chain of CAD command is as follows: Work is passed from a design engineer, who may do little more than a rough sketch of a product or part, to the CAD draftsman who translates that hard copy into an electronic design. There may be several levels of CAD draftsmen—those who search the data base for components and assemble them (research), those who do the first drafts, and those who finalize the CAD rendering for the engineering department.

In the United States, as in many industrialized nations, the problem is to locate and hire enough qualified engineers and designers. For many companies the only way to meet productivity requirements is by using CAD/CAM techniques to enhance the capability of the people already available. The case of CAD/CAM at Grumman Aerospace in New York shows how employers are working their way around a CAD/CAM talent shortage. Russo of Grumman recently explained: "For future employees we are looking for some background in computer knowledge. We don't expect engineers to program but we hope they have the background. Having some form of computer science background can only help. But really what we are hiring are engineers. The CAD/CAM is just a tool."

CAD/CAM at Grumman is used in a wide range of aerospace product designs. On many new aircraft programs it is used from design to production. The models are designed electronically, and the parts made by robots that take their die cutting instructions from the original CAD/CAM designs.

Vocational training in CAD drafting is pervasive in technical schools around the country. The Glendale CAD/CAM Operator Training Program in Glendale, California, gives a good picture of what such a vocational degree entails. Located at the Glendale Community College the program is funded by the local Jet Propulsion Laboratory (JPL), a private, non-profit research and development laboratory at Cal Tech; Singer Librascope, a division of Singer Corporation; and Computervision, the largest producer of turnkey CAD/CAM systems in the country. The program that the group designed involves three-hour lectures at the college two mornings a week and laboratory training two evenings a week. All candidates are required to have completed the following college-level courses: one semester of basic mechanical drafting, one semester of advanced mechanical drafting, one semester of descriptive geometry or equivalent work experience. The students receive 12 weeks of classroom instruction and 6 hours of terminal training per week. The curriculum is designed to include introductory material plus three Computervision customer courses: (1) basic mechanical design; (2) advanced mechanical design; and (3) basic printed circuit/electrical schematic design. Students are given an examination following each work segment. Successful graduates begin worksite training at JPL and Singer. After 200 hours of worksite training, an average of 7 out of 11 candidates are hired for full-time employment at these two companies.

Advanced placement in these careers is only achieved, however, with training in related fields as well, particularly architecture, drafting, product design and industrial graphics.

Salary: CAD's biggest application is in the manufacturing sector. Entry-level positions run the gamut from $20,000 to $30,000 per year. CAD designers with only a few years' experience earn $40,000. The new JPL CAD/CAM operators received entry-level salaries of $6–7.50 per hour. Singer employees begin with starting salaries of $6.25–7.25 per hour. CAD salaries vary depending on the job, the company and industry. Here are broad ranges for several existing job titles in the operations category:

CAD Production Clerk: Responsible for supplying CAD operators and engineers with support materials and information, for instance, the computer tapes, they need to do their job. A high school education is necessary, and they make $10,000–13,000.

CAD Operator, sometimes known as a **CAD technician, CAD terminal draftsman** or **CAD product designer:** Two years of college is needed, and they make $14,000–28,000.

CAD Product Engineer, also known as a **CAD engineer** or **CAD product designer:** Four years of college is needed, and they make $15,000–35,000.

The fast growing CAD/CADD industry also needs skilled and professional workers. The needs of the CAD companies for chief scientists, researchers and product developers are similar to those in the computer industry. (See Chapter 4.) Beginning with entry level, some CAD titles and salary ranges are the following:

CAD Programmer: Two to four years of college. $15,000–25,000.

CAD Software/hardware Designer: Four years, preferably in electrical or manufacturing engineering. $20,000–40,000.

CAD Training Specialist: Two to four years of college. $15,000–30,000.

CAD Sales Representative: Four years of college. $20,000–50,000.

Key employers within the vendor community include not only the specialized CAD firms, many of which are being opened by corporations but general purpose computer manufacturers as well. Large users of their own systems, these firms are excellent training grounds.

CAE: COMPUTER-AIDED ENGINEERING

Both prior to and after the product design of CAD, engineers get involved in the process to assure the product is sound and does what it's designed for. This is the traditional bailiwick of the industrial, mechanical or design engineer. Now, computers are also being applied to this work.

Engineers in research and development and product development groups work on CAD or computer graphics-based systems. In addition, once all the detailed blueprints and designs have been completed, test engineers turn to computers. They use them to simulate the conditions the product may be exposed to. In a simple example, they simulate the winds experienced by the Space Shuttle on re-entry into the earth's atmosphere. A mock-up prototype of designs is still built, but only after simulations have ruled out those least likely to succeed. Only after passing the computer tests are prototypes built. This has resulted in considerable cost savings.

CAE experience is increasingly being asked for in job advertisements. Requirements and salaries for such manufacturing engineers are much the same as for CAD engineers.

CAM: COMPUTER-AIDED MANUFACTURING

Engineers are but one part of the future manufacturing work force. There will be CAM mechanics, CAM superintendents and CAM inventory controllers. In addition, programmers will design the automated systems, write the software and design the computer networks of the new manufacturing and design systems.

Although CAD/CAM acronyms are often lumped together, they are quite different pursuits because CAM refers to the manufacturing process. This may include robots, lasers, machine presses, lathes and other machine tools, all of which are automated and computer controlled.

One way to look at this is an actual example. The Luken Steel Co. in Coatsville, Pennsylvania has installed two production control systems: Materials Tracking and Expending (Matrex) and Status On Line (Statline).

"Prior to Matrex and Statline . . . 200 people worked in production control. These people tracked 650 to 700 orders per month and coordinated 22,000 pieces of steel (in various stages of completion) through 900 acres and 50 different buildings and operation locations. The primary task of these workers was to communicate order status to salespeople and customers. A customer who called to insure about an order got his information two days later, at which point it was two or three days old and often incorrect."[9]

A robot technician or repairman might well fit under the CAM job heading, but still other responsibilities need to be considered, all of them with one common denominator. There is an extreme shortage of trained personnel, so much so that IBM recently donated $50 million to 12 universities for CAM engineering programs.

Case Study: Bringing Good Things to Life

General Electric is a leading employer of CAM engineers. Its Edison Engineering Program in Schenectady, New York, is recognized as a "fast track" by design and conceptual thinkers. It combines on-the-job training with graduate-level academic degrees. GE hires 1,500 entry-level engineers a year. Half of them go into training programs, many specifically for CAM applications. In all training programs, according to E.J. Clark, GE manager of educational communications, engineers are exposed to robotics and computer-aided manufacturing systems. "We don't expect people coming out of school to have expertise in CAM. It is the type of thing they can work their way up to as a specialty while at GE." He adds that engineering schools shouldn't be responsible for preparing students specifically for careers in CAM or robotics. "They should take a more interdisciplinary approach, though for our needs we are looking for people with some degree of electrical engineering training."

Salaries for B.A. engineering graduates at GE range from $26,000 to $30,000 depending on their skills. "Electronics and computer science types" are in short supply and thus "get better salaries than industrial and civil engineers."

The following is a listing of opportunities in the field of CAM.

CAM PARTS CONTROLLER

In the past this job was called a traffic controller, responsible for making sure that parts inventory matched production. This crucial manufacturing balance is controlled exclusively by computer in the factory of the future, and easily adjusted so that inventory doesn't outweigh production needs at any given time. Since this is primarily a clerical task, entry-level salaries are usually in the $15,000 range, and require a junior college or vocational school degree.

This job is similar to that of the CAM production supervisor, who specifically regulates and inspects the production speed of the automated assembly line. CAM production supervisors make several thousand dollars more than controllers.

CAM FOREMAN

This is another job title that has its roots in a previous responsibility on the plant floor. The CAM foreman supervises the other CAM workers. In the future he will most likely oversee their jobs from a single terminal that can look in on any other terminal at any time. Because of the supervisory role of this occupation, entry-level positions reach $17,000 and demand no more than a two-year vocational training program.

CAM MAINTENANCE/CAM TECHNICIANS

These people are responsible for the day-to-day maintenance and repair of CAM machinery. They install and make adjustments on the robots and automated systems. Entry-level positions requiring only two years of vocational training, pay in the $15,000 range.

CAM technicians require similar training and receive similar salaries. The difference is that their job descriptions are more flexible, and are usually required to work closely with system designers, programmers or engineers.

CAM PROGRAMMERS

CAM programmers require an extensive background in computer programming and CAM design. Their responsibility is to adjust the production schedule by either accelerating assembly line progress or creating automated short cuts. Since the fully automated factory requires constant adjustments from a central computer, their job is a crucial one in the factory of tomorrow.

Properly trained individuals gain jobs with only junior college degrees and expect starting salaries of $22,000.

CAM ENGINEERS

At the top of the CAM employment pyramid is the CAM engineer. He or she is ultimately responsible for designing and redesigning the CAM system. Though the number of individuals a given factory needs with these skills is limited to a few, salaries are commensurate with the responsibilities.

Individuals with engineering degrees in CAM or post-graduate degrees in CAM specialties make as much as $40,000 after only several years.

ROBOTICS

Robots, computer-controlled machines programmed for a variety of tasks, used currently on the assembly lines, are truly double edged. Many see them as threats. Robotics, the use of these robots, is both ending and creating jobs. Many U.S. companies squeezed by foreign competition and outdated manufacturing plants are rushing to robotics for everything from product assembly to quality control, albeit not as rapidly as some would like.

Although at first the rise of robotics will increase blue collar unemployment, in the long term it will double factory productivity and create a demand for robot installers, technicians, engineers and maintenance crews. The bad news is that fewer jobs will exist in the factory of the future.

The demand for high tech hardware is spurring an entirely new industry dedicated to building, designing, selling and enhancing industrial robots. Both the U.S. and Japan are developing robots that see via optical sensors, robots that touch surfaces for brittleness or fluidity, and robots that walk.

Of course, Japan is far ahead of the U.S. in the robot race. According to the latest Robot Industries Association (RIA) figures, the Japanese have 41,000 robots, the Europeans, 13,000, and the U.S., 9,000. This prompts some industry watchers to ask the obvious: Why is the U.S. so advanced in the use of computers but so behind in the use of robots? One pro-robotics consultant writing in an industry trade newspaper answers: "The Japanese want to use robots! Americans seem to be more interested in robot technology than in using robots in production."[10]

U.S. manufacturers have hindered the introduction of robots simply by never being satisfied. Robot manufacturers are never able to please. "The bottom line is that U.S. manufacturing management doesn't want to install robots."[11]

Steel Collar Workers: The Workerless Factory

Automation is coming, and the union fear of the "workerless factory" may soon become a reality. Since assembly workers constitute 17% of the U.S. work force and inspection workers another 10%—two areas in which robotics is expected to make its biggest impact—bold challenges lie ahead. As many as 4 million production workers will lose their jobs over the next 20 years because of changes now afoot.

The debate of the pros and cons of automation will continue to rage for years. At the same time major manufacturers are increasingly replacing blue collar jobs with steel collar workers—robots. One school of economics says that throughout history automation has reduced jobs in some sections and created entirely new job categories. They point to an Ontario

Manpower Commission study of a Canadian Singer Company plant. When the company replaced 350 mechanical parts in a sewing machine with a single microprocessor in the late 1970s, assembly labor dropped dramatically. The report indicated, though, that a simultaneous increase in clerical and support workers offset the layoffs.

Automation such as that embodied in robotics projects is the only way for the U.S. to remain competitive in new world markets, argue automation proponents. Robot Industries of America (RIA) indicates that the future is bright for factory employment. "The industry position is that there are lots of new career opportunities in manufacturing. Somebody has to install, maintain and program them [robots]. Since they make companies more productive, in turn, they'll be able to hire more people," said Jeff Burnstein, RIA manager of public relations.

A look at factory employment in the 1990s can best be envisioned by a look at the changes already underway at the nation's largest auto maker, General Motors. GM has committed $120 million annually for retraining any workers who lose their paychecks to a robot. According to Richard Huber, assistant director of labor relations at GM, automotive manufacturing employment in the future will break down into the same two categories as it does today—skilled and non-skilled trades. "Going into the 1990s, the new jobs will require a good knowledge of electronics, especially as it relates to programmable devices. Lasers are also coming on, as they apply to welding and inspection." He emphasizes that job descriptions always evolve. "This does not mean that skilled workers are replaced." The trend he observes is one of retraining the work force to adapt to new trade positions opened by high technologies. "An electrician who once used to wire a box might now be retrained to use programming tools. Existing jobs evolve, as the tasks change relative to the function."

Such retraining is now underway in GM-UAW training centers in Flint, Michigan, and Buffalo, New York, and involve thousands of employees. For plants that are in the midst of automation on-site retraining is the rule. Huber admits that new job opportunities in the non-skilled trades are diminishing, but adds that skilled opportunities have never been stronger at GM.

The most common applications of industrial robots today are as follows: material handling, machine loading/unloading, spray painting, welding, machining and assembly. According to the Society of Manufacturing Engineers (SME) the demand for robotics workers over the next ten years will be in the following industries: automotive, aerospace, cosmetics, military, mining, nuclear energy, oil, plastics and textiles.

What will those jobs be? According to the Robot Institute of America the biggest career opportunities in robotics today are the following:

1. Robot technicians
2. Robot repairmen
3. Robotics programmers

4. Robotics engineers
5. Robotics supervisors
6. Robotics sales engineers

ROBOT TECHNICIAN

Of all these categories that of robot technician is expected to be the biggest growth sector. It reflects the general upturn in technician employment throughout the computer and information processing industries. Growth of the number of skilled technical workers is expected to grow an unprecedented 147% by 1990, and industry analysts expect a shortage of at least 100,000 robot technicians by that year. That includes a four-fold increase in robot technicians by the end of the decade.

Most robot technicians are hired after extensive retraining within the existing factory population. In Detroit, for instance, thousands of automotive employees are enrolled in community colleges to become robotics technicians as a result of a UAW retraining agreement with the Big Three auto makers. There will be, however, ways to enter this lucrative career from the outside.

Switching production jobs is not as easy as it seems. For one thing the robotics technician requires high levels of skill—particularly in computer electronics. For a company to hire someone with some computer proficiency is easier than to retrain someone from the existing work force. Present employees must learn new skills. They have to develop a new attitude toward their job under an entirely new pay scale. Those employees for whom technology is a foreign domain where they are afraid to tread will lose out.

What is the role of the robot technician? What is the best way to prepare for the job that some analysts are calling the "backbone of the 21st century"? Technicians work in both the creative and manufacturing ends of the factory. They often end up as assistants to those in research and development. The robot technician tends to the robots on the production line, makes sure they function properly, replaces worn parts, installs factory hardware improvements, customizes the robot motions, and checks them repeatedly for malfunctions. These "tenders" require a basic understanding of the way robots work and how computers are programmed to administer their commands.

Their responsibilities break down as follows:

1. Assembling robotic prototypes. The technician works from an engineer's CAD/CAM blueprints and creates the first working model of the robot.
2. Troubleshooting system malfunctions. The technician may not necessarily repair the robotic equipment, but is responsible for identifying malfunctions that occur in the manufacturing system.
3. Evaluating retooling requirements for new products. The technician may be called on to create cost analyses of adapting automation systems for new product designs.

4. Testing and calibrating electronic test equipment. The technician is trained to test and adjust computer and electronic test gear in order to evaluate the functioning of a particular robot or CAM system.

Of course, there are supervisory levels of employees who manage both robotics repairers and technicians.

Requirements: This skilled trade includes an interest in and a practical understanding of electronics design; mechanical aptitude; two-year vocational school study; ability to work closely with engineers and other professionals; keen problem-solving sensibilities; and welding skills.

Many skills required are gained from two-year vocational colleges, especially those in the industrial centers of the Midwest where much of the demand for robot workers currently exists. Because of the regional nature of robotics training the meaning of robot technician varies from state to state. In Detroit the robotics technician is considered a skilled tradesman like a plumber or an electrician. This city is a tough nut for technical school trained workers to crack since employment is based mostly on retraining programs, which offer existing employees job placement priorities. In Detroit robot technicians have usually served the company for at least 10 years.

On the other hand, robot technicians in the Sun Belt wear the same white collars as management. They serve mainly as manufacturers' sales reps, service engineers and installers.

The job of the robot technician differs from other robototics jobs in the degrees of responsibility. The lower paying jobs are robot VDT operators who spend their days monitoring on-screen activities of a series of robots under their command. This is largely a clerical assignment and doesn't bring more than assembly line wages.

On the other end of the pay scale are robot engineers who design and install the robots and computer-aided manufacturing systems. This job requires at least four years of college education and possibly graduate degrees for further advancement. Robot engineers make $40,000 after 10 years of employment. A robot engineer whose innovations result in cost savings to the corporation becomes indispensible in their progression toward an automated future.

A robot repairman, like other skilled tradesmen, will be in great demand. His or her ability to get a robot up and running quickly determines the profitability of a day's work at the factory. The ability to ensure that all electronic, pneumatic and hydraulic devices are working as they should makes the robot repairman an invaluable staff member.

Salary: Robotics International, a division of the Society of Manufacturing Engineers (SME), indicates that robot technicians with extensive experience in electronics or mechanical repair receive $25,000–30,000 their first year. This was confirmed recently with interviews at Macomb Community College in suburban Detroit. It offers an associate degree program in robotics. Most of its 50 students are quickly snatched up by nearby motor makers at salaries of "more than" $30,000. (These figures are based on the salaries recently paid to 4 Macomb graduates installing a new General Motors auto paint robot line in Georgia.)

As the industry settles salaries of $15,000–25,000 might be more realistic. Experienced supervisors should earn $15,000–30,000.

ROBOTICS PROGRAMMERS

One robotics career that doesn't appear to be as promising as it should is robotics programming. Starting salaries are $12,000 and usually peak at $25,000. Why such a relatively low pay scale for a programming professional who easily makes double that in computer- and information-based industries? Most robots on the market are programmed with the "teach-repeat" method. Robot engineers claim that anyone from a production worker to an electrician can program a robot by leading it manually through the motion sequences that the robot's memory records and then instructs it to repeat. Robot programming thus doesn't require special personnel.

Newer robots are instructed by off-line computers. A terminal or PC is attached to the robot's memory and is used to key in instructions. This code is usually predesigned by the CAM engineers in a series of easy-to-follow on-screen menus and mechanical drawings. Robot programming is thus a low skill task that could become the equivalent of the assembly line tasks with more user-friendly and intelligent programs and CAM systems in the years to come.

Salary: If this comes to pass salaries will suffer. A robot programmer might start at $12,000 and reach $20,000 at mid-career. Much depends on how the robotics industry develops. As with all robotics occupations, geography and supply of available workers will play a major factor in pay scales.

ROBOTICS ENGINEER

The robotics engineer is a position that promises to be in great demand in the years to come. Those with specific robotics engineering training will be particularly in demand. The robotics industry is facing the same engineer shortage of other electronics related industries. This persists despite the fact that the number of bachelor's degrees in electrical engineering and computer science has grown 12% per year for the past 10 years. According to the American Electronics Association (AEA), American corporations are facing a severe shortage of electronic engineers going into the 1990s. The AEA states that industry will demand 23,000 more engineering graduates than the existing supply by 1995. This will affect the development of the robotics industry. Robotics requires an entirely new category of engineer. The UpJohn Institute has estimated that Detroit auto makers alone will require 3,500 robotics engineers by the end of the decade.

According to personnel managers at leading robotics concerns like Cybotech and Unimation, the main factor constraining the automation of American factories is the limited amount of trained engineering talent. This has become an especially tough problem because of a limited number of university robotics engineering programs. At a recent U.S. Department of Commerce symposium one of the 11 most important issues facing American industry today was described as the "need for better technical-scientific education to ensure supply of qualified personnel."

For universities much of the problem is in developing a robotics curriculum, since the career is a hybrid that demands equal parts of mechanical engineering, electrical engineering, industrial engineering and computer science. For advanced robotic development a working knowledge of artificial intelligence is also necessary. This diversity is what keeps many current engineers from making the shift into robotics.

Robotic engineering programs are growing, though, thanks to a working relationship with industry, but even these major universities are suffering from severe shortages of instructors and equipment. The demand for trained robotics engineers is so high in industry that university scientists are frequently snatched up from the classrooms. University engineering departments are hard pressed to find teaching talent, for they cannot pay the top salaries now offered by industry.

Furthermore, the universities claim that there aren't enough funds for robotic training equipment. A sophisticated robot costs $100,000. The average robotics engineering program requires an initial investment of $500,000 in equipment. For this reason the Robot Institute of America proposes that the federal government offer robotics companies tax incentives for equipment donations to educational institutions. With preconditions some such donations are already being made. For instance, Rensselaer Polytechnic Institute has successfully solicited over $2 million from GM, Boeing and GE for a new manufacturing technology program. A new robotic arc welding lab at Ohio State University has been financed by outside business contracts. Robot maker Cincinnati Milacron has six of its robots on loan to colleges around the country and has dozens of requests from other institutions. The Emhart Corporation of Farmington, Connecticut, has entered into a joint program with the Worcester Polytechnic Institute of Worcester, Massachusetts, for the development of factory automation systems. In exchange for financial support WPI tests and develops the systems, and Emhart is allowed to take the products to market.

This corporate-college connection raises questions of academic independence that have been raised in other areas, but the demand and start-up costs for university robotic training is so high, however, that colleges may have no other choice but to become dependent upon industry donations. The corporations benefit from a pool of robotics engineering candidates. The candidates themselves have virtually guaranteed jobs, and possibly the opportunity to work their way through school with outside consulting and design work during the school year and summers.

Salary: Starting salaries at Unimation, a leading Danbury, Connecticut, robotics firm, reach the $30,000 mark for engineering school graduates.

ROBOTICS INDUSTRY JOBS

One of the most successful U.S. robot manufacturers has gained that success by jumping into the Japanese robot market. American Robot of Pittsburgh has a 7-year, $10 million licensing agreement with a Japanese robot maker for American's Merlin system. Unlike most of the Japanese stand-alone robots the Merlin system (programmed in Unix software) handles many of the white-collar inventorying processes and is integrated easily into a CIM assembly chain.

An ideal robotics industry job is a sales representative. The responsibilities are similar to a computer salesperson but with different applications. Sales representatives earn $23,000–50,000.

Small companies are ideal employers of new robotics-attuned workers. Here's a breakdown of staffing for a robot manufacturer:[12]

Engineers (23.7%)
Engineering technicians (15.7%)
Other technical workers (4.2%)
Office managers (6.8%)
Sales (3.4%)
Clerical (13.9%)
Skilled craft workers (8.4%)
Semiskilled craft workers (4.2%)
Assemblers (19%)
Laborers (0.7%)[17]

NUMERICAL CONTROL MACHINES

Dating back more than 20 years to manufacturing in the aircraft industry, numerical control (N/C) machines have been a growing part of American industry. Their importance has heightened with the introduction of computer controls. N/C machines are large machines that create a particular part based on numerical instructions which have been programmed and fed into the machine.

NUMERICAL CONTROL MACHINE OPERATOR

Now that companies realize the need to improve manufacturing processing they're adopting N/C machines faster. "Employment of numerical control machine-tool operators is expected to increase faster than the average for all occupations through the mid-1990s."[13] There are currently

70,000 such jobs and because many operators have been working on these systems for 20 years, the growth projections don't include replacements for retirees. Industries employing the most N/C workers are aircraft and heavy manufacturing.

Here's what a N/C operator does:

"Working from written instructions or directions from supervisors, operators must position the workpiece, attach the necessary tools, and load the program into the controller. The machine tool cannot 'see' the workpiece; it moves and operates in relation to a fixed starting point. Therefore, if the operator positions the workpiece incorrectly, all subsequent machining will be wrong. Operators also must secure the workpiece to the work table correctly, so the piece does not move while it is machined. When setting up and running a job, operators must install the proper tools in the machine. Many numerically controlled machines are equipped with automatic tool changers, so operators have to load several tools in the proper sequence. The time an operator needs to position and secure the workpiece and load the tools may be only a few minutes or it may be several hours, depending on the size of the workpiece and the complexity of the job.

"The way a program is loaded into a controller depends on how it is stored. If the program is stored on tape, it must be run through a tape reader that transmits the program to the controller. Increasingly, machine-tool controllers are connected to minicomputers. Operators load programs that are stored on disk or tape directly into the controller via the computer.

"Programs must be corrected, or debugged, the first time they run. If the tool moves to the wrong position or cuts too deeply, for example, the program must be changed. Some employers have numerical-control machine operators debug the program. Others have tool programmers monitor the first run.

"Once a job is properly set up and the program has been checked, the operator monitors the machine as it operates. Some jobs require frequent loading and unloading, several tool changes, or constant attention to insure that the machining is proceeding properly. For other jobs, the machine can run unattended for hours."[14]

Training: N/C operators do not require college educations. Most work in other jobs prior to graduating to the more sophisticated machines. Courses in shop math or blueprint reading as well as good work attitudes help land N/C jobs. N/C operators work initially as trainees with other operators. If they do the programming, they often attend classes for this. Those with special aptitudes may be able to move into this higher paying specialized programming field.

Salary: N/C operators receive an hourly wage in the $8.70–10 range. "This rate is about the same as the average hourly earnings for all production workers in manufacturing but slightly lower than the hourly rates of skilled machining workers such as machinists and tool-and-die makers."[15] N/C operators often belong to labor unions. (See Appendix 1 for N/C associations.)

LASERS

In sci-fi movies lasers are those super-duper guns used to shoot 'em up. In the real world these high-powered, computer-controlled light rays are the latest industrial tools. Commercial sales of lasers are expected to increase 5-fold between 1980 and 1990. Lasers will replace spot welding, tool and die manufacturing and all sorts of machine work. They will also strongly influence the health services. (See Chapter 11.) Lasers will play a part in new printing technologies, although perhaps to the detriment of workers. "Although employment in some occupations will be adversely affected, the increasing use of laser technology is expected to result in overall employment growth," reports BLS, on the need for skilled scientists and engineers and semiskilled assemblers and technicians to work with lasers.[16]

Expect laser technology to grow in the 1990s for a good reason: The government is behind it 100%. The military spent $3 billion on laser research and development in 1983. That expenditure is expected to jump to $10 billion by 1990. These developments will apply not only to space age weaponry, but also to the factory, graphics, printing and space laser communications. Other laser applications include atmospheric research, chemical analysis, fiber optics communications, holography, light shows, measurement, metal working, optical scanning and recording.

Two trends appear to be simultaneous. Jobs expected to be extinguished by laser technology are all projected to increase by 1995. Quality control supervisors will increase by 319,000 jobs, machinists by 58,000, press and plate printers by 35,000, tool and die makers by 32,000 and millwrights by 30,000. The number of welders and flamecutters is expected to rise by 105,000. According to the BLS report, "The majority of machinists, tool and die makers, and millwrights in durable goods manufacturing, which declined during 1980–82, is expected to recover and grow." At the same time, they projected 600,000 new openings for laser technicians by 1990.

LASER is an acronym for Light Amplification by Stimulation of Energy Radiation. Light waves from various sources are concentrated in a resonant circuit and then reflected through lenses and mirrors into one very intense, narrow beam of light. Laser uses are plentiful but have one thing in common: They are controlled by computers and by people trained to use computers. They are finicky electronic devices that have to be repaired, adjusted and maintained.

The emergent laser factories depend as much on its laser technicians as others now do their quality control supervisors, tool and die cutters and millworkers. Technicians who run or repair industrial lasers are responsible for machinery and parts manufacture for the product cycle. They drill holes, cut and weld hardware and ensure that the machinery runs correctly. For example, a machine tool operator using a laser may complete an intricate machining job more rapidly and precisely. A sheet metal worker may work more quickly. Lasers affect the existing production jobs of heat treaters, pattern makers, drill press operators, welders, sheet metal workers and machine tool operators. The result is an increase in programmers for the computers and the numerical control tools in which the new lasers are embedded.

Within the laser industry technicians are required to test and assemble lasers, service the equipment, and train both users and new technicians. On the laser production line semiskilled assemblers are also needed to build the complicated machines.

Lasers will also be heavily involved in quality control and inspection. Laser/holographic inspectors will use lasers and optical fibers to sense dimension and stress points in order to match them with a computer model. This will be done throughout the assembly cycle.

The greatest need for laser experts will be at the scientist/researcher/ engineer level. "Although engineers and physical scientists constitute less than 2% of the total work force, they make up over 20% of the work force in some laser manufacturing firms," reports the BLS. Also needed will be sales engineers and safety engineers first to sell and then safeguard workers from blindness and other injuries.

Laser/holographics specialists will largely be a VDT-bound job with the inspector trained to observe holographic images of a "perfect" example of the product and compare them to the real thing on the robotic assembly line.

Laser technicians will also operate and repair laser-based measuring devices such as interferometers, spectrometers and spectrophotometers.

Requirements: Regardless of the ultimate job descriptions, someone interested in becoming a laser technician should have an electronics systems experience; computer background; interest in lasers and/or electronics; skill or aptitude for detail measurements; and good close-range eyesight.

Salary: Those with a vocational, college or a post-graduate degree in laser technology will fare well in the factory of tomorrow. In fact, someone with 2 years of vocational training in laser technology can expect to start at $30,000 per year, according to the Laser Institute of America. Someone trained in laser/holographic specialities can expect a similar salary although these positions require two years of college.

1. R.C. Reeve. "Where Are the Robots?" *Computerworld*, June 10, 1985, p. ID/25.
2. Ibid. p. ID/26.
3. Michael Stanton. "Computer-Aided Design." *Occupational Outlook Quarterly* (U.S. Department of Labor, Bureau of Labor Statistics, Washington, DC), Spring 1985, p. 2.
4. Ibid. p. 6.
5. George T. Silvestri, John M. Lukasiewicz, and Marcus E. Einstein "Occupational Employment Projections Through 1995." *Monthly Labor Review* (U.S. Department of Labor, Bureau of Labor Statistics, Washington, DC), November 1983.
6. Karl Marx, *Capital* (London: Lawrence & Wishart, 1974) Vol. 1, p. 174.
7. Stanton, op. cit.
8. Mike Cooley, *Architect or Bee? The Human/Technology Relationship* (Slough, Great Britain: Hand and Brain Publications, Langley Technical Services, 1980) p. 100.
9. Lee White, "Automation Heats Up At Lukens Steel." *Computerworld*, June 19, 1985, p. 33.

10. Reeve, op. cit.
11. Ibid, p. ID/26.
12. 1982 Upjohn Institute estimate.
13. Ibid. p. 14.
14. Tom Nardone. "Numerical-Control Machine-Tool Operators." *Occupational Outlook Quarterly* (U.S. Department of Labor, Bureau of Labor Statistics, Washington, DC) Spring 1985 p. 13.
15. Ibid.
16. Arthur Gartaganis. "Careers in the New Technologies." *Occupational Outlook Quarterly,* Winter 1984, p. 23.

8
ARTIFICIAL INTELLIGENCE

"The computers of the future will make those of today look like idiot savants," says Ray Kurzweil, Cambridge, Massachusetts, inventor. Like many computer entrepreneurs he is racing to apply the next generation of computer technology to commercial products. His machines will do more than just calculate in megaseconds and transmit messages over the phone. They will be thinking machines. Computers processing artificial intelligence software and programs will replicate the thought patterns of human beings. These systems will be used to make decisions, serve as expert consultants or to create a new generation of products. Reading machines for the blind, voice activated typewriters and digital keyboard synthesizers that produce the sound of an aged Steinway grand. Kurweil's ambitious hardware is but a tip of the burgeoning business of artificial intelligence, most commonly known as AI. Computers that achieve high levels of problem solving that is equal to or better than the best human performance are already being applied in business, government and science.

It's impossible to say where artificial intelligence and all the related software tools, programs and hardware will ultimately end up. There is much debate about AI and whether or not it's even possible to create "smart" machines. Many suspect that expert systems, AI's most popular rendition so far, do nothing more than take advantage of the tremendous number crunching capabilities of the supercomputers.

EXCITING CAREER HORIZONS

Precisely because this technology—still very much in the conceptual stage—is evolving, it's critical for the career evaluator to know about. AI will become less of an art/science and more of an underpinning for many other new projects and businesses. "AI has probably created the most interesting growth surge for people in all of the liberal arts," finds Chick Bisberg, a senior consultant at Halbrecht and Company in New York, who recruits AI professionals. "There are so many things going on that we won't recognize as AI until they're in the market. I can't think of a single business I am in that is not going to incorporate AI." Computer-based typesetting, magazine page make-up systems and numerically controlled sheet metal machines are ideal applications for AI techniques. A magazine could be entirely designed and assembled by the system. The military is already investing heavily in AI-based defense systems such as tanks and submarines that do not require human on-board controllers. AI techniques will be used in computer-based systems that recognize speech, decipher visual pictures, communicate with humans using colloquial language and even learn from experience. Why not a computer that would tell you where to invest your money, or which company is the ideal one for your firm to merge with and on what terms?

All these unknowns make for an ideal situation for the career seeker. It's a shrewd move to take advantage of voids and vacuums in a new technology. But remember: AI requires tremendous talent and long preparation. There may not be that many AI jobs although technology predictions are often notorious for missing the mark. One expert sees a market for 8,000 knowledge engineers (the powerhouses of most AI efforts) working at about 150 companies by 1990. Another AI industry observer guessed that only 3,000 AI jobs existed in 1985. This is tiny compared to the 200,000 persons who currently work as systems analysts in data processing.

What about professionals already working in traditional data processing? Is there any hope for them getting involved in AI projects despite a lack of formal AI training? Bisberg urges present DP employees to "go to the fringe," to get involved with leading edge technical projects within the organization where you're already working. If there's an AI project, so much the better.

Projects are not all with trendy AI firms. Metropolitan Life Insurance is applying AI expert systems techniques to its bread-and-butter applications such as underwriting screening, risk assessment, dividend calculation for group insurance and medical pre-admission review (for doctors to determine if an illness is covered by an individual's policy). In such applications, Metropolitan uses its existing expertise towards developing expert systems to take over much of the work. Metropolitan is using about a dozen of its own employees on the AI development project.

Part of the problem is that the industry is not growing as rapidly as the technology, although venture capitalists continue to invest money in new AI firms. A recent report from the Gartner Group of Stamford, Connecticut, on the behavior of AI users stated: "Development costs for expert systems are still quite substantial, due to the relatively high cost of the specialized hardware involved, the scarcity of expert systems programmers and relatively long development cycles."

The employment situation is equally promising but yet unfulfilled. A computer industry research firm surveyed 28 major corporations, all with a recognized interest in artificial intelligence, and found the following:

- 21% of the companies surveyed have at least one staff person working full time on AI related systems.

- The remaining 79% said no personnel were working on any AI projects at the time.

- One-third said that some staffers were engaged in only part-time AI systems development.
- The average number of AI researchers in this survey group was eight.

FIFTH GENERATION

AI applications run on a computer, but not just any computer. AI applications require special systems, an assortment of which are being designed, improved or discarded constantly.

Modified thinking computers exist today. Computers programmed in languages called LISP and Prolog provide a reliable, though expensive, "expert system" that does everything from prospecting for oil to diagnosing human ailments.

Knowledge-based expert systems seek to mimic human thought patterns in order to solve questions in a specific field of inquiry. Such systems solve complex problems by duplicating the decision-making processes of human experts. In some instances they outperform human experts. Expert systems encode knowledge symbolically and draw conclusions through logical or plausible inference, not by calculation as previous computer generations did.

The next generation of computers to be associated with AI and related applications is known as the Fifth Generation. An international race is on to develop and build this next generation. In 1981 the Japanese government launched its Fifth Generation project in order to create a human reasoning computer by 1990. The Japanese, who take such efforts seriously, will have 10,000 workers familiar with AI processes and computations. In the U.S. a conglomerate of 21 corporations called the Microelectronics & Computer Technology Corporation (MCC) has a similar aim. That effort is headed by retired admiral and former CIA director, Bobby Inman. Participating companies—interestingly IBM not among them (IBM has its own $4 billion research program.)—buy into various MCC research efforts such as the popular Advanced Computer Architecture project. Developments made will be licensed to the participating companies. As many as 70 Fifth Generation projects are underway at U.S. universities and corporations.

Who will win the Fifth Generation race? The jury is still out: "Basically, both countries are starting out even in the era of parallel computing for AI. We both have the same number of ideas, which is very little. They have extraordinary focus and momentum. We have extraordinary diversity and almost intentionally unfocused activity,"[2] reports Edward A. Feigenbaum of Stanford University. He co-authored the classic book on AI, *The Fifth Generation: Artificial Intelligence and Japan's Computer Challenge to the World,* and is a founder of one of the early AI companies, Teknowledge.

True diversity of opinion exists, as others are not even convinced the obstacle lies in hardware know-how. "There is lots of hardware available to run Prolog or anything else you want to run. The real obstacle is that the AI software has not been intelligently enough written yet."[3] offers William F. Zachman, vice-president of International Data, a Framingham, Massachusetts, market research firm.

GROWING INTELLIGENCE

Artificial intelligence is expected to be a high growth field:

- International Resource & Development Corporation (IRD) of Norwalk, Connecticut, put the total "knowledge systems market" including hardware, software and services at $220 million in 1985. The research group predicts that the 1993 market will reach $8.5 billion.

- A market is growing for software that allows expert system software to be built—software that creates other software. The research group expects this submarket to grow to $1.8 billion by 1993.

- Venture capitalists who fund new technology-based companies continue to inject millions of dollars into at least 40 small companies bent on commercializing artificial intelligence.

- More than 30 U.S. corporations and some smaller companies, particularly in the computer industry, have invested in AI efforts. For example, Lotus is funding an AI company founded by a Lotus former employee.

AI did not emerge overnight. Artificial intelligence dates back to the early 1950s when three computer pioneers—Marvin Minsky of MIT, John McCarthy of Stanford and Alan Newell of Carnegie-Mellon—made a revolutionary joint breakthrough: If computers could manipulate symbols instead of numbers, they reasoned, they could also manipulate symbols for words, musical notes or any other complex assemblage of detail. Following this breakthrough was the development and creation of computer languages that could accommodate words and symbols and not just numbers. LISP and Prolog were those languages and remain the cornerstones of the current boom in artificial intelligence applications.

In the late 1980s AI work consists of these primary disciplines:

1. Expert systems: software that attempts to mimic human decision-making processes in certain expertises.

2. Natural language: software that allows the user to pose questions in close to conversational English to the computer and receive answers and data back. No computer languages are required.

3. Visual recognition: software, typically coupled with hardware such as robots, that identifies specific shapes, sizes and objects. This enables a robot to discern a part arrayed or passing before it.

4. Voice recognition: hardware and software that analyzes and identifies speech, and allows for both voice input and output from the computer.

5. AI languages: programming languages, of which LISP and Prolog are in the forefront, used to develop software that mirrors human thought patterns by manipulating symbols.

6. AI computers: hardware, which usually takes advantage of symbolic processing, customized for AI software and applications.

7. Government contracts, almost entirely defense-related.

ARTIFICIAL INDUSTRIES

Where are artificial intelligence and expert systems being used? Expert systems aren't just figments of academics' imaginations, but are here today. Though there are ambitious applications in mind—including computers that can develop themselves—companies currently depend on AI applications for more mundane pursuits ranging from research and decision-making to quality and management control. Expert systems diagnose diseases or machine repair problems, search for minerals and oil deposits, and make megabuck financial moves.

Such systems don't come cheaply. The AI application has to deliver tremendous cost savings in order to return the often million-dollar investments required to develop a computer product that replaces a person with 50 years of experience.

PROSPECTOR is the best known AI product used by industry. Developed by SRI, formerly Stanford Research Institute, this program has the collective knowledge of 9 different geologists programmed into its memory banks. The program has been able to locate an iron ore deposit that none of the experts found on his own, a find worth $100 million. Because of such windfalls energy interests have become some of the biggest AI investors. Schlumberger, a multinational oil services company, has invested heavily in AI prospecting programs. El Aquitaine, a company that explores the North Sea for oil, commissioned an AI expert system to determine why their drill bits got stuck in the sea beds. This is an important question since downtime on offshore rigs costs $100,000 per day.

The most exciting thing about artificial intelligence careers is that they are found in a variety of industries and professions. What follows are several projects that are on the cutting edge of this new technology.

AI in Medicine

Applications of expert systems for medical diagnosis has been one important use. Stanford University's MYCIN program was one of the ground breakers in this growing software genre. Originally designed to examine evidence for 100 diagnoses, the program relates its body of medical knowledge to diseases. Another program, HELP, is used in two hospitals in Salt Lake City and Elmira, New York. Built by Control Data, the program took 15 years and $30 million to develop. It integrates all the data on patients from doctors, labs, pharmacists and nurses, and suggests possible diagnoses and treatments.

Since AI specialists in medicine are especially difficult to find, hospitals usually train their own. According to Phillip Marting, vice-president of Health Care Services at Control Data: "We feel some obligation to provide training to fill the void. We need people to bridge the medical and computer domains."

William J. Tritter, vice-president of Arnot-Ogden Memorial Hospital in Elmira, New York, where HELP has been used, explains that several levels of employees are needed to operate the AI/diagnosis system. On the first level are the technical people who write the code. The second level includes systems people who make the programs "idiot proof." Finally "some highly motivated person with an interest in the topic and a discipline in detail," a knowledge engineer, usually comes from a medical related profession—nurse, pharmacist, medical technician. He or she understands medical terms and has professional insight into how doctors think. Adds Tritter: "There are unbelievable employment opportunities for young doctors with computer science training."

AI in Finance

When millions of dollars are at stake, the ability to spot even minute savings or profits realizes huge windfalls. Prudential Bache Securities has contracted with Interactive Financial Services of Marietta, Georgia, to devise a system that will perform a stock watch for brokers. The system includes a monitor and alert capability that tells the broker when certain securities or markets reach a predetermined level. Other financial expert systems have been developed to track several different markets simultaneously, as well as to help stockbrokers analyze their clients' portfolios and offer financial planning advice. Banks use AI programs to screen loan applications. A brokerage house might develop an expert system for stocks and bonds trading based on the instincts and talents of its most gifted traders. Then less-gifted traders could compare their decisions against the "expert."

AI in the Factory

AI will have an impact on robotics and the factory of tomorrow. Along with machine vision devices, AI-based robots will not only be able to handle repetitive manual tasks, but may be able to fill management duties as well. AI has already made an impact on CAD/CAM designs. Richard Greenblat, a former research scientist at MIT, recently established LISP Machine, which developed computer-aided drawing programming called New Draw. The company claims that the program has helped design products that would have taken up to 100 man-hours in 2 hours.

AI in the Office

In 10 years a computer receptionist may be built that handles the majority of incoming business calls. The system will have voice recognition, speech generation capabilities, and be able to field a variety of questions and recite the appropriate answers. A prototype of this system, the Phone Butler, is already in operation at MIT.

IBM has meanwhile devised the office answer to junk mail. Its EPISTLE system reads executive mail, screens it, reroutes to the appropriate office and even writes a synopsis of its content. For the latter reason it is already being considered by publishing houses for screening manuscripts.

AI in Science

The first real expert system can be traced back to 1965 to the AI lab of 3 computer pioneers: Joshua Lederberg, Edward A. Feigenbaum and Bruce Buchanan. Their first product—DENDRAL—an aid to organic chemists in determining the molecular structure of chemical compounds, remains in use to this day.

AI in Industry/Business

Other major industrial applications of artificial intelligence-based systems include the following:

1. Seismic data processing
2. Financial forecasting and prediction
3. Geological and geophysical exploration
4. Industrial/factory quality control
5. Robotics
6. Data base management
7. Design, testing and layout of sophisticated integrated semiconductor chips

AI in Defense Systems

Much of the work in and funding for AI efforts is coming from the Defense Department, primarily through private companies on contract to the government. The Defense Advanced Research Projects Agency (DARPA) is committed to spending $600 million in contracts to industry and universities on three AI projects.

- Autonomous Land Vehicle (ALV) is for development of unmanned aircraft, submarines, tanks and land vehicles. Such crafts would navigate themselves, plan routes from digital (computer-readable) terrain data, and change plans as new weather, visual or other data that doesn't agree with input data becomes available. As fun as that sounds, it requires scores of complex sensory, visual recognition and expert decision systems.

- Battle Management System, an expert system originally focused on an aircraft carrier, will help the combat team fuse information, develop options, follow what's going on, and make battle decisions that involve many contingencies such as large numbers of men, ships and aircraft. In addition, it will have to handle the complicated communications between all the parties, where natural language queries to the computer would be most desirable.

- Pilot's Associate, another expert system, will duplicate the cockpit crew helping the pilot exploit the numerous weapons and systems on board. Because of the increasing complexity of the cockpit, this system would take over lower-level decisions.

LEARNING HOW TO LISP

Despite current excitement about LISP programming this programming language (short for list processing) is one of the two oldest programming languages still used today. (The other is Fortran, the scientific programming language.) LISP, one of the key tools of artificial intelligence, allows its programmers to link symbols the same way the human mind assembles and structures knowledge. For instance, in LISP the term "monkey" could be stored in lists along with terms like "banana" or "jungle." (In comparison, the Japanese are developing their Fifth Generation computer on an AI language called Prolog.)

These languages give programmers the ability to make symbolic relationships in the same way researchers believe that the human mind organizes its data to issue decisions. Tracing exactly how those decisions are made has proved to be the most formidable task in the race toward a thinking machine. No matter how smart the new computers may be, they are not yet smart enough to teach themselves. Just as today's computers need programmers to tell them how to function, the next generation of AI machines will need experts to tell them how to think.

This programming process will be far more complicated than the current assemblage of code. The coding process will remain part of the picture with future computers, but beind every code will have to be the distilled thought processes and information data bases that are currently stored in the cerebral cortexes of the world's leading authorities. In order to create thinking computers, computer programmers will have to logically distill human expertise, organize it, reinforce it with the appropriate information data bases and create a decision-making "system."

Because AI is germinating, job titles, descriptions and salaries are in the development and shake-down phase. Although there's much variation, the key working job categories are AI researcher, knowledge engineer, AI programmer, and AI technician.

AI RESEARCHER

The job of AI researcher or AI expert is the province of academics. The American Association for Artificial Intelligence (AAI) consists of 7,500 members, mostly university professors, academic researchers and students. "There are probably only 200 AI experts in the U.S. today," maintains Raymond G. Koerner, manager of human resources for the Carnegie Group, one of the new AI companies. Just as biotechnology researchers spawned new biotechnology companies in the seventies, the academic millionaires of the eighties will come from this core of 200 experts. In fact, rare is the university AI department whose chairman and teachers aren't stockholders in the local businesses devoted to AI applications. Such experts/academics are an elite who do the original conceptualizing about AI systems, directions and new study. They have advanced or Ph.D. degrees in computer science, mathematics or physics. They've worked at the growth edge of AI.

"Training for AI starts with a solid grounding in computer science, a field that goes well beyond basic programming skills," explains Pamela McCorduck, author of *Machines Who Think*. "In essence the researcher in artificial intelligence needs to learn how computers accumulate and manipulate information in general, not just how to get a certain model to perform a particular task."

Herbert Halbrecht notes that AI salaries have skyrocketed. Two years ago $50,000 was the tops this prestigious recruiter could garner for a leading AI expert. That is now the least he will receive for a moderately qualified candidate. He recently placed one chief scientist for a salary of $100,000. "Superstars come in six figures," he adds, "and they expect stock in the company." In more cases than not, these AI stars do receive stock in the company, if in fact they are not already the founders.

KNOWLEDGE ENGINEERS

The initial AI programming process is the most crucial. An entirely new profession has recently emerged, knowledge engineering, for the purpose of interviewing, and organizing the decision-making processes of human experts. The knowledge engineer's responsibility is to collect the knowledge data base—everything from expert interviews to statistics—and store it in the computer's memory banks. AI program development is not routine in nature. Knowledge engineers are required to collect the ideas and methods necessary to make decisions that can make or break millions of dollars or even human lives.

The skills involved, despite the use of the word engineer, parallel that of project manager or senior systems analyst in data processing shop. Both systems analysts and knowledge engineers are involved in scoping the project, determining user needs, and then designing, implementing and evaluating the system that will accomplish this. With AI the users are "experts" in the field who contribute information, and the system is called an "expert system."

Whether in the field of anthropology or linguistics the knowledge engineer is asking, "How do we learn?" offers Bisberg. "How can we take experience and translate it, framework it, format it? Knowledge engineers work out the logic so that the computer can become the 'expert'."

Employment for all AI experts and knowledge engineers specifically is promising, according to Howard Dicken, president of DM Data, an AI industry research firm. He estimates by the end of the decade there will be 8,000 knowledge engineers, all will be employed by at most 140–150 companies. Small companies, with under $5 million in sales, will account for about half of the employment. The other half will comprise in-house AI employment at companies like IBM and Xerox.

Hunting for Heads

With such an extreme shortage of AI experts corporations have to rely primarily on word of mouth for the appropriate candidates. Unfortunately, many of them aren't properly qualified. "We are inundated with job hunters. But headhunters often are just trying to place people who aren't qualified," explains Karen Prendergast, administrative office manager at MIT's AI lab. According to Halbrecht, the major employers for AI talent at present are major weapons suppliers. Minimum qualifications include at least a master's degree in computer science and preferably a Ph.D. and several years of AI research. "I know one client who needs 14–16 knowledge engineers in the next three months," he relates. "I told him respectfully, 'best of luck.' The best people are already taken. The better people are leaving the universities before they are fully trained. The professors are all starting their own companies. Everybody wants to be a millionaire."

Training: Digital Equipment Corporation (DEC) has an internal AI training program that educates its own knowledge engineers. This program includes both classroom and practical application assignments in-house. DEC is also involved in university apprenticeship programs with MIT and Carnegie-Mellon, and has taken an aggressive management position in regard to this growing specialty. "Our goal is to have an ongoing source of thoroughly trained knowledge engineers ready for assignments throughout the corporation," states an annual report. DEC has about 20 active artificial intelligence-related projects in various stages of development. So far 80 people, most of whom already had programming skills, have gone through the two-year-old program, according to Arnold A. Kraft, AI marketing director at DEC. The DEC AI curriculum has three basic parts: project management, LISP programming and interpersonal skills. According to Kraft, "I look for a sense of raw talent, rather than a resume full of the appropriate courses."

Few corporations can afford to groom their own knowledge engineers like DEC. As a result career counselors are predicting a wave of openings for qualified knowledge engineers in the years to come. Knowledge engineering is a specialized discipline that requires at least a four-year B.A. degree and most likely post-graduate training. However, someone experienced at writing computer code is not necessarily qualified for the job.

At this point in time all the leading candidates for AI appointments in both academia and industry come from the following universities: Carnegie-Mellon, Stanford and MIT. Candidates are increasingly being trained for advanced placement in knowledge engineering at other institutions of higher learning: University of Pennsylvania, Rutgers, University of Texas, University of California at Santa Cruz, Yale, University of Illinois, Champaign-Urbana and Ohio State University.

Expert systems degree programs are few, but other than the need to be able to grasp concepts and theories with LISP, few other educational requirements are needed for the aspiring knowledge engineer. There are certain personality characteristics that employers look for and expect in knowledge engineers.

Requirements: "Knowledge engineering needs the type of personality who can extract information from somebody," reports Julie Harris, information specialist at Teknowledge. Says Kenneth P. Morse, vice-president of marketing of Applied Expert Systems (Apex). "Most productive knowledge engineers are Phi Beta Kappas, regardless of what they study. They are usually found in areas of study which emphasizes right and wrong answers. You'll find that most have their MBAs and are fluent in another spoken language." Apex currently has 20 knowledge engineers on staff. Anyone who is adept at "symbol manipulation" of any kind would qualify for a career in knowledge engineering, said Eleanor Van Campden, director of administration at Intelligenetics. She lists computer scientists, electrical engineers, linguists and anthropologists as qualified candidates.

Koerner of the Carnegie Group lists the following personal qualifications: Achievement rather than power or recognition oriented; someone who seeks responsibility, assertive not aggressive; self-starter. He downplays the need for specialized AI training by mentioning the fact that the founders of the Carnegie Group recently brought in a cognitive psychologist from the University of Colorado to join their knowledge engineering team. The need for psychologists to apply their expertise to knowledge engineering is obvious, since the most essential part of the programming process is to design a computer program that can replicate a human expert's thought process. As a result Koerner says that the ideal knowledge engineer combines the instincts and information of the software developer, cognitive psychologist and linguist.

The degree of expertise required for knowledge engineering has led to an extreme shortage of qualified personnel. Teknowledge founder, Lee Hecht, was led to proclaim recently that "the limit to our industry's growth will be our ability to clone our own expertise growth."[3]

Salary: Because of these shortages high salaries are paid in this emerging field. Entry knowledge engineers, or AI assistants, with master's degrees in computer science start anywhere from $27,000 to $30,000, according to Jerrold Kaplan, director of technical marketing at Teknowledge. Experienced knowledge engineers (sometimes termed AI researchers) with advanced degrees and knowledge of either LISP or Prolog earn from $50,000 to $70,000. The top salary for well-qualified knowledge engineers/AI researchers is $75,000.

AI PROGRAMMER

Once the expertise is extracted and the system designed, coders or programmers are needed to fill in the machine instructions required by the computer. Artificial intelligence programming doesn't promise the escalated salaries of knowledge engineering. This is because of a range of easy-to-use knowledge engineering software tools that reduce the time and skill required to build a knowledge system. In fact, these tools are the first viable products of the artificial intelligence industry.

Building a knowledge system in a language like LISP previously required 10 to 50 man-years of programming. With the new generation of tools this task is handled by standard programming staffers in about five man-years. This dramatic time savings has been matched by a reduction in the level of training and experience required to build working expert systems. Knowledge engineers no longer need years of study to understand AI fundamentals. A competent data processing programmer can usually be productive with just a few weeks of AI training. As a result one of Teknowledge's leading products is AI training. Their training courses cost $2,250 for one week and up to $38,000 for a six-month course.

Salary: Depending on education, expertise and experience, salaries for programmers who work on AI applications range from $20,000 to $50,000. Job titles and responsibilities are so undefined, changing and dependent on the specific operation, that salaries vary greatly. They're not too far above those for programmers in mainstream DP, although qualifications are more stringent.

AI TECHNICIANS

A common lament is that too few experienced knowledge engineers exist. There is an equal shortage in field engineers who are required to do day-to-day program maintenance. This position equates to the systems engineer in the present data processing environment. This technical job category could prove lucrative and may require only several years of community college training. The bad news is that there's no such job. These jobs will only emerge with the increasing application of AI in industry in the years to come.

WHERE THE JOBS ARE

The start-up company is now the lifeblood of the AI industry. If any company characterizes the current state of commercial applications of artificial intelligence, it is Teknowledge in Palo Alto, California, also home of Stanford University, one of the AI wellsprings. Founded in July 1981, Teknowledge's principals were all computer scientists from Stanford University, MIT and Rand Corporation. It is currently staffed by 90 knowledge engineers.

The company was started to exploit the growing commercial interest in knowledge engineering. Its initial activities were strictly educational, but it has since taken on other commercial knowledge engineering projects, including a knowledge-based expert system for NCR called OCEAN, which lets factory personnel maintain an electronic encyclopedia of computer components and ways they can be interconnected. This program has eliminated component configuration problems for NCR.

Teknowledge was responsible for the El Aquitaine project. It brought in-house a drill bit expert who spent six months with Teknowledge's knowledge engineers who ultimately produced a set of 250 "if/then" rules that the expert used to determine problems causing oil bits to stick or drag.

In 1984 Teknowledge announced the first AI product for the IBM PC, an AI training and knowledge engineering software development package. Potential AI users may have to wait for more powerful PCs to take advantage of such AI products.

General Motors has a $3 million equity investment in return for 10% of Teknowledge, since AI is expected to be an important component in GM's fully automated factory. Besides its knowledge engineering videotapes Teknowledge products include a professional system for reasoning problems that is operational on Xerox 1100 series computers and DEC's VAX.

View from the Top

Not just small start-ups are dominating the emerging AI industry. DEC, the world's second largest computer manufacturer, has been supporting university artificial intelligence projects for the past 20 years. In 1964 it introduced the first AI workstation with its PDP/6. Today much of its work is being done on the VAX line of minicomputers, found in many scientific and technical environments.

DEC builds its own expert systems. Its XCON system claims to be the first to be used routinely in an industrial environment. This AI system assures quality control managers that all VAX system components are configured accurately and are identical throughout DEC's worldwide manufacturing network. Developed in 1980 in conjunction with a research team at Carnegie-Mellon, this joint venture resulted in the development of a second expert system called XSEL, now in the final stages of implementation. XSEL helps international sales representatives define customer machine configurations, analyze site preparation requirements and estimate delivery dates.

DEC employs a staff of about 100 AI experts housed at its Artificial Intelligence Technology Center in Hudson, Massachusetts. It has hired few AI specialists and knowledge engineers from outside the corporation. Just as the computer industry did in the 1960s, AI start-up companies have settled in California and Massachusetts, according to DM Data, a research firm that specializes in AI companies. The Scottsdale, Arizona consulting firm revealed that 90% of all individuals involved in new AI firms are located in the following 7 states, in order of employment level: California, Massachusetts, New York, Michigan, Florida, New Jersey and Texas. The study indicated a strong correlation between employment levels and the number of engineering graduates per state. According to the report, "AI companies are even more strongly concentrated near centers of higher learning than other computer companies. For instance, most firms are located in California adjacent to Stanford and most Massachusetts-based AI companies are in the Cambridge area around MIT."

The leading AI corporations include DEC, Fairchild Camera, Hewlett Packard, Machine Intelligence, Schlumberger, Teknowledge, Texas Instruments and Xerox.

AI Vendors

Just as AI requires a whole new standard of programming skills and its own programming languages, it requires its own hardware as well. One good indication of AI's promising future is the fact that its hardware is rapidly dropping in price.

The AI market leaders include the following computer makers and their products:

1. Symbolics, Cambridge, Massachusetts, offers the Symbolics 3670 for $85,000. Symbolics single-user systems are called the Cadillacs of AI hardware and cost as much as $150,000.
2. Xerox produces at its Palo Alto Research Center (PARC) the 1108, a LISP processor that now starts at $22,000.
3. LISP Machine, Los Angeles, offers the Lambda for $89,000.
4. Texas Instruments, Dallas, has the Explorer at $53,000.
5. Tektronix, Beaverton, Oregon, sells the TEK 4044 for $15,000.

Ask the Experts

Because AI is in the embryonic stage it's difficult for the career seeker to know how excited to get about it. How should a career prospector approach AI? Let's ask the experts:

Frederick Hayes-Roth, chief scientist, Teknowledge: "Will it change our lives in 5 to 10 yars? I doubt it. The computer didn't change our lives in 5 to 10 years, and this won't either. It will make a lot of companies money."[4]

John McDermott, principal scientist in the computer science program at Carnegie-Mellon: "There's nothing special about expert systems now. As increasingly powerful techniques are discovered, however, they will be exploited in applications programs so that through an evolutionary process, in 20 or 30 years, we'll have some truly impressive machines."[5]

Roger Schrank, professor of computer science and psychology, Yale University: "AI has as its goal something so complicated and difficult that it will never be here. By that I don't mean that AI is impossible. I just mean there will always be more to do."[6]

1. "The Race to the Fifth Generation: Does Japan Have the Inside Track?" *Computerworld,* May 6, 1985, p. Update/8.
2. Ibid. p. Update/9.
3. *Venture,* March 1983.
4. Glenn Rifkin. "Toward the Fifth Generation." *Computerworld,* May 5, 1985, p. Update/14.
5. Ibid.
6. Ibid.

9

COMPUTER GRAPHICS

Computer graphics uses a computer to generate charts, graphs, three-dimensional drawings, designs and, at the most sophisticated level, digitized photographs. These graphics are usually drawn on a computer screen, a plotter or other specialized peripherals. Initially the bailiwick of engineers in the complex fields of defense, space and automobile design, computer graphics is now becoming more accessible to more users. Although it still requires tremendous amounts of processing, computer graphics is used more as the cost of computing drops and capabilities increase. As in other technologies, the IBM PC is popularizing the computer graphics applications for the personal computer.

At a fun and fantastic level computer graphics techniques are being used in futuristic movies, in film animation, and even in lively television weather maps. At this intersection of animation and engineering graphics it's easy to be confused about computer graphics. There are differences between the computer-controlled graphics used by artists and filmmakers and the computer-generated graphics used by engineers, designers, architects and business users. Only recently are these two processes coverging, and the combined techniques (generation and control) being used by both artists and engineers and business users.

The easiest way to view computer graphics techniques is to play an arcade video game, which might as well be called a computer game. Arcade games use at least one of the computer simulation or computer graphics or "paint" techniques described below.

With all this excitement and development on the two fronts, there are many career opportunities. Remember—computer graphics is one of the growing number of fields where dual expertise is often needed. For example, at the conceptualization and design stage, developing computer graphics systems for architects requires an understanding of both computer graphics and architectural work. One estimate states that by 1990 there will be 600,000 jobs in CAD/CAM systems, 150,000 in the graphic arts industries, and as many as 300,000 in the preparation of presentational, educational and training materials. This chapter looks at several applications of computer graphics.

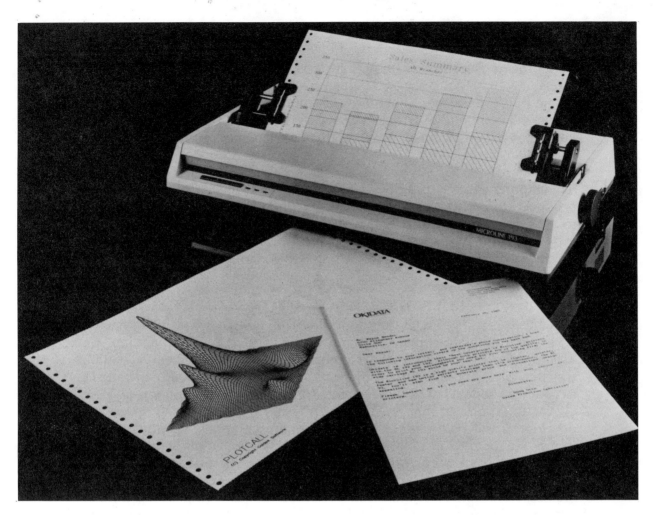

The use of graphics in business is opening up new ways not only of making sales presentations but of doing business in general. Hard-copy printer technologies are just beginning to catch up with the fantasy of one picture—or chart—equalling 1,000 words. (Courtesy of OKIDATA®. OKIDATA and Microline® are registered trademarks of OKI AMERICA, Inc.)

COMPUTER ANIMATION

Futuristic science fiction movies have provided some of the most exciting and expensive examples of computer graphics possibilities. The movies, *The Last Starfighter* and *Star Wars*, have used the most sophisticated computer graphics, which are developed only on supercomputers. In the case of Digital Productions, one of—if not the—leading digital image producer, it's a multimillion dollar Cray X-MP computer (which is so big it has a bench around it to sit on). Until recently supercomputers (cooled by liquid freon circulating inside the hot circuitry) were reserved for such scientific and military calculations as simulating atomic reactions or wind currents on aircraft.

This process is complex. Photo film has a resolution of 3,000 × 4,000 pixels and 10 bits of color (see below) per each 35mm frame—and 70mm movie film even more. Generating just one second of film (3000 × 4000 pixels × 3 colors at 24 frames per second × 10 calculations/color pixel) takes 8.64 billion calculations to produce one second of film. The Cray at 200 million instructions per second takes from 3 seconds to 10 hours to generate just one second of film. *The Last Starfighter* included 21 minutes of computer-generated images. Needless to say, only a few movies get produced this way each year. Not every film effort needs to be created to such demanding specifications, though, and less ambitious projects are shown on our screens every day. Short television commercials seem especially popular applications of computer-generated graphics.

Painting by Computer

A simpler, although equally amazing to the eye, process is "painting" on a computer VDT usually via a digitizing tablet. The images are then transferred to a color hard copy printer. Paint programs allow the user to color or shade what's on the screen, for example, an animation cartoon character. Such systems are frequently used to enhance and speed the development of both animation and other presentations. Working with a mouse cursor control or a joy stick the paint user colors what's on the screen as if using a coloring book and crayons. The artist draws in full color electronically and has the capability to manipulate the two-dimensional images. He or she stores and retrieves them along with any text and/or lettering. The images may then be captured on slides, film, video film or hard copy. With sophisticated software images may be repeated automatically or reflected elsewhere on the screen—all useful techniques in animation production. Most systems have drafting functions as well as lettering capabilities.

Since the technology behind coloring in the spaces is considerably less complex and expensive than the actual generation, paint systems are now available for personal computers. In fact, IBM announced one for less than $100 in 1984 for the ill-fated PCjr.

Computer-controlled Production

Film animation can also be controlled by computer. In fact the personal computer is an ideal device for tracking the tedious process of linking still drawings, each slightly changed—how most animation is still done. The computer clicks off the frames as they are shot, and tilts table tops or other devices to reposition the object or drawing for the next shot. Compared to Cray image simulation this is a primitive system, but it is used far more often.

Production is growing in video, in which the systems available for computer graphics are being developed to do video film (as in the video tapes used on television) and to bring movies into the home. This is sometimes called digital video. Animation and lettering for video requires somewhat different techniques, but the results are already being seen in sports coverage, weather graphics and program introductions.

ENGINEERING GRAPHICS

The original computer graphics were done during the course of development of computer-aided design (CAD) systems. (See Chapter 8.) First came the two-dimensional drawings that resembled stick figures; today's CAD designers have systems which provide three-dimensional representations on the screen. Computer graphics are developed on a computer or terminal screen. The simplest of screen technologies is the raster screen or television monitor. Any image, whether it be on film, on a newspaper page or on a TV, is composed of dots clumped together at varying levels of density. In computer graphics the electronic dots that compose the screen, known as pixels, are manipulated. Like color television monitors, computer graphics screens have different resolutions and herein lies the challenge of computer graphics. For instance, the IBM PC standard graphics screen provides a resolution of only 640 × 400 pixels per square inch. Translating that image to film requires higher resolutions—perhaps 2,000 × 2,000. So the race is on both to develop screen technologies that produce more precise colors and resolutions and to find interim processes to convert today's screens to higher resolution images.

Coincident with the resolution question are the color demands of graphics systems. Producing colors is a matter of combining several color dots at each pixel point. Simple graphics monitors work from a palette of 16 color choices that allow combinations of 1,028 colors. Sophisticated graphics terminals provide thousands of colors.

Storing all these "bits" of screen color instructions within the computer requires tremendous memory. Driving, or manipulating, the colors requires powerful computer engines. Lower memory costs and more powerful processors have opened up technical possibilities in computer graphics. Once the image is generated on the screen, operators then use various devices—a mouse cursor controller, light pen, joy stick, 10-key numeric pad or the typewriter keyboard.

At the most basic level the CAD terminal is a drafting tool. By using it CAD operators are 4 times as productive as with paper and pencil. Revisions, extremely time consuming on paper, are done on the screen at the touch of several buttons. The more sophisticated systems allow engineers and designers to "fill in" the product designs beyond the two-dimensional drawings. Some systems allow them to design minute details of an integrated circuit, to design cars, to model a human body sitting in a car or even to simulate the impact on that body in a crash. The design on the screen can be zoomed in on or panned as in television

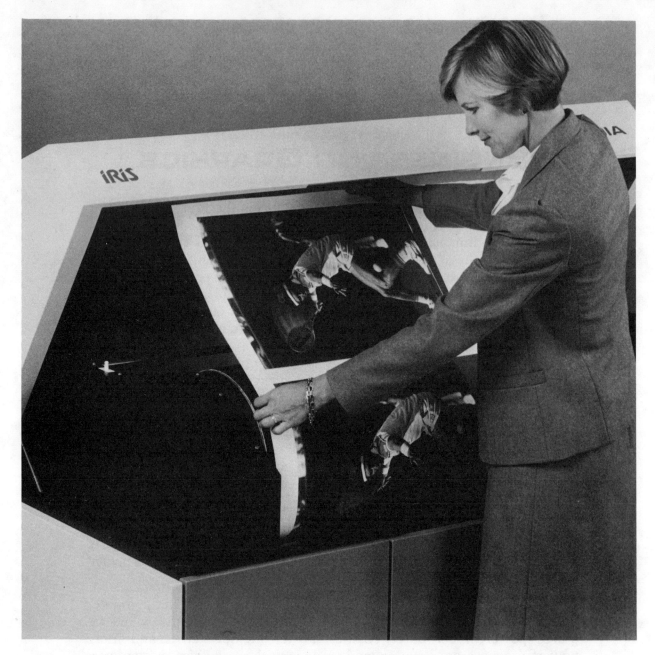

High quality color prints—more than one yard square—can be produced from ink jet printers without the expensive interim step of film and color separation. Printers such as this are attached to computer graphics systems used in scientific data plotting industries or by large commercial printers who need to check layout and color on projects before actual printing. (Courtesy of Iris Graphics)

coverage. These systems allow for processes such as layering; dimensioning; graphic operations such as translation, rotation, mirroring and copying; and computing analyses such as area, volume and distance. The advanced systems also handle freehand sketching so that the user actually draws ideas into the computer.

If these systems are connected to larger computers the information that the design generates may be passed to the administrative departments that prepare parts orders. This replaces expensive and time-consuming materials handling processes of the past. More exciting uses for these computer graphics systems are in architecture and cartography.

Computer graphics systems have traditionally been based on minicomputers shared by many users. The graphics workstation cost $25,000. All this is quickly changing with the arrival of the IBM PC. In the mid-1980s CAD systems for the PC were selling at the rate of about 2,000 a month and are expected to continue booming at growth rates of 60% a year, considerably above the number of mini and mainframe based systems. Although it costs $10,000 for an entire personal computer CAD system, many companies already have PCs running other applications. One estimate says designers spend only one-third of their time on design and analysis tasks. In addition, the versatile personal computer systems are sprinkled around an operation or connected to the larger systems as another input terminal.

Business Presentations

Salesmen used to walk around with large rolls under their arms—their sales presentations to be hung on an easel during their flip chart pitches. Then came the photographic slide presentation in a slide projector carousel—easier to carry but expensive. Even a simple marketing show might cost $10,000 for generation of the artwork and subsequent transfer to slides. The more prestigious the audience, the more expensive the slide show became. Despite the bother and expense, the flip chart and slide presentations worked. Sales representatives found pictures more effective than stacks of written reports. As the use of computers grew executives and sales representatives wanted to use the numbers generated on computers in their reports and slide shows. This was especially true of the computer literate MBAs who were eager to share their financial spreadsheets and related graphs. Getting the slides produced from the charts proved to be the bottleneck. Several equipment manufacturers developed $50,000 systems that connected to mainframe computers to produce high-quality color transparencies or the actual slide film itself. Even then a 10 person mechanical art staff, hand-cutting and preparing acetates, was needed for the financial presentations of the 150 financial whizzes at one large auto maker—and an additional staff of 6 to actually shoot and produce the 35mm slides.

About 500,000 of these mainframe based graphics systems have been sold, but by 1984 the personal computer was making inroads. Between 700,000 and 1,000,000 personal computers sold that year were equipped with graphics capability (typically a graphics adapter circuit board allowing a color monitor to be connected to the screen instead of a monochrome one). Adding this graphics capability costs as little as $2,000 on top of the price of the micro. Once again, the PC moved to the front.

Users running spreadsheet software on their personal computers design charts either with spreadsheet software or additional packages. That data and chart are then output either to a special camera that produces slides

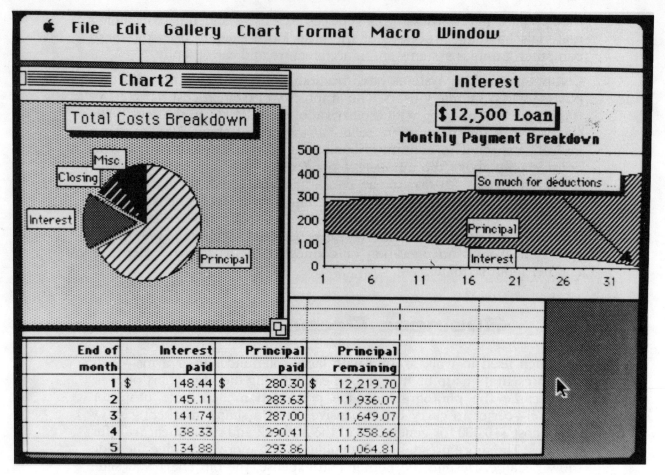

As personal computer users have come to appreciate the power of the small machines, they want to work on several work segments at the same time. Sophisticated software now allows them not only to prepare an accountant's spreadsheet but also to view the data in graph form. (Courtesy of Microsoft Corporation)

from the digital data or to a plotter. A drawing plotter produces with points—sometimes resembling colored pencils—the graphics or charts. The cost of such systems has become pennies per slide versus dollars, and they're relatively easy to use. Graphics for the PC remains a developing technology. New techniques are introduced regularly for less cost and at higher resolution.

GRAPHICS JOBS

Because computer graphics is growing fast and the emphasis is shifting to micro-based systems, there are many job and career opportunities. Artists skilled in the new technologies will be needed to create graphics for business presentations, reports and projects. They will also be needed in publishing. With the ease of use improvements, graphics artists working at computers no longer need to be programmers or computer scientists, a common complaint in the past. One estimate says 30,000–50,000 computer graphics layout/artists jobs will evolve in respective industries as computers are introduced. Graphics artists have either an associate or four-year degree. Entry-level salaries are expected to be in the $12,000–20,000 range.

The next level of computer graphics operator will be the user who implements the artist's concepts on the graphics system. Graphics terminal operators will work on detail such as typeface selection, total package design and integration of the various elements within a project—photographs, drawings and typeset lettering. A two-year associate or vocational degree will be standard. Salaries for the graphics operator are expected to range from $15,000 to $35,000 depending on the level of responsibility.

Computer graphics engineers will be needed in animation studios and in engineering and business shops. They'll be responsible for tailoring the system to the artists or product designers and for handling the programming and technical determinations. Such engineers will need not only computer and graphics know-how, but must also understand the work of their associates. They will usually have a four-year degree in engineering, probably electrical, and exposure to graphics work.

Similar to pay scales for BSEEs in other high technologies, entry-level salaries for computer graphics experts may run as high as $25,000–32,000 and continue upward with experience. Experts are currently much in demand. Computer graphics professionals work in a variety of environments: universities, research labs, Hollywood movie animation studios, television news departments, government and military agencies or private businesses.

This growth in computer graphics is reflected in a booming manufacturing industry, especially for the many companies incorporating personal computers in their products. Besides engineering, service and sales positions available within any high technology company, computer graphics companies need savvy employees who identify additional areas for graphics applications. Many new high tech jobs require dual expertise to carry the technology to new vistas, and this need is urgent in computer graphics work.

Because the computer graphics industry is still emerging its members have formed a more cohesive group than other high technology industry segments. The National Computer Graphics Association (NCGA) is one of its most active and focused associations. There's also an active academically based group of computer graphics developers in the Special Interest Group of the Association for Computing Machinery (SIGGRAPH). Both groups hold important trade shows throughout the year. (See Appendix 1 for the Associations' addresses.)

10

NEW MEDICINE, BIOTECHNOLOGY AND LASERS

The new technologies are affecting medicine, often in unexpected ways. It's high tech versus high touch versus high costs. In the late 1980s highly skilled surgeons supported by the most sophisticated equipment based on computers and lasers are performing astonishing operations: implanting artificial (plastic) hearts, re-attaching severed limbs, removing cataracts.

At the same time, terminally ill patients ask not to be sustained artificially, "pull the plug" on life support systems themselves or ask loved ones to do it for them. Authors such as John Naisbitt of *Megatrends* argues the return of the age of "High Touch." That is, as medicine adopts more high tech medicine, patients crave more human warmth in their medical treatment. The federal government, which through Medicare pays a large proportion of the country's medical costs, has begun clamping down on high costs and unnecessary procedures.

With both high tech and high touch emphases, however, the need for workers grows. One scenario for the hospital of the future sees a campus-like environment with a variety of services—exercise centers, nutrition centers, counseling offices, outpatient clinics, clinics—to treat every ailment; in other words holistic hospitals addressing the entire body. Such campuses will be more friendly surroundings in which to recover from illnesses. Staffing such campuses will be a diverse group of workers, physical fitness coaches, dietary aides, and scientists and doctors specializing in radiation therapies or laser surgery.

Despite pressures to cut health care costs, the increasing proportion of the elderly and the growing emphasis on health care assures many jobs, at all levels, in the new medicine. Developments are forthcoming in genetic engineering and molecular recombination that will have a great impact. This is the area of biotechnology. The new jobs in the physical and health sciences will be in medical technology; biotechnology; lasers and related technologies; and computers in medicine and health care.

MEDICAL TECHNOLOGY

Medical technology is the application of technology to medical challenges resulting in the development of new procedures and practices. The

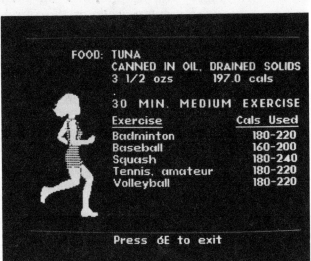

Personal computers running health-related programs are being enlisted in the fitness push in the U.S. as well as in the hospital operating room, laboratory and administrative offices. (Courtesy of Bantam Electronic Publishing)

obvious example is the use of radiation for early diagnosis of disease and treatment of cancerous growths. Other technologies include ultrasound (sonography) and systems such as dialysis machines duplicating human body functions outside of the body.

Despite the growth in the use of technologies, the impact has not always been positive. This has been especially true in the allied health professions discussed below. When a new piece of equipment was developed in the late 1960s and 1970s no one questioned its value—someone was just trained to operate it. That lead to a great deal of on-the-job training. This training, however, did not produce enough operators with adequate credentials. The certification or licensure process that followed created a monopoly of these professionals, and allowed officials to control how they were used in hospitals. This isn't working anymore. "Assistants" are now being brought in to run the equipment. With shorter hospital stays and emphasis on costs there's not the great need for these practitioners. In medicine it's a time of tremendous change.

Salaries for operators of this new equipment do not compete with those available in other technologies such as data processing, and are not advancing as fast. The American Medical Association acknowledges this: "A comparison of the average entry-level incomes for 1981 and 1984 suggests that many allied health occupations are not keeping pace with national average increase in entry-level income for the health care occupations."[1] Individual responsibility and stress on the job is much greater. Nursing professionals are among the most stressed groups in our society. The discrepancy in salaries is due to a number of factors. The major reason may be because the health care profession has been around for a long time. The health care profession seems more routinized and ritualized with an emphasis on exams and certification. This is less the case with industries centered around the newer technologies.

The AMA survey of educational program directors within the allied health field also was disturbing. Here are some of their concerns:

1. Decline in enrollment and difficulty in recruitment of new students
2. Expanding curricula due to new skills required by new technology and the need to train in supervision
3. Continuing emphasis on competency
4. Increased competition in the job market as more knowledge and skills are needed
5. Reduction in employment opportunities
6. Moderate but increasing disenchantment with some occupations
7. General budget tightening[2]

Here's a look at the major job categories.

DIAGNOSTIC MEDICAL SONOGRAPHERS OR ULTRASOUND TECHNOLOGISTS

Sound waves, a form of mechanical energy, can be converted into pictures of the human body because high frequency sound waves produce echoes when directed at a body's internal organs. The amount of time for and strength of these echoes provides information about the size, shape, consistency and distances between human organs. Sonographic equipment records these results both visually and on read-outs. Persons who operate this equipment and who usually specialize in one area of the body are diagnostic medical sonographers. Formerly employed in radiology or x-ray departments, sonographers have recently begun to work in other hospital areas.

Sonograms are used in obstetrics to check development of a fetus and during labor to monitor heartbeat and blood flow. Echoencephalogy pinpoints masses or tumors and is mostly used in cancer work. Echocardiography scans the heart, measures the chambers and evaluates how heart valves are functioning. In opthalmology sonograms detect detached retinas or internal eye hemorrhaging. A special form of sonography, doppler sonography, may be used to uncover vascular problems or monitor the flow of blood to the heart.

At a physician's instructions a sonographer selects the equipment to be used for each test after checking what other tests have been or will be performed. On the day of the test the sonographer explains the procedure to the patient and conducts the test. As the scanning device moves across the body the sonographer watches the viewing screen for abnormalities, obstructions or changes in shapes or density of any organ. Spotting and identifying growths or positioning of organs requires a high degree of skill and knowledge of anatomy and physiology. The sonographer is a detective using the sonogram to provide information. Part of the detective work is recording all the equipment settings, patient's positioning and other details that must be considered in relation to the measurements. Along with the sonographer's technical notes this is encapsuled in the test results package. During the course of their work sonographers also maintain a log of all examinations done in the radiology department so that different tests can be compared for validity. They also monitor their equipment for malfunctions and readjustments, and are often involved in evaluating new equipment.

The need for ultrasound technologists will continue, but the recent cutbacks by the government are affecting the need for diagnostic medical sonography technologists. In addition, because patient loads are dropping in some hospitals, ultrasound technicians may work part-time or be expected to have more than one technical specialty. As the job market becomes saturated the need for specialization and advanced education increases. At the same time the technology itself continues to diversify, putting a greater burden on the practitioner. Since more physicians want the equipment in their own offices, some sonographers work outside the hospital environment. Research centers and universities also require sonogram experts.

Requirements: Training in sonography is growing. About 80 schools offer training programs in it, but less than a dozen have been accredited by the Committee on Allied Health Education and Accreditation (CAHEA). Programs run from one to four years. One-year programs are offered by hospitals and lead to a certificate; junior colleges offer two-year associate programs. Both of these typically accept applicants who already have some health training. Additional health background is unnecessary for the bachelor of science sonography specialty offered by four-year colleges. A list of programs in ultrasound technology, "Allied Health Education Directory of the American Medical Association's Committee on Allied Health Education Accreditation," is available for $3: Order Department, American Medical Association, 535 N. Dearborn Street, Chicago, IL 60610. Program directors are reporting an increasing need for on-the-job training as part of schooling. No licensing or certification program has developed, although the American Registry of Diagnostic Medical Sonographers does offer a voluntary written and practical certification exam.

Sonographers are technical specialists foremost, but in working with patients they must also give care. They need good hand–eye coordination for working with and monitoring the equipment, particularly the ultrasound images. They must be strong enough to lift and position patients, and stand for long periods. A strong background in math and science (chemistry, physics, biology) is desirable for sonography work. In echocardiography, which requires additional calculations, math is especially useful.

Salary: Depending on the employer and the size of the community, salaries for ultrasound technologists range from $15,000 to $32,000, according to the Society of Diagnostic Medical Sonographers. The above cited AMA study found an average salary of $18,769 in 1984 with the range from $15,000 to $23,000.

RADIATION THERAPY TECHNOLOGISTS

With the increasing success of radiation treatment of cancerous masses or tumors radiation therapy technologist positions have grown. (Prescribed minute doses of radiation treatment break up the cancerous cells without permanently harming healthy tissues in the same area.) Radiation therapy technologists operate the radiation administering equipment at the direction of a radiation oncologist who prescribes the treatment, usually a series of them in combination with surgery and/or chemotherapy. (Titles within the health professions are often confusing. The technician generally has less training than the technologist and is better prepared to operate the equipment and handle day-to-day care and emergency situations. The technologist or therapist, on the other hand, has more training and is more concerned about the long-term implications and interconnections of the treatment.)

The radiation therapy technologist first takes a general x-ray to help define the area to be treated and the proper dosage. The actual radiation treatment is much like administering an x-ray in that equipment must be properly angled and spaced in relation to the patient. Special filters and wedges are added to distribute the radiation beam properly within the treatment area. The patient is then immobilized with molds, which the technologist has customized. The patient must remain absolutely still for several minutes during the actual treatment. Depending on the severity of the cancer and the exact location technologists assist in making the precise calculations so that only the diseased cells are treated. This is critical if the diseased area is next to a vital organ.

Because other therapies are not necessarily suspended during the radiation therapy the technologist may also function as a nurse. He or she may monitor intravenous treatments of fluids or oxygen, and check blood pressure, sample, pulse and respiratory rates. During the radiation treatment the technologist must constantly monitor the patient's condition in the event of breathing difficulties, shock or cardiac arrest. In the course of treatment radiation produces side effects such as nausea, vomiting, hair loss and redness of skin. The technologist must watch for and keep the physician informed of these changes.

The radiation technologist must keep extremely careful records of each treatment—radiation doses, equipment settings, patient reactions, amount of radiation received and amount yet planned. If the physician chooses to implant a small dose of radioactive material in an affected area, the technologist prepares that capsule.

In a new development combining technologies, radiation therapy treatments are now being planned on computer-assisted programs. The CAT scanner, which uses a computer to generate images of the brain or other parts of the body, is the most sophisticated radiologic equipment used today. With the advanced technology the patient is exposed to less radiation with a CAT scan than traditional x-rays.

Because of the extreme dangers of radioactive materials safety is a major concern for technologists. They must wear special badges that measure the amount of radiation exposure, and use safety devices to keep radiation exposure within safe levels.

Radiation therapy technologists often work for hospitals or clinics. A few are employed in research institutes or as sales representatives for equipment manufacturers.

The demand for radiation therapy technologists is expected to grow. Shortages of technologists shift from region to region of the country, according to a survey by the American Society of Therapeutic Radiologists. The AMA study found a "critical manpower shortage" of radiation therapy technologists because of the increased demand for certified technologists.[3] About 40% of those working in radiation therapy have no formal training, but have transferred from other hospital areas, a situation that has compounded the need for more education.

Requirements: There are 120 accredited institutions for radiation therapy technology education, ranging from one- to four-year programs. The schools are listed in the American Medical Association (AMA) directory. High school students with good preparation in math and science enter the two- and four-year courses without additional training. One-year programs are usually for students with experience, such as a radiologic technologist, or with coursework in a related subject such as radiation physics. Students from the four-year programs have the most successful career tracks. Well supervised on-the-job training is critical for students in radiation therapy. Health employers prefer employees with associate level degrees rather than certificates from hospital sponsored programs.[4]

Radiation technologists may take a certification examination through the American Registry of Radiological Technologists of the American Society of Radiologic Technologists. (See address in Appendix 1.) States are increasingly requiring licensing as concern grows over the use of radioactive treatments. In addition to the necessary training radiation technologists must be good communicators with physicians, other medical personnel and patients and their families. During cancer treatments the patient is going through an extremely difficult period and is anxious, upset and/or depressed. The technologist must be understanding and able to deal with this. The technologist also must keep good records, be well organized and have good manual dexterity and hand–eye coordination.

Salary: Perhaps because they've been around longer than those working in other new technologies, radiation therapy technologists are less well paid. Starting salaries are $13,500–15,000 and the average experienced technologist earns $22,000–25,000. The AMA study in 1984 found an average salary of $18,925, with the low $16,000 and the high $24,000. In 1981 the range was $13,500–22,200, the average $16,300.[5]

NUCLEAR MEDICINE TECHNOLOGISTS

Another variant of the use of radioactive materials is nuclear medicine. In this case gamma rays emitted by radioactive materials are injected into the body and traced in diagnostic tests. Certain radiopharmaceuticals introduced into the body either by injection or orally accumulate in specific organs and tissues of the body. Using special equipment the nuclear medicine technologist measures and records these gamma rays as they pass through the body, through organs and to the detecting device.

The technologist either samples the level of material collected in a specific internal organ or takes pictures of the organ using a gamma ray camera. The amount of radioactive material distributed in the body show on a screen the status of organs, glands and body systems. This is useful in detecting cancer, strokes, blood clots, heart conditions and metabolic problems. The technologist may subsequently measure the level of radioactive material in specimens taken from the body such as blood or urine. Radiopharmaceuticals, as these radioactive materials are called, may be used for treatment as well as for diagnosis, and accumulate in the diseased organ and then destroy cells.

In both instances the nuclear medicine technologist meets with the patient and outlines the procedure. After the physician has determined the treatment the technologist determines the dosage. In administering treatment internally the patient must also be positioned and immobilized during the equipment monitoring.

Safety in the radiation area and with patients is critical. Nursing care and record keeping are also important parts of this job. Besides logging and recording radiopharmaceuticals the technologist records each procedure, amount of radiopharmaceuticals given and subsequent results and observations. After meetings with the treating physician the technologist typically works alone. In nuclear medicine work the technologist usually is responsible for monitoring and checking equipment and calibrating instruments.

Requirements: There are 135 programs in nuclear medicine technology in one- to four-year courses. The one-year certificate programs are for persons already working in the field such as registered nurses, x-ray technologists or other allied health professionals. However, the rapid growth that marked this field has ended, according to an AMA study of program directors, which found that hospitals are holding back on filling nuclear medicine technologist openings. Graduates now must go to where the jobs are. Nuclear medicine technologists are also expected to be trained in a related field, since newer technologies are being used in place of the nuclear medicine tests. There's also a decline in the number of procedures performed.

Nuclear medicine technologists often are working with very sick patients and their families; which requires great sensitivity. Record keeping and good oral communications skills are important. Nuclear medicine technologists must be good at observing and concentrating on their work.

Salary: Entry-level salaries for nuclear technologists range from $15,000 to $19,000. At the experienced supervisory level they range from $25,000 to $30,000. Most of the work is in hospitals, although opportunities exist in research and private industry. The AMA study found 1984 entry salaries averaged $17,760, with the low $13,000 and the high $26,000. This compares to a $15,799 average and a range from $12,000 to $22,200 in 1981.[6]

PERFUSIONISTS

With the increasing experimentation in heart surgery, heart transplants and artificial heart implants, the work of the perfusionist who operates the heart–lung machine during surgery is growing in importance. The heart–lung machine takes over blood and oxygen circulation during the operation and is used during most types of organ transplant operations.

Perfusion is called an extracorporeal, outside of the body, technology. The patient's blood leaves the body through a catheter tube and circulates to the heart–lung machine in which carbon dioxide is eliminated and oxygenated blood is pumped back to the patient. Originally operated by physicians, technologists highly trained in human physiology have taken over the process.

The proper operation of the heart–lung machine is critical. The perfusionist is responsible for the machine being in top condition, and often repairs or adjustments must be made during an operation. Prior to an operation the perfusionist meets with the doctor to select the equipment, and perhaps modifies available equipment or makes something new. When meeting with the patient the perfusionist collects data about the patient's blood such as the amount of oxygen, since the heart–lung machine must be adjusted in order to mimic this.

During surgery the machine must be adjusted to the patient's physiological needs. The perfusionist may need to administer drugs and/or anesthetics prescribed in advance by the physician in order to stabilize body temperature, for example, in the course of surgery. The perfusionist must decide what drug is needed, when it is needed and the proper dosage. Constant recording of patient information, calculating drug dosage and checking the patient's condition must be ongoing.

It's standard procedure for the various responsibilities to be divided among a team of perfusionists. Many perfusionists are now employed at centralized medical centers so that their expertise is used to its fullest. This staffing trend is expected to continue. The market demand for perfusionists is moderating. Employers want certified clinical perfusionists.[7]

Requirements: Perfusion training is still growing. Only two dozen programs exist in the U.S. and competition for places is stiff. One-, two- and four-year programs are offered by hospitals, medical schools and universities. The one- and two-year programs prefer students with college or work experience in related health fields such as respiratory therapy or medical technology. Because of the competition most students in perfusion training have a four-year degree.

Training includes extensive study of anatomy and physiology, pharmacology, perfusion technology and surgical techniques. Supervised clinical training is crucial. Certification or licensing is not necessary, but a certification program is offered by the American Board of Cardiovascular Perfusion. (See Appendix 1.) Perfusionists must be quick thinking and able to make good decisions under the grueling pressure of the operating room. Record keeping and the ability to concentrate for long periods are also vital.

Salary: In 1984 perfusionists earned on the average $25,500, with the high at $26,000 and the low at $25,000, according to the AMA survey.[8]

CARDIOLOGY AND CARDIOPULMONARY TECHNOLOGISTS

As advances have been made in the treatment of heart ailments and the lungs and vascular systems, many new jobs have been created in the field known as respiratory therapy. Cardiology technology refers to cardiac testing. Cardiopulmonary technology is concerned with diagnosis and treatment of the pulmonary system, the lungs, or the cardiovascular systems, the heart and circulatory systems. Many of the new technologists are former respiratory therapists. Job titles and responsibilities depend on the equipment used in the test and treatment.

In cardiology treatments the job titles are focused on the type of cardiac test administered:

1. EKG technicians administer an electrocardiogram test, in which a patient is attached by electrodes to an electrocardiograph machine in order to obtain readings on heart action.
2. Phonocardiography is the testing for abnormal heart sounds or murmurs.
3. Vectocardiography records the heart's electrical activity.
4. Holter monitoring is a 24-hour monitoring test.
5. Stress testing records heart action during physical activity.
6. Echocardiography, a sonogram variation, uses ultrasound to "see" heart chambers and valves.

When a substance or instrument, a chemical substance, dye or a catheter, is inserted into the body to diagnose heart and cardiovascular problems, this is an invasive test. As in the cardiac catherization, a physician usually inserts the catheter through a vein into the patient's heart with a cardiac catheterization technologist assisting.

Cardiopulmonary technologists measure cardiovascular functioning by checking blood flow, blood pressure, heart sound, and by analyzing various gases displaced by the body. During such tests or in the operating room and intensive care unit the cardiopulmonary technologist is responsible for hemodynamic (blood circulation) monitoring. Based on this information a heart valve may or may not be replaced. This is the responsibility of the cardiopulmonary technologist.

Although they may specialize in one, cardiopulmonary technologists are trained in both cardiovascular and pulmonary procedures. Cardiopulmonary work is the diagnostic procedures as distinguished from respiratory therapy, the ongoing treatment of lung and circulatory problems. With the growth of heart and lung treatment the demand for cardiology and cardiopulmonary technologists is expected to grow.

Requirements: Until recently most persons in cardiopulmonary technology (besides those who'd worked as respiratory therapists) were trained on the job. Now the National Society for Cardiopulmonary Technology has approved eight programs for coursework. There are also two-year associate degree programs and four-year university programs, as well as shorter post-college training programs. Coursework emphasizes basic sciences, physics, math, chemistry, anatomy and physiology, along with special courses in cardiovascular pharmacology, medical electronics, medical instrumentation and cardiovascular physiology. Often as many as 1,000 hours of clinical experience in cardiopulmonary technology are required. These technologists must have a firm understanding of how the body works, and have excellent care skills.

Cardiopulmonary technologists must also be good observers and quick thinkers, and be accurate, thorough and careful with details. The scenario is much the same with cardiology technicians and technologists. On-the-job training is common. Training is longer and more demanding for administering invasive tests.

Formal one- or two-year training programs are being developed at hospitals, community colleges, universities and some technical institutes. Neither specialty has a licensing procedure, although there are voluntary certification programs through the National Society for Cardiopulmonary Technology. (See Appendix 1.)

Salary: Cardiopulmonary technologists on the whole are better paid than cardiology technicians. Starting salaries are $16,000–21,000, and experienced workers earn $20,000–26,000. The director of a cardiac department may earn $30,000–37,500.

Cardiology technicians begin at $12,000–16,000, and at the supervisory level earn $15,000–22,000.

DIALYSIS TECHNICIANS

The great strides made in the treatment of kidney disease and disorders have dramatically increased the need for technicians to operate dialysis machines. These machines function as artificial kidneys, cleansing the patient's blood of waste products. This increase has been helped in the 1970s by the extension of Medicare coverage to pay for expensive dialysis treatments. Caring for a patient with a kidney disorder, often related to other problems, requires many professionals, and so the dialysis technician often works as part of a team with a nephrology (study of kidneys) nurse and/or renal physician or nephrologist. The dialysis technician carries out the dialysis treatment, which like the perfusion heart–lung machine works outside of the body.

In setting up the treatment the dialysis technician weighs the patient and takes the pulse, blood pressure and a blood sample to determine blood clotting time. The latter determines dosage of anti-clotting drugs to be used, under the nurse's supervision, during the blood cleansing procedure. In the treatment the technician inserts one needle into an artery and one into a vein in the patient's arm or leg; the needles are attached to tubes carrying the blood to and from the artificial kidney. The impurities are purged and vital chemicals added.

Dialysis takes 4–6 hours, during which time the patient must be carefully monitored for complications. The machine can cause additional problems and must be carefully watched, too. Either case calls for immediate action. After the treatment the technician must check the patient's vital signs, remove the needles, apply bandages and sterilize and restore the expensive equipment.

Requirements: Dialysis training programs are usually short, 6 weeks to 6 months, and offered in conjunction with hospitals with dialysis equipment. A high school diploma is the minimum requirement, and a background in biology is desirable. Certification or other requirements are not yet formalized.

In addition to understanding the kidney treatment process the dialysis technician must be thoroughly familiar with the equipment, a process that takes about a year on the job to acquire. In an emergency the dialysis technician must respond quickly under stress and observe subtle changes in the patient and/or the equipment. Manual dexterity and organizational and recordkeeping skills are also important.

Salary: Salaries range from $11,000 to $23,000 depending on experience and level of responsibility, according to the recently formed National Association of Nephrologist Technologists.

BIOMEDICAL EQUIPMENT TECHNICIANS

There are yet more medical machines that must be operated and maintained: CAT scanners, radiation meters, microscopes, defibrillators. The persons who monitor and maintain this equipment are Biomedical Equipment Technicians. Working in hospitals and clinics, they maintain and repair electronic equipment used in diagnosis and treatment, including complex machines such as heart–lung or dialysis. They must have a thorough understanding of how each machine functions and be able to repair it. Regular preventive maintenance is critical in order to prevent breakdowns occurring during operations or treatment.

Basic maintenance includes taking equipment apart for cleaning, oiling, replacement of worn parts and then reassembly. Technicians must also calibrate instruments so that they run at the correct ratios. They inspect and test equipment such as blood gas analyzers, radiation monitors, spectrophotometers and microscopes, and replace defective parts or modify them.

Working with the manufacturer's representatives, biomedical equipment technicians install new equipment. All activity is recorded in a log that tracks expenses, shows compliance with safety precautions and helps evaluate a machine's performance over time. With a new machine a technician may train the rest of the staff in its use and provide troubleshooting tips for working with the equipment.

Some biomedical equipment technicians have entered this work from other equipment repair jobs, especially if they have been working for a manufacturer. Some manufacturers have training programs for persons already experienced in electronic instrumentation.

Requirements: Most biomedical equipment technicians are trained formally either in one of 50 programs across the country or in the U.S. military. These programs, often associate degree courses, provide classes in anatomy and physiology, electronics, math, biomedical instrumentation, chemistry, physics and communications. There's also a practicing clinic where a student works with an experienced equipment technician or a biomedical engineer.

The biomedical equipment technician must be expert at repairing equipment. Good "bedside manners" are necessary when the work must be done on the spot in the operating room, treatment room or ward. Technicians may be called in after workday hours if a problem develops. Technicians move from machine to machine, from problem to problem. This requires a great deal of flexibility while remaining efficient under pressure. Manual dexterity and good communications and organizational skills also count.

A voluntary certification program is offered by the International Certification Commission for Clinical Engineering and Biomedical Technology administered by the Association for the Advancement of Medical Instrumentation. (See Appendix 1.) Passing the test requires a combination of experience and/or an associate degree.

Salary: Entry-level salaries range from $12,000 to $14,000. Experienced technicians earn $18,000–22,000.

BIOTECHNOLOGY

In the early 1980s Wall Street investors, to say nothing of the media and futurists, trumpeted biotechnology and the dream that no one would ever be sick again. The potential of using biology and genetics, specifically genetic engineering, to create marvelous organisms and disease fighting antibodies that would do everything from preventing cancer to better, cheaper drugs created great excitement.

Whereas most of today's chemicals are made from petroleum or natural gas, biotechnology promises microorganisms that turn coal or biomass (waste agricultural residue such as leaves, stalks and wood) into chemicals. This is the concept behind manure and animal wastes being used to generate methane gas. Animals and food crops might be improved genetically to yield faster growing or disease resistant hybrids. Plants might be bred to grow in salty soil or to be resistant to certain insects.

Although developments since have hardly matched the dream and investors are disillusioned, work goes on, albeit more slowly and on more practical and focused levels. Observers are still waiting to see what impact biotechnology will have ultimately on medicine and jobs. Only 5,000 persons worked in biotechnology in the mid-1980s, according to the Bureau of Labor Statistics. Other prognosticators are more optimistic: The U.S. Department of Technology Assessment estimates the need for 30,000 to 75,000 workers in biotechnology in the next 20 years.

Biotechnology companies started by a couple of Ph.D. biologists quickly offered public stock sales that sold out in a minute because they were believed so hot. Hundreds of companies in the medical field went public. Then nothing happened. No breakthrough products were delivered. Just as quickly as the flash in the investment community had ignited, it died. Investors found that the start-up company's efforts were impeded by government regulations, conservatism on the part of doctors and poor management by ex-academics with little experience running a high risk company. The dream has not died in the hearts of biotech researchers, but even they have come to realize that tremendous investments in time and resources are needed to bring about the exciting miracle drugs and treatments.

Nevertheless, advances are forthcoming. Home testing kits such as those for pregnancy testing use antibodies developed by biotechnology procedures. The growth in popularity of these tests is expected to continue. A version of human insulin needed by diabetics is also produced by a recombinant DNA process.

What Is Biotechnology?

Biotechnology uses biology to create new products. The two most used phenomena are recombinant DNA (deoxyribonucleic acid) and monoclonal antibodies. DNA is the double-helix structure found in the chromosomes of cell nuclei. DNA carries the genes responsible for passing hereditary "instructions" from one cell generation to the next. In recombinant DNA scientists graft genes onto a simple organism, and this then synthesizes the protein coded for by the newly introduced genes. For instance, in insulin production, the human gene that encodes for the protein of insulin is inserted into the e. coli bacterium, a single cell organism that normally

Biomedicine today is a combination of sophisticated equipment and methodologies to discover the unknown. Small, entrepreneurial, risk-taking firms like Biomatrix are creating new technologies that are revolutionizing the science of health care. (Courtesy of Biomatrix, Inc.)

lives in the intestine. The insulin gene then causes the e. coli to produce insulin.

Monoclonal antibodies are developed in a similar "grafting of cells" fashion. Antibodies, an important part of the body's immune, or disease fighting system, are proteins that are generated in reaction to foreign proteins, and neutralize them. By attaching these antibodies to extracted myeloma cells (which grow rapidly in the body), scientists create a hybridoma that grows rapidly outside the body. Antibodies are produced that are identical to those fighters within the body. Because the antibodies are all clones of the original cell they're called monoclonal.

BASIC RESEARCH: THE NEED FOR PH.D.S

Biotechnology has had a limited effect on employment in the medical and research professions, and fewer than 5,000 persons are employed in biotechnology research and development. Most of these hold sophisticated scientific research positions in biology, biochemistry, bioprocess engineering and related fields such as immunology and molecular biology.

Although jobs in the production of these new substances exist, such production uses the latest in both computer and production technology, which means less demand for production workers. The use of biotechnology products will not spur employment as computers have. Biotechnology products will simply be alternatives prescribed by physicians just as any other drug.

The critical need in biotechnology is still for scientists, basic researchers and laboratory technicians. More biotech products need to be discovered and developed. Academic researchers (most with Ph.D.s in biology or biochemistry) and biologists (also preferably with advanced degrees) are needed. These biologists specialize in molecular biology—the chemistry of the cell—or in immunology and the manipulation of genes. An estimated one-third of all technicians in biotechnology are molecular or immunology specialists.[9] Most molecular biologists specialize in animal molecular biology because of its applicability to medicine. Immunologists often get involved in drug research. In the future, plant molecular biologists may be more in demand as biotechnology turns toward agriculture.

Ph.D.-level experts have historically been required in the beginning phases of any new technology. A Ph.D. or advanced-level degree plus a special interest in biotech is the best entry requirement. In certain cases these researchers move into management, but the skills that make for a good scientific researcher do not necessarily make for a business leader or good manager.

Several universities are geared to the emergence of biotechnology opportunities. One four-year program at Rochester Institute of Technology offers this course work: First year—introduction to biotechnology, biology, general and analytical chemistry, calculus, statistics, liberal arts and

English composition; second year—plant and animal tissue culture, molecular biology, organic chemistry, chemical separations, liberal arts; third year—microbiology, immunology, hybridoma techniques, genetics, plant physiology, biochemistry; fourth year—microbial and viral genetics, industrial microbiology, cell physiology, genetic engineering.

BIOPROCESS ENGINEERS

As more biotechnology-created products move into production, so will bioprocess engineering. Biochemists, microbiologists and bioprocess engineers with a bachelor's degree will formulate the methods of large quantity production. Bioprocess engineers are currently involved in such tasks as designing fermentation vats, today for beer and wine, tomorrow perhaps for microorganisms that will produce biotech products. The work will be much more complicated than managing the yeasts needed in beer. Microorganisms grow only in highly sophisticated, temperature controlled, computer monitored systems. Although several universities currently offer bioprocess engineering courses, this is one of the few fields that could grow markedly because of biotechnology.

Biochemists will be needed to study the chemical processes of living organisms, to develop the subsequent production processes and to aid in production recovery, purification and quality control.

Microbiologists will be needed to isolate, screen and select the microbes and environment best suited for each production process. Enzymes will be used to enhance these production processes, requiring the skills of enzymologists and cell culture specialists. Researchers already know that biotechnology processes are speeded up considerably by the presence of certain enzymes. The minimum requirement will be a Bachelor of Science degree and a demonstration of expertise in biotechnology.

As these systems are developed and installed, process control personnel will be needed to monitor and control production. Jobs will be similar to process control jobs in the chemical, drug and food industry today. As industries grow around these biotech products, the necessary sales and support personnel will also be needed. None of these occupations will be new, just new variations on jobs that already exist in related industries.

Growing Industry

There are a limited number of employers in biotechnology. Currently, only several hundred companies dabble in biotechnology research. Some large companies are adding biotechnology subsidiaries or departments, or simply buying smaller existing companies. Universities and research centers are the other big employers of biotech specialists, but universities find that their budgets rise and fall with the availability of government research contracts, especially in defense work. The U.S. National Institute of Health also sponsors biotech research.

LASERS

The use of lasers in surgery is one of the bright spots in today's medicine. A beam of intense light removes tumors in the body, clears blocked arteries or releases the fluid build up in the eye caused by glaucoma. For an increasing number of operations the laser beam is proving more effective than the scalpel. It has special properties. Since it can't penetrate water surgeons destroy tumors or make fine incisions without damaging nearby tissues. As researchers experiment with different kinds of laser beams the possibilities expand. Carbon dioxide lasers create a beam of light so intense it is invisible and vaporizes tissues. Light from an argon laser is absorbed by tissue pigments and removes disfiguring birthmarks. With the combination of lasers and optical fibers doctors treat internal injuries such as bleeding ulcers without incisions.

Doctors are currently experimenting with computer-controlled lasers in surgery and the possible use of lasers to treat cancer. In the future, doctors may be able to target a single myeloma cell within the body. Lasers may ultimately stimulate the growth of the body's own healing cells so that wounds could literally be knitted back together. As the art and science of microsurgery grows (painstakingly reconnecting severed tissues under the microscope), additional uses for lasers may be found. One estimate says that the laser market may grow to $300 million a year by 1990. Companies are already aligning themselves in the laser market. Larger medical equipment companies are buying small medical laser makers. Smaller firms are combining to gain a stronger toehold in this fast paced market. There are exciting advances in several areas of microsurgery.

In opthalmology surgeons use lasers to repair the eye without entering it. They remove membranes that develop around secondary cataracts. Certain types of glaucoma are also treated by lasers.

In dermatology and facial plastic surgery argon lasers coagulate or cut off the abnormal blood vessels that create wine-red birthmarks, warts, skin cancers and disfiguring scar tissues. There would otherwise grow back if removed by a scalpel.

In microsurgery and gynecological procedures surgeons looking through a microscope aim the beam to reconstruct blocked fallopian tubes or reconnect severed organs. The beam is manipulated via the joy-stick (like controls on video games).

Lasers beams are used to vaporize cancer and other tumors. The laser is directed at a catalyst substance that has been injected into the diseased area in order to collect cancerous tissue. Exposed to lasers this catalyst substance turns into a poison that kills the malignant cells.

In heart surgery doctors continue to experiment with lasers to open blockages in the veins and arteries, which now require bypass surgery.

Additional breakthroughs may come as researchers harness lasers and computers. Some day procedures first outlined by a surgeon on a three-

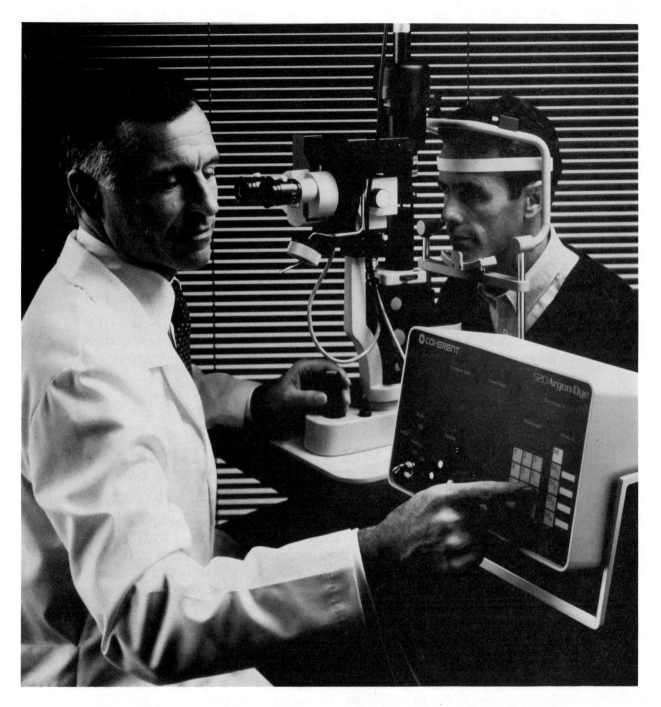

Sophisticated lasers, including an argon and a dye laser, are being used in delicate eye surgery and treatments never before possible. (Courtesy of Coherent Medical)

dimensional imaging screen may be performed by a robot-like controller, providing all the precision and steadiness that implies.

As with any new technology acceptance has been slow. In the case of laser surgery there are two counterforces: the federal Food and Drug Administration (FDA) and the conservatism of a medical profession already inundated with new techniques. In addition, a laser is considerably more expensive—$30,000 to $200,000—than a scalpel. Although most laser work is done by highly trained professionals, as laser use becomes more widespread related job opportunities with lasers will evolve. By 1990 all the major (more than 200-bed) hospitals are expected to use lasers in surgery, compared to about one-quarter currently.

Seeing the Light

"The field is developing rapidly and it will not be long before laser medical technology is part of our medical school curriculum," reports Dr. Ellet H. Drake of the American Society for Laser Medicine and Surgery. The society serves as a clearinghouse for short courses on lasers and laser biophysics for doctors, surgeons and nurses. Such courses are sponsored by associations such as the Laser Institute of America. (See Appendix 1.)

For those primarily interested in lasers, with medicine secondary, the laser/electro-optics technician position is lucrative. Students need either a two-year technical course or major in optics within a university physics program.

COMPUTERS IN MEDICINE

Just as computers are being applied to almost every other facet of our society, they are being adapted in medicine. Hospitals use computers like any other large organization for record keeping, billing, staff scheduling, etc. Large service bureaus that specialize in processing insurance paperwork and other procedures in the health care business have been especially successful in utilizing computers. Customized computer systems are helping medical professionals not only in the laboratory and the special treatment areas discussed above, but are also helping diagnosticians in the form of expert systems.

In the laboratory computers run the research equipment for analyzing and reading data such as blood cell counts or in automated chemical analysis. Laboratories are information systems that process data, often specimens to be tested. A computer is the ideal tool to manage all this information, especially since time is often critical.

A laboratory computer does the following:

1. Allows clerks to call up a patient's previous records, thus eliminating the need to search for and then copy records
2. Prints many labels for various samplings and specimens
3. Allows specimens to be more easily tracked through the various tests
4. Compiles results of an archival analysis over a period of time

Because of the discreteness of laboratory analyses, personal computers have been used effectively in some data gathering processes. Scientific and laboratory software for microcomputers is predicted to be one of the next large market growth segments. Such software packages for the personal computer will be used in hospital laboratories and other research facilities as well.

A laboratory project leader is in charge of the computer operation, especially in the initial stages. That position requires expertise and understanding of laboratory work and data processing.

Medical Experts

Doctors and health care professionals are becoming swamped with new technological and treatment developments. Hospital computer systems collect both thorough histories and treatment data on their patients. Adding these facts together, one computer manufacturer has developed an expert system that aids doctors in diagnosis, and takes into consideration a patient's complete medical history. Control Data Corporation (CDC) distributes the HELP system, the first to evaluate a patient's hospital history against a vast data base of medical knowledge and then suggest diagnoses and patient care procedures. Terminals distributed throughout the hospital have access to HELP, and in more than one case it has saved a person allergic to penicillin or morphine from being administered those drugs. HELP has the potential to significantly affect the quality of medical care, particularly in areas that don't have access to the latest medical technology. HELP's data base of therapy and treatment results for thousands of patients is readily available for research. "Few technologies have grown faster or are destined to have a greater impact on the health care field than the computer," observes Robert M. Price, CDC president.

Health care is just one of the growing uses of expert systems. A classic expert system is Eliza, which functions as a psychotherapist. The program is instructed to pick key words from the previous sentence and combine those with appropriate canned responses. Using Eliza at a terminal does give one the sensation of talking with a non-committal psychotherapist.

Biomedical Computing

Training for the new medical careers is in the early developmental stages. One program training students to develop computer systems for medical and diagnostic tests is Biomedical Computer, offered by the Rochester Institute of Technology. The four-year course combines training in science and biomedical sciences (biology, biochemistry, physiology and anatomy, medical technology and management) with courses in computer science. Students also participate in a co-op work program as part of their study over five years. Other universities are developing similar programs.

1. Robert B. Parks. "A Report of Surveys: Impact of PPS on Clinical Education and Perspectives of Program Directors." January 1985, Committee on Allied Health Education and Accreditation of the American Medical Association, p. 6.
2. Ibid.
3. Ibid. p. 9.
4. Ibid. p. 9.
5. Ibid. p. 3.
6. Ibid.
7. Ibid. p. 9.
8. Ibid. p. 3.
9. Douglas Braddock. "Biotechnology: Careers in the New Technologies." *Occupational Outlook Quarterly* (U.S. Department of Labor, Bureau of Labor Statistics, Washington, DC), Winter 1984.

11
TECHNICAL WRITING

Microchips and megabytes, operating systems, parallel processing, fourth generation languages and systems operators, MIPS, MAP, bit-mapped and MOPs. All this technology makes you dizzy. If the engineers and scientists who dream up these words, and the technologies and concepts underlying them, communicate with others who speak their special language, all is well. Sooner or later, though, technical ideas must be translated into terms understood by users, decision makers, and the general public. What's needed is a go-between or translator in this communication between the non-technical public and the technician, scientist and engineer—the technical writer.

Only a decade ago technical writing was largely aimed at technical readers, for instance, in manuals that dryly set specifications for electronics devices or in journal articles addressed to fellow specialists. In the last five years, particularly with the advent of the personal computer, technology has moved into the mass media and through the media to the general public. Computer and related technologies are faster, smaller, cheaper, thus enabling thousands of computer devices and software packages to make their way into homes and offices daily. Bar-code systems that read cryptic combinations of thick and thin black lines help control inventories in local supermarkets. Electronic banking centers appear on every corner. Behind each system is a technical writer whose job is to explain the technology to those who operate and maintain them.

The audience for technical writing has expanded to include more *non-technical* people than ever before. Not only is the demand for their services increasing, the qualifications for technical writers are changing. Large firms still hire writers with technical training to write traditional proposals, reports, instructional materials and manuals. The need to explain technology is so great that small software companies, consulting firms, and even advertising agencies are specializing in technical writing. Because of the shortage of trained and experienced technical writers, these companies are hiring people with little or no technical experience as writers. An informal survey of help wanted ads shows that communications skills more than technical understanding are often the most important qualifications for today's technical writers. A documentation writer for one of these independent firms says, "Teaching a writer how to run a computer program is a lot easier than teaching a programmer how to write."

WHERE THE JOBS ARE

Technical writing came into its own as a profession during World War II. Before then engineers and specialists themselves wrote manuals and guides for other experts who understood the technology involved. The problem was that these experts rarely had the desire or the ability to write well. With the increased use of technical writing during World War II and the subsequent surge in technology afterwards, technical writing became a specialty, although one that received limited attention.

Technical writers have worked in large industrial firms. They have covered manufacturing, telecommunications, aerospace, medicine, research and development and consulting. Tech writers in these companies prepare specifications manuals, reports or proposals for clients and government regulatory agencies. They write guides to the installation, operation, repair and maintenance of the company's products.

Because these documents are often aimed at a technical audience—those who will be operating and taking care of the equipment—these companies require tech writers to have a degree in physics, chemistry, electronics or whatever the line of work. The job might entail writing brochures, press releases, catalogs and articles for specialty publications. Typical employers in this category are AT&T/Bell Laboratories, Eastman Kodak, McDonnell Douglas or Mobil Oil.

The federal government is also a big employer of tech writers. Many government agencies need writers to prepare bulletins, research reports and pamphlets on a wide variety of subjects. The Environmental Protection Agency (EPA), for instance, might use a tech writer for a report describing emissions standards for cars or a bulletin detailing recent legislation.

SOFTWARE DOCUMENTATION

With the tremendous growth in the development of computer systems within large organizations to do everything from traditional payrolls to complicated international banking transactions, users found they needed clear explanations of how the systems worked. They also needed detailed explanations of how the computer code was written because code is, by its nature, indecipherable. The programmers wanted to move on to other challenges and had no desire to document their work. Companies were forced to hire technical writers who knew something about programming to document these complex, software systems. These software documentation specialists often worked right along with the programmers, and often were freelancers. Although freelance programmers working on the system might earn $60 per hour, the technical writer was earning $25.

PUBLICATIONS WRITERS

Technical publications also need technical writers. As technology marches into offices, homes and industry, the press (the trade press and newsstand magazines and newspapers) keeps readers up to date on the latest developments. The public is interested in new developments. There's even a newsstand publication entitled *High Technology*. Technical magazines and journals report on hot topics in the field they cover, interview key members in industry and give readers the inside story on the business side of high technology. Since these publications often address a wide audience, their writers may be journalists familiar with the industry and its products rather than people with formal technical training.

Advertising and public relations agencies also need technical writers. The job involves writing copy for brochures, magazine and newspaper ads, press releases and catalogs that sell their clients' products. This side of technical writing has become more important in recent years as more companies develop technology-based products and compete for customers who may not be technically oriented.

A unusual side of technical writing has also developed. Because of the increasing complexity of today's systems such as the ones used in defense installations for systems control, manuals are necessary to operate the systems. However, the educational level of the operators may be such that a traditional technical manual is of little use. The military and its contractors have come up with what are called "comic book manuals" detailing the systems in comic book style panels and drawings. Today's technical writer working on such a system may end up writing a "comic book."

MANUAL AND TUTORIAL WRITERS

Anyone using a personal computer for the first time knows what a struggle it can be. It's even more frustrating if you have to trudge through a manual that makes a poor attempt at explaining how a piece of hardware or software works. Firms that specialize in writing computer documentation and manuals are sprouting and growing quickly. This industry segment is one of the hottest areas for writers who want to tackle technical subjects. A software developer, for example, may engage such a firm to write a user's manual and tutorial for a new word processing program.

A tutorial is the initial training material for the person who will use the system. Some fall in the first pages of the product manual; others are embedded in the software so that it appears on the VDT screen. As consumers cry for easier-to-use software, many companies are intertwining the "help" information with the product itself. Users push help buttons or enter the word "help" and get explanatory information for where they are in the program. (A goal is for such "help" information to jump ahead and inform the user of short cuts to processes that he or she may be doing awkwardly: "You've been using the Ctrl key and Del key to erase sentences; do you also know you could use one Alt key.") Writing such tutorials requires communications skills, an understanding of educational psychology and how people learn. Former teachers are sometimes enlisted on such projects.

Before the personal computer boom a computer company sent a training team to a customer's office or plant to teach employees (usually technicians themselves) how to operate the equipment and iron out any early bugs in the system. Nowadays so much computer hardware and software is being dispatched to so many people that manufacturers, especially small ones, don't have the resources to personally train their customers. The result is that user manuals must be written to do the job that trainers used to do. Technical personnel remain a phone call away to help with unusual problems. The quality of documentation may make the difference in whether or not someone buys a product in the first place. In the competitive computer business manufacturers are turning to specialists—technical writers.

For more complex systems that require special explanation, training manuals are necessary. Trainers are often used as intermediaries in presenting new technical systems to users. Training manuals are initially used by these trainers, who in turn present the material to the users and work with them in learning the new systems. This is the more traditional way of introducing new technology. Training manuals require the same ability to break complex theories and procedures into easily understandable ones and communicate them in words and illustrations.

FREELANCE WRITERS

The greater demand for knowledgeable writers has opened the technical writing field to new horizons. Established technical writers can take a crack at freelancing. Small technology companies may not have enough work to hire a full-time writer, and "job out" writing assignments to qualified freelancers. These assignments may take a few days or several months. Freelance assignments are usually found through word of mouth. Full-time tech writers may come into contact with firms that need their services from time to time.

Publications also hold rich opportunities for freelance writers. Sometimes they are assigned to cover trade shows or report on newsworthy industry topics. Technical books, especially in the personal computer industry, are often written by independent writers.

Writing About Technology

The technical writer's job is to translate technical information into a document that can be clearly understood by a target audience. Typical documents include the following:

1. Reports—Reports are usually aimed at company decision makers and give an objective look at the way things are—the status of a developing technology, for instance.
2. RFPs (Requests for Proposals)—These highly technical documents outline in detail a company's needs for a special service or product. A corporation that wishes to install a new telephone

switch will send to the top 4 or 5 telecommunications firms an RFP describing what new functions it needs for the telephone system. Companies that want the business respond with their own bids or proposals.

3. Proposals—The firms that respond to an RFP will prepare a detailed proposal showing how they will meet the requirements stated in the request.

4. Instructional materials—These run the gamut from do-it-yourself tutorials on how to run a computer software program to very technical training guides for complicated manufacturing process control systems.

5. Letters—Writers for high-tech companies are called upon to write business correspondence or sales letters about the company's products or services.

6. Manuals—Technology companies need all kinds of manuals—user manuals, maintenance and repair manuals, installation manuals. Depending on the audience these may be either non-technical "how-to" guides or highly technical documents describing the workings of a piece of equipment. In the defense and aviation industries operating instructions fill thousands of pages.

7. System and user documentation—Every computer system is accompanied by documents that tell what its components are, how to operate it, what to do when something goes wrong and so on. Banks have large computer systems tracking account balances that are used by customers, bank tellers, managers, archivists and systems analysts. The documentation is a reference guide telling the various users what makes a system run and what it can and cannot do.

8. Periodical or journal articles—Writers for technical periodicals observe technology as it happens and report it to specialists or to the general public.

What a Tech Writer Does

A technical writer's job varies depending on the company, the audience and the document, but it always requires two things: research and writing.

First, the writer researches the topic. This may mean going over blueprints or other specifications for a product, visiting the library and searching through recent publications or conducting interviews with programmers, designers, managers and other sources. It may mean visiting laboratories and development centers and talking with the researchers and/or designers on a project. Often the writer tests first hand the piece of equipment or software he or she is going to write about. This is a growing trend with the popularity of the personal computer. On PC projects the technical writer is expected to be familiar with the hardware and software in order to explain it better to the audience. Writing about a word processing package is difficult if one hasn't worked on a word processor. Researching takes hours or months depending on the publication and the topic being investigated. For long-term projects involving sophisticated machinery or software the tech writer may be part of the team of engineers designing the product. He or she may sit in on meetings, study competing products, tour the company's manufacturing plant and test the product to gain complete familiarity with it.

The second step is the actual writing of a first draft. This draft should give an accurate presentation of the topic in an organized fashion. The focus of the writing is established at the beginning of the assignment. A publications manager or editor tells the tech writer who the audience is and what should be covered, what its level of expertise should be and how long to make it. Almost always this work must be done by set deadlines. While the publications manager is setting the guidelines, the tech writer may get information from the product's designers that disagrees with what the manager wants. This is where diplomacy comes into the writer's job, making compromises between the manager and the technical experts.

For technical writers who work on tight deadlines at newspapers or magazines, that might be the end of an assignment. The technical article is passed in to an editor and prepared for publication. At most other organizations the first draft goes through at least one revision before it's ready for publication. This is especially true with longer documents or promotional material that a marketing campaign is riding on. The drafts are often reviewed by technical experts, managers and editors who make suggestions for further changes. The document does not reach final form until it meets with either the approval or consensus of all involved. This may take many days and meetings.

The tech writer may also need to collect and prepare charts, diagrams, photographs and other artwork to supplement the written material. Once these elements are in order the writer may be responsible for following the document through to final production—getting the document set in type, printed, bound and ready to go to the readers. Constant monitoring of documents for accuracy is critical because dropped sentences or words or lines of computer code shut down the entire program and possibly the system.

Prospects for Tech Writers

Almost all technical writers agree that their specialty is growing rapidly. One of the many documentation writing companies that have popped up in the Northeast hired 15 new technical writers in one year, and they're looking for more. In major metropolitan areas the number of newspaper advertisements for technical writers indicates the demand exists and is growing. On the data processing side recruiters Source EDP reports: "Demand will grow due to a continued broadening and diversification of systems fundamentals, software, and hardware. Positions will require increased knowledge of sophisticated documentation techniques as well as technical knowledge of hardware, applications and programming languages. Awareness of various advertising techniques will be an asset to companies marketing data processing services and hardware."[1]

Tech writers find job openings in any city, especially those with a concentration of technology companies. New England, Texas and California's Silicon Valley are especially promising areas, as are cities and towns with high tech headquarters.

Training: Formal training is a big boost in starting a technical writing career, but is not essential. Educational programs in tech writing have sprouted in the past 15 years in response to an increasing demand in the job market, but technical writers have been around much longer. A listing of these programs is available from the Society for Technical Communication, Inc. (See Appendix 1.)

For career changers—those with training in journalism, English, or almost any technical field—there are two ways to become a technical writer. Companies are always eager to find former engineers or people with engineering degrees working in other fields who are interested in writing. Switching to a writing career is an excellent path for an engineer who is bored or who's been made technically obsolete. It's a rewarding switch for both the engineer and the company. Many advertisements for technical writers request engineering training.

Almost any writer who's familiar with a certain technology can take the plunge into technical writing by studying target publications, talking to editors and getting editorial calendars and submitting well thought out story ideas or even finished articles. Published writers have an edge in this situation and may only need to submit a story idea. Inexperienced writers or those with little experience in a field are better off sending a detailed query letter or a complete article. In the same vein many companies seeking technical writers require no more than training or experience in journalism. These companies expect that the technical part will be learned on the job. Breaking into any field is difficult and technical writing is no exception. Submitting articles or ideas on a freelance basis is a time-consuming and discouraging experience, and takes self-confidence and motivation.

For a college student who wants to go into technical writing the best approach is to plan a curriculum that has a balanced mix of writing and technology or science. More than 20 four-year colleges offer undergraduate degrees in either English/journalism or engineering with a specialization in technical writing and editing. Many community colleges offer two-year programs for earning a certificate in technical writing. A smaller number of graduate programs recruit English majors and students with training in technology, engineering or science for their master's programs in technical communication.

Requirements: A survey of 200 industrial firms that hire technical writers found that employers consider three qualifications especially important for technical writers: skill in writing for clarity at the reader's level, skill in dealing diplomatically with engineers and management and a knowledge of the technical field in which the company is engaged.[2]

First and foremost, technical writing requires the ability to write clearly, concisely and accurately. Interpersonal skills are a must for interviewing, working with management to set schedules, gathering information from engineers or developers and in some cases guiding graphic artists and others to complete a document on schedule. A knowledge of the technology is also important for clear, accurate writing on a technical topic.

Tech writers have schedules. Writers for newspapers or magazines have more deadline stress than those who work on long-term projects, but every tech writer must be able to organize and pace his or her work within a time frame set by others. This takes self-discipline as well. Organizational skills are also necessary, since one of the most important aspects of the job is to assemble a mass of information from interviews, technical specifications, published material or product tests into a whole. If the document is long or needed in a rush, the writer may need to collaborate with other writers.

Technical writers frequently advance into management and supervisory jobs in a variety of areas. An intermediate job may be as a technical editor supervising the work of other technical writers. The top job on this career track is the publications manager in charge of all the documents a company produces. Tech writing positions in advertising and publishing may lead to management jobs in those fields. Experienced tech writers may freelance their way into these fields.

Salary: Starting salaries for technical writers range from $20,000 to $30,000 a year, depending on qualifications and experience. It's not unusual to see help wanted ads for experienced tech writers with salaries up to $40,000 a year. Experience counts in technical writing. In data processing Source EDP found that entry-level writers and editors earn $20,700–30,800, with the mid-point at $25,400. With 2–4 years' experience the range was $23,500–36,700, with the average, $30,400; 4–7 years, $26,700–38,900, with an average of $34,200; and over 7 years' experience, $28,300–40,000, with $34,900 average.[3]

Those who specialize in describing software programs earn $20,500–28,000, according to a Robert Half survey. The technical translator who writes about software and hardware earns $25,000–31,000; the technical writing manager $33,000–43,000.[4]

Freelancers are paid by the hour, earning $20–40 an hour, or by the document. It's not unusual for a software specialist to spend a year freelancing or consulting with a company on a project producing a variety of documents and manuals.

1. Source, op. cit. p. 11.
2. John A. Walter. "Education for Technical Writers." *The Journal of the Society for Technical Communication.*
3. Source, op. cit. p. 16.
4. Half, op. cit. p. 24.

12

PUBLISHING TECHNOLOGIES

Electronic publishing is the dissemination of information electronically via either broadcasting or hard wires. Almost every day another technology is enlisted in the dissemination of information. It's fast becoming the Information Age that author Alvin Toffler prophesied. Coming on strong is computer-aided publishing (CAP), in which computers, especially PCs, are harnessed to typesetters and laser printers.

In the late 1980s the major electronic publishing fields include: videotex and teletext, on-line data bases, cable television and its variants, and CAP. This chapter reviews those topics. Employment will come in those sectors that prove most commercially viable because the jury is still out on several of these technologies, especially videotex-like ones.

VIDEOTEX, TELETEXT AND VARIATIONS

There are two names for the dissemination of text electronically: Teletext is one-way sending, and videotex allows for two-way communications between the sender and receiver. The two approaches often are lumped together under the name videotex. Videotex, developed in the United Kingdom and France and brought to the U.S. in 1976, is the display of text on a video screen. Usually in color and viewed on a television screen, it includes words, numbers and pictures and is called up on a special receiver box or on a computer keyboard.

Teletext systems are distributed two ways, either broadcast like the running screens of listings available on cable television or over telephone lines or other hard wire. Both teletext and videotext are being studied for the home and office.

With teletext the receiving user has less control over which information is broadcast. He or she reads only what is sent across the screen at a given point, and can decide "yes" or "no" on reading the material. Length of text is limited by the number of lines that can be carried over the data transmission, typically less than 100 on a screen.

By contrast, videotex allows the user to call up almost unlimited quantities of information from the system at any time via a special terminal or specially rigged computer. The information is stored on huge computer disks, from which the user selects at his or her convenience. Videotex is distributed in either over telephone lines or over dedicated lines on a cable television line. The receiver is able to also send messages back to the sender/transmitter. The best example of this is a shopping service in which the viewer sees something he likes, pushes the necessary buttons to order the item and charges it to his account or credit card.

Videotex was originally conceived to both bolster the use of the British telephone system and allow the British Broadcasting Company (BBC) to caption television programming for the deaf. Indeed, one system that delivers phone book listings has been successful in France. Videotex falls in and out of favor with major potential vendors. For the most part the many new companies and pilot videotext systems in the U.S. market have not found the dollar returns they wanted.

Optical Disks and Videotex

Videotex has taken on a life of its own. The most viable uses on the horizon may be a variation of videotex in which the interactive terminal is connected not on-line to a huge computer that has access to hundred of disks, but in which a PC is connected to an optical or video disk. The PC would provide the interactive capability. The optical disk, which stores millions of bits of data such as those used for stereo recordings, would provide the data base of information. In fact, most data that users want to access over on-line data bases—legal case and citations, for example—do not change every day. Such data bases stored on video disks could be updated quarterly or semiannually, especially if the cost per disk is under $10 as it's expected to be.

Photographs of homes for sale could be stored on disks connected to PCs with videotex capability. The potential home buyer could call up properties to look at by delineating price ranges or neighborhoods. Such disks and PC-based systems are also being used in exhibits and visitors' centers to inform viewers of events and directions.

JOBS IN VIDEOTEX

Many who got involved in early videotex efforts have found their careers stifled because the technology went nowhere. No one is interested in their skills. These were the ambitious systems designed for the home but with high price tags [say $600–900] on the service and the special receiver.

Videotex does create new jobs, but the question is whether they will survive as the technology matures—if it does. Entrepreneurs are needed to start these videotex firms. Such start-ups will need the same software developers, computer experts, business developers and marketers as any high technology company. Two new job categories will be:

Videotex editors: Select and edit what is available on the huge data bases.

Videotex artists: Design the screens and add charts and illustrations, which also would be stored on the computer data bases. Videotex offers many design possibilities because the text is delivered on a color screen.

The question is whether these new assignments will create more jobs than they displace in the traditional publishing and information industry—in newspapers, at magazines and in book publishing, primarily. Because of the reliance on computers, fewer workers will be required in the videotex operations.

Most of the persons displaced by a move to videotex would be lesser skilled workers such as clerks and production workers. There's no way of knowing if they wouldn't be displaced anyway because of other incoming technologies or changes. The experts are hard pressed to predict the final impact.

A videotex industry would necessarily sell more computers, software, communications hardware and lines. This would further offset the employment numbers, although it would probably not affect the clerical-level workers.

On-line Data Bases

For anyone who's ever spent time in a library searching for an article or researching old newspapers, one of the most astonishing uses of computers is on-line data bases. On-line means the information/data is stored on computer disks and accessible to a terminal or personal computer. The terminal or PC is either hard-wired to the computer or connected over telephone communications lines (including lines used only for data transmission).

The growing use of PCs equipped with modems has considerably expanded the use of on-line data bases, especially by users in their home, although the customers that the on-line services are after continue to be corporations. Such large users have libraries equipped with terminals or PCs and information specialists who find information over the on-line systems with the least amount of searching.

One of the best ways of appreciating on-line data bases is reviewing a list of what's available. Here are just a few of the offerings on Dialog, one of the most comprehensive, reliable, although sometimes expensive services:

BLS Consumer Price Index	Foreign Traders Index
Chemical Industry Notes	Harvard Business Review
Coffeeline	ICC British Company Financial Database
Economic Literature Index	Moody's Corporate Profiles
Electronic Yellow Page	Pharmaceutical News Index

Chemical Abstracts Search
Chemical Exposure
Drug Information Fulltext
Health Planning and Administration
Medline
American Statistics Index
Chemlaw
Criminal Justice Periodical Index
Congressional Record Abstracts
Federal Index
Laborlaw
Food Science and Technology Abstracts
Geoarchive
Mathfile
Meteorological and Geoastrophysical
  Abstracts
World Aluminum Abstracts
World Textiles
Canadian Business and Current Affairs
National Newspaper Index

Washington Post Index
Aquatic Sciences and Fisheries
Electric Power Database
Environmental Bibliography
Oceanic Abstracts
Books in Print
Academic American Encyclopedia
Encyclopedia of Associations
Foundation Grants Index
America: History and Life
Child Abuse and Neglect
Mental Health Abstracts
Middle East: Abstracts and Index
Philosopher's Index
Religion Index
Sociological Abstracts
American Men and Women of Science
Career Placement Registry
Marquis Who's Who

The Dialog bargain version most popular with PC users is Knowledge Index, a reduced-rate evening and weekend service with 26 data bases and an electronic mail service. The only problem with Dialog is cost. There are monthly use charges, the meter is always running, and the rate depends on which data base is accessed. Rates range from $0.30 to $5 a minute with most in the $1–1.60 range.

Besides Dialog Information Services (a subsidiary of Lockheed, headquartered in Palo Alto), a few of the many other major data bases are the following:

1. Nexis/Lexis from Meade Data Central, Dayton, Ohio. Nexis is primarily news clippings. Lexis is legal citations and cases.

2. Dow-Jones News/Retrieval, Princeton, N.J., by the publishers of the *Wall Street Journal*. A data base of stories and news in the *Wall Street Journal*, *Barron's* and Dow-Jones Financial News Service dates back to June, 1979. Users search for company names, chronological periods, subject areas or stock quotes. Dow-Jones is billed by usage, ranging from $1.20 per minute during prime time to as little as 10 cents a minute.

3. The New York Times Information Service, New York, New York. *The New York Times*, complete, and related services.

4. Disclosure, Bethesda, Maryland. Contains filings of the Securities and Exchange Commission (SEC). Disclosure is an example of a data base being available through several delivery mechanisms, directly from the company or through Dialog. Disclosure's services stem from documents filed with the Securities and Exchange Commission (SEC) and the financial statements that companies are required by law to file.

Other variations are microDISCLOSURE software for the IBM PC and Disclosure II Online, which can be accessed (dial-up) through DIALOG

Information Services, The New York Times Information Service and Control Data Corp. services. The microDISCLOSURE software (linking with Disclosure II) allows for modeling and "what if" questions based on information extracted from the data base on 110,000 companies dating to 1968.

One of the most cost-effective ways to access these on-line data bases are special telephone-like lines dedicated entirely to transmitting data. Tymnet and Telenet are two key examples. These networks use a special transmission technology, packet-switching, that packs data onto the lines and is accessed via local or regional phone numbers that then tap into the giant computer-based networks.

The growing trend is toward communicating either over these networks or voice lines via personal computers equipped with modems. This speeds the digital signals over the voice networks. These modems dial into access computers that in turn transmit to the large data bases.

Data Base Variations

Services such as The Source and CompuServe provide a panoply of services, including some data bases. These special communications services are best known for providing current information such as airline schedules, weather information, investment information including stock market quotes, shopping services and breaking news. One group even offers a weekly newsletter on the computer and PC industries.

These electronic communications utilities allow users to communicate with others on the network in a variety of ways, including electronic mail. Users can all tune in on regularly issued newsletters. Users can access an on-line on-going conversation via computer, a technology called computer conferencing. This works on the same idea as a bulletin board, where passersby add comments on to a message or request posted on the board. A computer conferencing group can be formed to comment on a draft report. It's proving an increasingly popular way of communication among group members.

INFORMATION SPECIALISTS: DATA BASE JOBS

Most of the jobs working with data bases and communication networks are the same as those working with software or communications—especially for the providers of these services. The job unique to data base work is that of the information specialist. In the past these workers were known as librarians working for corporations and public and school libraries. Today they must be expert at dredging information from electronic networks. The discipline called library science is now information science, although this term varies with institutions. Many schools offer four-year degrees in information science. More advanced degrees may be required soon.

Salaries for information specialists, at least at large companies, are in the $18,000–25,000 range—not nearly as high as in data processing, although the practitioners are often as well if not better prepared.

COMPUTER-AIDED PUBLISHING

The possibility of adding a computer to a typewriter or a drafting board has opened up new technologies of office automation and computer-aided design. Computer-aided publishing (CAP) and computerized typesetting (with the ubiquitous personal computer, especially the IBM PC) are connected to the actual typesetting system or photocompositor.

Despite the electronics revolution the hunger for printed documents is not going to go away. In fact, it's mushrooming: Every day American business creates 370 million pages of new business document originals, generates 1.9 billion pages of computer output and makes 19 billion copies. With a growth rate averaging nearly 5% per year through the mid-1990s, the total number of new documents produced annually will grow from about 1.6 billion pages today to 1 trillion in 1995—a 60% increase.

Typesetting is not the only existing technology that is being threatened by computers. Microfilming and photocopying are being integrated into sophisticated publishing systems. One of these innovative systems combines a VDT workstation, a printer of generated paper copies of microfilm images, a central computer controller, a robot-controlled autoloader for the rolls of microfilm, a local area network and software to tie it all together. (A six-station system is about $450,000.) With such a sophisticated system, an individual controls the creation of an entire document; he or she merges photographs and artwork with text and headlines to produce reports, manuals and publications that look professional.

Experts predict that we are on the verge of a typesetting revolution. Every top executive will demand a typeset-quality memo like this book page rather than one from a typewriter or computer printer. Typeset-quality documents will become de rigueur and secretaries will have their personal computer workstations connected to huge typesetters, similar to those now used only within the printing industry.

Typesetting is the highly detailed process of preparing documents to high-quality standards—hyphenating, justifying the columns of type, adjusting the white space—that make the page look attractive to the eye. Typesetting once was a jealously guarded craft of unionized workers, but then minicomputers were introduced.

The PC-based systems offer small publishers and job print shops new business opportunities. For example, a publisher of newsletters can own

Entire technical documents, including charts or line illustrations, are produced on the latest high-quality typesetting and page make-up systems with the boom in computer-assisted publishing. (Courtesy of Eastman Kodak)

for $7,000–10,000 a typesetter that on a minicomputer-driven system was at least $25,000. The PC-based system is just as powerful and has as much capacity. On a small networked system several operators work on multiple documents. Corporate headquarters can have their own PC-based typesetting systems. Document writers (or originators) prepare reports and pass them over the network to their bosses or to other involved departments for approval. Changes and corrections may be made at any point of the network, and even draft copies printed.

Just as we today have walk-in photocopying shops, one consultant sees while-you-wait printing shops on the horizon. Customers will walk in off the street with their resumes that will quickly be typeset, positioned on the page and printed. If they have a personal computer with communications capability, they will transmit their computer files to the typesetter over the telephone lines.

The availability of desktop laser printers has opened up many of these typesetting possibilities. In 1985 laser printers became cost effective for the personal computer, with most in the $3,000–4,000 range, although some with additional features, including built-in computers, are $7,000. These printers produce documents of almost typeset quality and users configure their text in the form it will take coming out of the printer. Many companies and small publishers don't need professional quality and are satisfied with the laser-printed copy, which often resembles an offset-printed original.

Large typesetters will also benefit from the capabilities of the PC and new printing technologies. These manufacturers are already including a personal computer as an input terminal for their larger systems. As noted above larger companies will continue to need the big typesetting systems with this new consciousness of typeset quality documents. There will remain some applications that are either too big or complex to be handled on the small systems.

PC typesetting is just part of the CAP revolution. Because of the cost and the increased capabilities of the new equipment, more typesetting and document preparation will be done within companies rather than sent out to third-party typesetting firms. Included in this CAP trend are the following:

1. Text document systems, such as the PC-based ones above, allow some graphics—simple charts, for instance—to be included in the document.

2. Technical documentation systems with higher-quality graphics capabilities produce sophisticated technical manuals, such as those required in the defense and aerospace industries.

3. Sales and executive reports systems prepare reports such as slide-presentations or color charts on paper needed by sales representatives and executives in their work.

Desk top laser printers connected to PCs or other computer-based typesetting or page processing systems are opening new opportunities for individuals publishing newsletters, company in-house production departments, as well as the corner job shop printer. (Courtesy of Eastman Kodak)

4. Executive quality presentation systems prepare reports of the highest quality for chief executives and board of directors. (Much of their work is currently done outside of the company, usually at high expense, because of the special equipment that's been required up until now.)

5. External communications systems will produce newsletters, brochures and advertisements used by public relations and advertising departments to impart the company's message. Again, much of this work has been done by third party services.

This computer-aided publishing market is expected to grow from $1 billion in 1983 to $12 billion in 1987. An estimated 15,000 companies will automate their publishing functions. In many cases these companies already have in-house publishing capabilities, but as islands of automation. Computer-aided publishing is connecting the islands, to use the terminology popular in computer-aided manufacturing. The goal is that all the text, digitized photographs and illustrations will be stored in gigantic computer data bases, and users will call up only what they need—a page of a parts catalog—instead of rummaging through stacks of old catalogs.

JOBS IN CAP

Jobs in the publishing and printing industry are undergoing several changes. Operators increasingly use computer terminals or PCs rather than typesetting keyboards without video screens. Work is increasingly being done in-house. The new jobs will be at the old places. It's anticipated that the number of jobs lost will be replaced by jobs created in the new CAP, although persons with old skills may not immediately transfer to the new jobs.

The good news is that many new vendors are entering the business at the PC level; it's an opportunity for entrepreneurs who want to start their own companies because so many products are involved that no one manufacturer can supply it all.

Because the work on a computer requires less specialized skills and knowledge, persons with less training will operate the new equipment. Long apprenticeships are no longer necessary. Many of the CAP workers will be promoted from within the company where they may already be working in office automation or computer-aided design (CAD) jobs. Especially in page make-up and composition many of the skills needed are the same as for CAD operators, discussed in Chapter 7.

Persons who enjoy the detail work of publishing will find many opportunities in the "new publishing" at the operations level. Many artistic jobs such as the magazine page make-up artist will also be transferred to either personal computers running page processing software or dedicated CAD-like systems. At the manufacturers, sales people, engineers, software developers and service technicians will be needed.

CABLE TELEVISION

The most glamorous jobs in the late 1970s and early 1980s were in cable television. Cable was the way to go, if one really wanted to be involved in the most trendy business. Some judged cable even more rewarding than network TV. Things didn't turn out, though, as the dream makers envisioned. Since the limited number of jobs were eagerly sought by talented, well educated college graduates, salaries remained low. The

American public did not embrace cable as much as the developers would have liked. A good number of the companies went off the air, if they ever got through the labyrinth of government regulations and public hearings in the first place. The specialized cable networks (arts programming, for example) failed to find an audience in the early 1980s and shut down their broadcasting facilities. As the dust settled, other cable programming caught on such as sports and rock video stations. The cable industry found its level and began to stabilize. These specialized cable channels such as Cable News Network or Entertainment and Sports Program Network (ESPN) each have 25–30 million subscribers.

Cable is an intriguing technology that combines many electronic capabilities. Cable television signals are broadcast over the airwaves—either via satellites or microwave dishes or hard wires—like television signals. Once they are received by the local station, however, there's a major change—the signals are then processed and converted for transmission on a coaxial cable direct to the receiver's home.

Cable television was initially developed for residents of remote areas (specifically those surrounded by mountains) who complained they couldn't receive television signals. The solution was a master antenna constructed on a nearby mountain, and the signal piped by wire to the houses in the valley. As the television industry flourished, these local master receiving stations started doing their own programming of community shows in addition to programs the rest of the country was not viewing.

The cable industry has multiple parts that operate on local, regional and national levels. At the local level are the individual franchises, companies approved by local governing boards to install the cabling, either underground or overhead. Government gets involved because of the jurisdictional issues in laying the cable and because of federal and state communications regulations. Cable companies (5,800 serve 31 million subscribers nationwide) also build a local station that includes the "headend," or electronic control center where the broadcast signals received by the antenna are converted into frequencies for distribution over the cable. Signals are transmitted from the programming providers—generally in New York City—via satellites to microwave dishes at the headend. This combination of technologies makes cable work demanding. Running a local cable company is much like running a local television station, but the cable company must maintain the lines, something the TV station doesn't need to worry about.

63,000 persons are employed in local cable stations. This 1983 figure is a 13% increase over the year before; in 1982 cable employment jumped 40%. In 1983, 15% of cable station employees were women and/or minorities.[1]

The American public is hooked on cable and job opportunities are expected to continue, although not at the rampant pace of the past. While the industry is no longer investing $1 billion a year in new systems—as it did at its 1982 peak—the investment continues, as do the new ideas and programs to win viewers.

JOBS IN CABLE TV

During the initial days of establishing the franchise, the following technical workers are needed:

Telecommunications officer: Works with local officials

Engineer: Supervises the construction of the headend

Electronics technician: Builds headend in conjunction with supervising engineer

Needed to build the system are the following:

Satellite technician: Installs, tests and completes the satellite connections.

Strand mapper: Plots the network, determining the layout of the cable both above and below ground.

Easement coordinator or **right-of-way coordinator:** Negotiates agreements and secures the necessary permits for the placement of the cable on private property.

Line installer and **cable splicer:** Lays the trunk lines and run feeder lines into neighborhoods. Once installation is complete and transmission underway, he or she is responsible for maintenance.

Once the system is up and running, technical operations experts are required:

Electrical engineer: Obtains and maintains necessary power for the far-flung system.

Electronics engineer: Plans, operates and analyzes performance of the special broadcast system.

The **chief engineer** is the most senior technical expert. He or she is responsible for all professional and technical concepts of cable system design, equipment planning, layout of the cable communications service, equipment, construction, installation and technical advice to the rest of the company. The chief engineer also must be ready to upgrade and improve service and equipment, making recommendations to management. Often the chief engineer must interact with the local officials, explaining the technical capabilities and limits of the system. The chief engineer is one of the top managers within the system, responsible for hiring and performance reviews.

Plant maintenance technician: Responsible for general maintenance of the system and broadcast center equipment.

Installer: Prepares the customer's home for the cable wiring, explaining the system and how to operate it, installing the home feeder lines and doing minor troubleshooting.

Trunk technician: Repairs line failure in main line or feeder lines (that can, unfortunately, shut down the entire system).

Service technician: Responds to customers' problems, usually electrical instead of systems (actual physical repair of the plant).

Bench technician: Repairs broken equipment at the systems repair facility.

Chief technician: Supervises the repair team and monitors and maintains the expensive, complex headend system and satellite receivers.

The chief technician's major concern is the quality of the signal received by the satellite and/or microwave and relayed to the headend. The headend contains many antennae which receive broadcast, microwave, and satellite signals that must be passed through a series of electronic devices that process and amplify them for further transmission to the subscriber's home via cable. Such equipment is highly sensitive to temperature, humidity and weather conditions and requires constant monitoring and adjustment. As the senior technical manager, the chief technician hires and fires, and supervises many employees.

Requirements: As in the telecommunications industry, engineering jobs require a four-year engineering degree. At the technician level—from installer to chief—a variety of training will do. Possibilities include the two-year vocational programs in electronics from either a private school or community college. Some two-year colleges offer programs that combine communications technology and business skills/administration, the right combination in the cable industry. Many of the installers and technicians currently in cable received their electronics training in the military. Positions in growing companies offer many opportunities for on-the-job training.

PROGRAMMING AND PRODUCTION

Some of the local cable service providers do their own local program development. In fact they must by law allow community residents to produce programs of local interest. The specialized theme networks require programming (program preparation, as opposed to computer programming) expertise. The local cable stations are located around the country. Several are operated by one larger company, identified as a multiple system operator (MSO). The specialized services, mainly package and market movies and sports programs, are headquartered primarily in the centers of the entertainment industry, New York and Los Angeles. Most of the jobs in these cities are in marketing and general business.

At the local stations opportunities exist for newcomers with no or little experience to break into cable television. The techie jobs are the same as a network television station: studio technician, lighting technician, sound technician. The requirements are usually a high school diploma and a background in electronics, television production or one of the specialties—lighting or sound.

The availability and popularity of video recording equipment (small and easy to handle and carry around on assignments), to say nothing of price, has enhanced the opportunities both for persons to move into production and for production itself. The fact that equipment is so portable encourages additional live filming done on site instead of staged in a studio—or not done at all. Such inexpensive, portable equipment is now within reach of the smaller cable stations.

1. Janet Quigley. "The Cable Job Guide." (Alexandria, Virginia: The Cable Television Information Center, 1984.)

APPENDIX 1

ASSOCIATIONS

Data Processing and Personal Computers

American Federation of Information Processing
  Societies (AFIPS)
1899 Preston White Drive
Reston, VA 22091

American Society for Information Science
1010 Sixteenth Street, NW
Washington, DC 20036

American Statistical Association
806 Fifteenth Street, NW
Washington, D.C. 20036

Association for Computing Machinery
11 West 42 Street
New York, NY 10036

Association for Women in Computing
407 Hillmoor Drive
Silver Spring, MD 20901
(14 local chapters)

Association for Women in Mathematics
Women's Research Center
Wellesley College
828 Washington Street
Wellesley, MA 02181

Association for Women in Science
Suite 1122
1346 Connecticut Avenue, NW
Washington, DC 20036

Association of Computer Programmers
  and Analysts
c/o Cate Corporation
Suite 808
1180 Sunrise Valley Drive
Reston, VA 22091

Association of Data Processing Services
  Organizations [ADAPSO]
Suite 300
1300 North 17th Street
Arlington, VA 22209
(software developers and computer services
  organizations)

Black Data Processing Associates
P.O. Box 7466
Philadelphia, PA 19101

Data Processing Management Association
505 Busse Highway
Park Ridge, IL 60068
(one of the largest DP associations)

Electronic Data Processing Auditors
  Association
373 South Schmale Road
Carol Stream, IL 60187

GUIDE
111 East Wacker Drive
Chicago, IL 60601
(IBM large systems users' group)

Independent Computer Consultants Association
P.O. Box 27412
St. Louis, MO 63141

Institute for Certification of Computer
  Professionals
Suite 268
2200 East Devon Avenue
Des Plaines, IL 60018

Institute of Electrical and Electronics Engineers
  (IEEE)
345 East 47th Street
New York, NY 10017

IEEE Computer Society
Suite 201
1109 Spring Street
Silver Spring, MD 20901

Instrument Society of America
Box 12277
67 Alexander Drive
Research Triangle Park, NC 27709

SHARE
111 East Wacker Drive
Chicago, IL 60601
(IBM mid-size systems users)

Society of Computer Simulation
P.O. Box 2228
La Jolla, CA 92038

Society for Industrial and Applied Mathematics
Suite 1405
117 South 17th Street
Philadelphia, PA 19103

Society for Information Display
654 North Sepulveda Boulevard
Los Angeles, CA 90049

Women in Information Processing
Suite 9
1000 Connecticut Avenue, NW
Washington, DC 20036

Technologies Industry

Computer and Business Equipment
 Manufacturers Association
1828 L Street, NW
Washington, DC 20036

Telecommunications

Empire Wo/Men in Telecommunications
P.O. Box 98
Elmont, NY 11003

International Communications Association
Suite 710, LB-89
12750 Merit Drive
Dallas, TX 75251

North American Telecommunications
 Association
2000 M Street, NW
Washington, DC 20036

Manufacturing Technologies

Computer and Automated Systems Association
One SME Drive
Dearborn, MI 48128

Computer Graphics & Applications
IEEE Computer Society
10662 Los Vaqueros Circle
Los Alamitos, CA 90720

Electronic Technician's Association
Route 3, Box 564
Greencastle, IN 46135

Laser Institute of America
Suite 103–West
5151 Monroe Street
Toledo, OH 43623

The Robotics Institute
Carnegie-Mellon University
5000 Forbes Avenue
Pittsburgh, PA 15213

Robotics International of the Society of
 Manufacturing Engineers
P.O. Box 930
One SME Drive
Dearborn, MI 48128

Artificial Intelligence

American Association for Artificial Intelligence
445 Burgess Drive
Menlo Park, CA 94025

Carnegie-Mellon University
Department of Computer Science
Schenley Park
Pittsburgh, PA 15213

Massachusetts Institute of Technology
Artificial Intelligence Lab
545 Technology Square
Cambridge, MA 02139

Stanford University
Heuristic Programming Project
Computer Science Department
Stanford, CA 94305

Computer Graphics

National Computer Graphics Association
Suite 601
8401 Arlington Boulevard
Fairfax, VA 22031

SIGGRAPH (Special Interest Group—Graphics)
c/o Association for Computing Machinery
11 West 42 Street
New York, NY 10036

Society of Computer Simulation
P.O. Box 2228
La Jolla, CA 92038

New Medicine

American Board of Cardiovascular Perfusion,
  Inc.
Suite 209
109 South 27th Avenue
Hattiesburg, MS 39041

American Cancer Society
777 Third Avenue
New York, NY 10017

American Cardiology Technologists Association
Reston International Center
Suite 808
11800 Sunrise Valley Drive
Reston, VA 22091

American Medical Association
Attn: Order Department
535 North Dearborn Street
Chicago, IL 60610

American Society for Medical Technology
Suite 403
1725 DeSales Street, NW
Washington, DC 20036

American Society of Radiologic Technologists
15000 Central Avenue, SE
Albuquerque, NM 87123–4605

Association for the Advancement of Medical
  Instrumentation
Suite 602
1901 North Fort Myer Drive
Arlington, VA 22209

National Society for Cardiopulmonary
  Technology
Suite 307
One Bank Street
Gaithersburg, MD 20878.

Society of Diagnostic Medical Sonographers
Building One, Suite 276
10300 North Central Expressway
Dallas, TX 75231

Society of Nuclear Medicine
475 Park Avenue South
New York, NY 10016

Technical Writing

The Association for Business Communication
University of Illinois/English Building
608 South Wright Street
Urbana, IL 61801

Society for Technical Communication, Inc.
815 15th Street, NW
Washington, DC 20005
(Publish *Academic Programs in Technical Communication*)

Electronic Publishing

The Cable Television Information Center
Suite 205
1500 North Beauregard Street
Alexandria, VA 22311

National Cable Television Association
1724 Massachusetts Avenue, NW
Washington, D.C. 20036
(Publish *Careers in Cable*)

The National Federation of Local Cable
  Programmers
900 Pennsylvania Avenue, SE
Washington, DC 20003
(Publish *Cable Job Guide*)

APPENDIX 2

PERIODICALS

A+
11 Davis Drive
Belmont, CA 94002
(Apple users)

Acute Care Medicine
149 Fifth Avenue
New York, NY 10010

Administrative Management
1123 Broadway
New York, NY 10001
(office)

American Clinical Products Review
P.O. Box 827
808 Kings Highway
Fairfield, CT 06430

American Health Care Association Journal
1200 15th Street, NW
Washington, DC 20005

American Journal of Cardiology
Technical Publishing Company
875 Third Avenue
New York, NY 10022

American Journal of Medicine
Technical Publishing Company
875 Third Avenue
New York, NY 10022

American Journal of Surgery
874 Third Avenue
New York, NY 10022

American Heart Journal
11830 Westline Industrial Drive
Saint Louis, MO 63146

American Medical News
535 North Dearborn Street
Chicago, IL 60610

Applied Cardiology
825 South Barrington Avenue
Los Angeles, CA 90049

Applied Radiology
825 South Barrington Avenue
Los Angeles, CA 90049

Assembly Engineering
Hitchcock Building
Wheaton, IL 60187
(management, design and manufacturing
  engineers)

Aviation, Space and Environmental Medicine
Aerospace Medical Association
Washington National Airport
Washington, DC 20001

Bank Systems & Equipment
1515 Broadway
New York, NY 10036

Broadcasting
1735 DeSales Street, NW
Washington, DC 20036

Business Communications Review
950 York Road
Hinsdale, IL 60521
(telecommunications professionals)

Business Computer Systems
221 Columbus Avenue
Boston, MA 02116
(for small businesses new to computing)

Business Week
1221 Avenue of the Americas
New York, NY 10020
(excellent information processing section)

Byte
70 Main Street
Peterborough, NH 03458

CATJ
Journal of the Community Antenna TV
  Association
Suite 106
4209 NW 23rd Street
Oklahoma City, OK 73107

CTIC Newsletter
Cable Television Information Center
Suite 1007
1800 North Kent Street
Arlington, VA 22209

Cable Marketing
352 Park Avenue
New York, NY 10016

Cableage
Television Editorial Corporation
1270 Avenue of the Americas
New York, NY 10020

Channels of Communications
Media Commentary Council, Inc.
1515 Broadway
New York, NY 10036
(cable TV)

Classroom Computer News
51 Spring Street
Watertown, MA 02172

Clinical Laboratory Products
P.O. Box 69
Route 101A
Amherst, NH 03031

Communications News
124 South First Street
Geneva, IL 60134

Communications Week
600 Community Drive
Manhasset, NY 11030
(communications industry)

Community Television Review
National Federation of Local Cable
 Programmers
Suite 109
3700 Far Hills Avenue
Kettering, OH 45429

Computer
10622 Los Vaqueros Circle
Los Alamitos, CA 90720
(monthly of IEEE Computer Society)

Computer Dealer
20 Community Place
Morristown, NJ 07960

Computer Decisions
50 Essex Street
Rochelle Park, NJ 07662
(DP managers)

Computer Design
11 Goldsmith Street
Littleton, MA 01406
(computer design engineers)

Computer & Electronics Marketing
820 Second Avenue
New York, NY 10017

Computer Graphics
c/o Association for Computing Machinery
11 West 42 Street
New York, NY 10036

Computer Graphics News
1515 Broadway
New York, NY 10036

Computer Graphics World
110 Russel Street
Littleton, MA 01460

Computer Pictures
330 West 42 Street
New York, NY 10036
(computer animation)

Computer Retail News
600 Community Drive
Manhasset, NY 11030
(computer retailers)

Computer Systems News
600 Community Drive
Manhasset, NY 11030
(weekly for computer manufacturers)

Computerworld
P.O. Box 880
375 Cochituate Road
Framingham, MA 01701
(weekly for computer users)

The Computing Teacher
International Council for Computers in
 Education
Department of Computer and Information
 Sciences
University of Oregon
Eugene, OR 97403

Contemporary Dialysis & Nephrology
Suite D
17901 Ventura Boulevard
Encino, CA 91316

Current Microbiology
175 Fifth Avenue
New York, NY 10010

Data Communications
1221 Avenue of the Americas
New York, NY 10020

Data Management
505 Busse Highway
Park Ridge, IL 60068
(DPMA monthly)

Data Training
176 Federal Street
Boston, MA 02110
(monthly for DP trainers)

Datamation
875 Third Avenue
New York, NY 10022
(DP managers)

Data Training
38 Chauncy Street
Boston, MA 02111
(DP trainers)

Design News
221 Columbus Avenue
Boston, MA 02116
(component designers)

Desktop Publishing
Suite 180
2055 Woodside Road
Redwood City, CA 94061

Digital Design
1050 Commonwealth Avenue
Boston, MA 02215
(electronics engineers)

Digital Review

Boston, MA

ECN (Electronic Component News)
Chilton Way
Radnor, PA 19089
(design engineers)

EDN
221 Columbus Avenue
Boston, MA 02116
(design engineers)

Electronic Business
221 Columbus Avenue
Boston, MA 02116
(electronics industry)

Electronic Buyers' News
600 Community Drive
Manhasset, NY 11030
(weekly for components buyers)

Electronic Design
50 Essex Street
Rochelle Park, NJ 07662

Electronic Engineering Times
600 Community Drive
Manhasset, NY 11030
(bi-weekly for electronics engineers)

Electronic Learning
902 Sylvan Avenue
Englewood Cliffs, NJ 07632

Electronic Media
740 North Rush Street
Chicago, IL 60601

Electronic News
7 East 12th Street
New York, NY 10003
(weekly on electronics industry)

Electronics
1221 Avenue of the Americas
New York, NY 10020

Government Data Systems
475 Park Avenue South
New York, NY 10016

Graduating Engineer
1221 Avenue of the Americas
New York, NY 10020
(engineering students)

Harvard Newsletter on Computer Graphics
P.O. Box 392
730 Boston Post Road
Sudbury, MA 01776

Health Care Systems
1515 Broadway
New York, NY 10036

Health Industry Today
454 Morris Avenue
Springfield, NJ 07081

High Technology
38 Commercial Wharf
Boston, MA 02110
(high tech for professionals)

Hospitals
211 East Chicago Avenue
Chicago, Il 60611

ICP Interface
900 Keystone Crossing
Indianapolis, IN 46240
(software users)

IEEE Computer Graphics and Applications
10662 Los Vaqueros Circle
Los Alamitos, CA 90720

IEEE Spectrum
345 East 47 Street
New York, NY 10017
(IEEE monthly)

Information & Records Management
101 Crossways Park West
Woodbury, NY 11797

Information Today
143 Old Marlton Pike
Medford, NJ 08055
(users and producers of electronic information
  services)

Information Week
600 Community Drive
Manhasset, NY 11030
(weekly for users on DP industry)

InfoWorld
Suite C-200
1060 Marsh Road
Menlo Park, CA 94025
(microcomputer users and industry)

Interaction
National Cable Television Association
1724 Massachusetts Avenue, NW
Washington, DC 20036

Interface Age
16704 Marquardt Avenue
Cerritos, CA 90701
(microcomputer users)

Intermedia
Tavistock House East
Tavistock Square
London WC1 9LF England
(cable TV)

Kidney International
175 Fifth Avenue
New York, NY 10010

Medical Care Products
13 Emery Avenue
Randolph, NJ 07869

Medical Electronics
2994 West Liberty Avenue
Pittsburgh, PA 15216

Medical Product Sales
550 Frontage Road
Northfield, IL 60093

Mini-Micro Systems
221 Columbus Avenue
Boston, MA 02116
(systems manufacturers)

MIS Week
7 East 12th Street
New York, NY 10003
(management information system
  professionals)

Modern Healthcare
740 North Rush Street
Chicago, IL 60611

Modern Office Technologies
111 Chester Avenue
Cleveland, OH 44114
(administrative, financial managers)

Multichannel News
300 South Jackson Street
Denver, CO 80209
(cable TV)

MULTIs
211 East Chicago Avenue
Chicago, IL 60611
(health systems management)

Nursing
1111 Bethlehem Pike
Springfield, PA 19477

The Office
1200 Summer Street
Stamford, CT 06904
(corporate, administrative managers)

Office World News
645 Stewart Avenue
Garden City, NY 11530
(equipment dealers)

Optimal Health
1842 Hoffman Street
Madison, WI 53704

PC Magazine
One Park Avenue
New York, NY 10016
(PC users)

PC Tech Journal
One Park Avenue
New York, NY 10016
(technical PC users)

PC Week
15 Crawford Street
Needham, MA 02194
(corporate PC users)

PC World
555 DeHaro Street
San Francisco, CA 94107
(PC users)

Personal Computing
10 Mulholland Drive
Hasbrouck Heights, NJ 07604
(microcomputer users)

Pico
Route 202 North
Peterborough, NH 03458–9995
(briefcase computers)

Savvy
111 Eighth Avenue
New York, NY 10011
(career advice for men and women)

Siggraffiti
ACM/SIGGRAPH
111 East Wacker Drive
Chicago, IL 60601
(SIGGRAPH graphics newsletter)

Software in Healthcare
323½ Richmond Street
El Segundo, CA 90245

Software News
5 Kane Industrial Drive
Hudson, MA 01749
(software users)

Southern Hospitals
Suite 125
2100 Powers Ferry Road NW
Atlanta, GA 30339

TVC
6430 South Yosemite Street
Englewood, CO 80111

Techline
National Cable Television Association
1724 Massachusetts Avenue, NW
Washington, DC 20036

TeleCarrier
5951 South Middlefield Road
Littleton, CO 80123
(cellular, paging and mobile phone systems
 management)

Teleconnect
12 West 21st Street
New York, NY 10010
(telecommunications users)

Telephone Engineer & Management
124 South First Street
Geneva, IL 60134

Telephony
55 East Jackson Boulevard
Chicago, IL 60604–4188

Television Digest
1836 Jefferson Place, NW
Washington, DC 20036

Television/Radio Age
1270 Avenue of the Americas
New York, NY 10020

Wall Street Computer Review
150 Broadway
New York, NY 10038–4476
(microcomputers in financial community)

Weekly Television Digest
1836 Jefferson Place, NW
Washington, DC 20036
(cable TV)

World Journal of Surgery
175 Fifth Avenue
New York, NY 10010

Working Woman
342 Madison Avenue
New York, NY 10173
(career advice for men and women)

APPENDIX 3

BIBLIOGRAPHY

Technology-related Careers

Butler, Diane. *Futurework: Where to Find Tomorrow's High-Tech Jobs Today*. New York: Holt, Rinehart and Winston, 1984.

Cardoza, Anne, and Suzee J. Vlk. *The Aerospace Careers Handbook*. New York: Arco, 1985.

———. *The Robotics Careers Handbook*. New York: Arco, 1985.

Cetron, Marvin J., with Marcia Appel. *Jobs of the Future: The 500 Best Jobs—Where They'll Be and How to Get Them*. New York: McGraw-Hill, 1984.

Hodgson, Jonathan. *Computer Operator Tests*. New York: Arco, 1985.

———. *Computer Programmer Tests*. New York: Arco, 1985.

———. *Data Processing Tests*. New York: Arco, 1985.

Strackbein, Ray, and Strackbein, Dorothy Bowlby. *Computers and Data Processing Simplified and Self-Taught*. New York: Arco, 1983.

Winkler, Connie. *The Computer Careers Handbook*. New York: Arco, 1983.

Careers in General

Beard, Marna L., and McGahey, Michael J. *Alternative Careers for Teachers*. New York: Arco, 1985.

Bolles, Richard Nelson. *What Color Is Your Parachute?* Berkeley: Ten Speed Press, 1985.

Corwen, Leonard. *Your Resume: Key to a Better Job*. New York: Arco, 1985.

Resume Service. *Resumes That Get Jobs*. New York: Arco, 1986.

Shykind, Maury. *Resumes for Executives and Professionals*. New York: Arco, 1984.

Turbak, Gary. *Action-Getting Resumes for Today's Jobs*. New York: Arco, 1983.

INDEX